TEACHING
AGAINST
THE
GRAIN

Critical Studies in Education and Culture Series

Critical Pedagogy and Cultural Power
David Livingstone and Contributors

Education and the American Dream: Conservatives, Liberals and Radicals
Debate the Future of Education
Harvey Holtz and Associates

Education and the Welfare State: A Crisis in Capitalism and Democracy
Svi Shapiro

Education under Siege: The Conservative, Liberal and Radical Debate over
Schooling
Stanley Aronowitz and Henry A. Giroux

Literacy: Reading the Word and the World
Paulo Freire and Donaldo Macedo

The Moral and Spiritual Crisis in Education: A Curriculum for Justice and
Compassion
David Purpel

The Politics of Education: Culture, Power and Liberation
Paulo Freire

Popular Culture, Schooling and the Language of Everyday Life
Henry A. Giroux and Roger I. Simon

Teachers As Intellectuals: Toward a Critical Pedagogy of Learning
Henry A. Giroux

Women Teaching for Change: Gender, Class and Power
Kathleen Weiler

Between Capitalism and Democracy: Educational Policy and the Crisis of the
Welfare State
Svi Shapiro

Critical Psychology and Pedagogy: Interpretation of the Personal World
Edmund Sullivan

Pedagogy and the Struggle for Voice
Catherine E. Walsh

Voices in Architectural Education
Thomas Dutton

TEACHING AGAINST THE GRAIN

TEXTS FOR A PEDAGOGY OF POSSIBILITY

ROGER I. SIMON

CRITICAL STUDIES IN EDUCATION AND CULTURE SERIES
EDITED BY HENRY A. GIROUX AND PAULO FREIRE

BERGIN & GARVEY
New York • Westport, Connecticut • London

Copyright Acknowledgments

The author and publisher gratefully acknowledge permission to reprint text from the following:

Roger I. Simon, "Jewish Applause for a Yiddish Shylock: Beyond the Racist Text." *Journal of Urban and Cultural Studies*, Vol. 1 (1990): pp. 69–86.

Roger I. Simon and Don Dippo, "What Schools Can Do: Work Education as Challenging the Wisdom of Experience." *Journal of Education*, 169 (3) (1989): pp. 101–116.

Library of Congress Cataloging-in-Publication Data

Simon, Roger I.
    Teaching against the grain : texts for a pedagogy of possibility / Roger I. Simon.
      p.   cm. — (Critical studies in education & culture)
    Includes bibliographical references (p.) and index.
    ISBN 0–89789–207–0 (alk. paper). — ISBN 0–89789–206–2 (pbk. : alk. paper)
    1. Education—Philosophy.   I. Title. II. Series.
    LB880.S539T43 1992
    370'.1—dc20   91–35246

British Library Cataloguing in Publication Data is available.

Library of Congress Catalog Card Number: 91–35246
ISBN: 0–89789–207–0
      0–89789–206–2 (pbk.)

First published in 1992

Bergin & Garvey, One Madison Avenue, New York, NY 10010
An imprint of Greenwood Publishing Group, Inc.

Printed in the United States of America

The paper used in this book complies with the
Permanent Paper Standard issued by the National
Information Standards Organization (Z39.48–1984).

10 9 8 7 6 5 4 3 2 1

For Wendy,
whose *ruach*
and practice of *tikkun olam*
have sustained this work for many years

Introductory quotations, or epigraphs, are often taken as emblems. If they assert a set of principles that seem to prick one's conscience, such quotations run the risk of being taken as symptomatic of a discourse of authority and arrogance. Rather than emblems, I like to think of introductory quotations as notes attached to a refrigerator door; reminders of things I too easily forget as I go about the business of everyday life. I've posted these here, in front of my text, for much the same reason; statements to be remembered but that are all too easily forgotten once the hard work of teaching has begun.

Justice . . . is not an abstraction, a value. Justice exists in relation to a person, and is something done by a person. An act of injustice is condemned, not because the law is broken, but because a person has been hurt.

—Abraham Heschel, *The Prophets*

Beware, even in thought, of assuming the sterile attitude of the spectator, for life is not a spectacle, a sea of griefs is not a proscenium, a man who wails is not a dancing bear.

—Aimé Césaire, *Return to My Native Land*

Sin has its source not in desire itself, but in desire's superstitious [mythic] surrender to fate.

—Susan Buck-Morss, *The Dialectics of Seeing: Walter Benjamin and the Arcades Project*

In real life we are happy, we love, and play, but *despite* the conditions in which we can become persons. The point is to change those conditions, not to make a virtue out of small personal triumphs over adversity.

—Shelia Rowbotham, *Woman's Consciousness, Man's World*

Contents

Series Introduction: Critical Pedagogy Without Illusions

Henry A. Giroux

In what follows, I am going to depart from my usual tradition as co-editor of this series of expanding on the theoretical and political implications of the book to be introduced. Instead, I want to provide some brief "snapshots" that not only contextualize Roger Simon's *Teaching Against the Grain*, but also situate this book within my own intellectual and personal encounter with Roger as both a colleague and a close friend. While I cannot flesh out the full implications of such an encounter, I do believe our longstanding friendship has been characterized by animated conversations, an attempt to work collectively as both writers and teachers, and a deeply felt need to develop a pedagogical project rooted in a politics of solidarity and hope. In part, this introduction is a reaffirmation of our ongoing friendship as well as the encounters and dialogue we have had regarding the politics of our own locations and how they fit within the social, cultural practices that surround them.

I first corresponded with Roger Simon in 1978. At that time, mainstream educational theory and practice was being challenged on a number of fronts, and the echoes of numerous radical discourses could be heard emanating from such diverse places as Teachers College, the University of Wisconsin at Madison, Ohio State University, and the Ontario Institute for Studies in Education. As a first-year assistant professor, I was trying to read as much as I could of the new work being written at the time on curriculum theory and critical pedagogy, while simultaneously attempting to make a modest contribution to the emerging radical literature. One of my earliest pieces was accepted for publication in *Cur-*

riculum Inquiry. Roger Simon was one of the co-editors and also served as one of the reviewers for the article. His review was favorable but exhibited a conceptual rigor that both challenged and invited me to become more self-reflective about the piece and the overall work I was doing. Soon afterwards, I met Simon at the 1979 American Educational Research Association Convention in San Francisco. I was immediately struck not only by his warmth and generosity, but also by his unique combination of brilliance and humility. My early impressions of Simon are conjured up in images of him engaged in endless discussions about critical pedagogy, but doing so in a way that ruptured and challenged not only the boundaries of traditional discourses but also radical perspectives as well. He seemed to move in and out of disciplines, raised questions that impelled conversations, and always did so with an attentiveness to listening to others that seemed extraordinary to me. He never missed a beat. The meeting in San Francisco began a long term friendship, dialogue, and collaboration that continues to this day.

Within the last fifteen years, Simon has produced a body of work that is as exciting as it is original. In an age of self-centered ideologies parading as the latest fashion in radical chic, his work always pointed to radical renewal and transformation. His writings on critical pedagogy, the pedagogy of possibility, the politics of representation and identity, and a number of other topics were always done with great theoretical precision and critical inventiveness. His work has always refused the safety of occupied theoretical territory, the determinism of master narratives, and the cynicism that relegated teachers to a place outside of power and struggle. What makes Roger Simon so remarkable as a scholar is that he has always been able to reinvent and reconstruct new spaces for engaging critical pedagogy as an ever-becoming relation of theory and practice. At the same time, he constantly worked toward implementing a pedagogy without illusions by being scrupulous in turning the tools of dialogue and self-criticism upon his own work. He was never satisfied with being in one place. His work was always shifting, moving, circling back on itself, pushing against its own discourse so as to extend and deepen its implications for critical pedagogy while tracing out a recognizable shape of the complexity that informed its underlying project.

Whenever an article written by Simon reached me, I always found myself attempting to remap and rethink the implications of his work for how I thought about the various fields in which I wrote. There was never anything ordinary about his texts; his work always pushed me further, it also opened up new avenues of analysis, and it began in the 1980s to have a wide impact in Canada, the United States, and in other countries.

In many respects, *Teaching Against the Grain* represents a series of inter-related essays that represent the best of Simon's thinking on pedagogy, cultural studies, and the politics of representation. I think the essays in this book set a new standard for engaging the problems and possibilities offered by critical pedagogy. To be sure, Simon makes no claims for an essentialist discourse of authenticity; in fact, every essay presents itself as an argument against such a logic. Instead, Simon presents a language of engagement and possibility that is rooted in a politics and pedagogy that takes the issue of solidarity seriously by placing it in the intersection of history, power, and social agency. This is a book that invites one to dream, dance, and confront how critical cultural and ideological analyses can connect with the material relations of diverse cultural workers engaged in pedagogical practices both within and outside the world of schooling. There are no easy answers in Simon's book. On the contrary, *Teaching Against the Grain* actively ruptures the binarisms that traditionally define critical pedagogy and the broader language of educational theory and practice. In doing so, Simon invites his readers to take up a new language, one that raises new questions and requires new formulations. The journey is as exciting as it is challenging. To use a phrase from Linda Brodkey, this is not a book for intellectual tourists, for those who wish to pass effortlessly through the complex social, ideological, and cultural landscapes, which any serious engagement with critical pedagogy must address. But it is a book for students, teachers, administrators, community activists, and other cultural workers who, as Simon states in his preface, are moved by the desire to "bring people together who share enough in the way of political commitments and educational perspectives to be able to learn together, refine our vision, and support our diverse efforts as educators." *Teaching Against the Grain* makes an important contribution to the Bergin & Garvey Series and to the wider fields of critical pedagogy and cultural studies. Simon's work establishes new theoretical standards for addressing the interaction and specificity of cultural practices, relations of power, and the politics of one's own location within them. This is a remarkable work that refuses a discourse of transcendence or exclusion, and in doing so offers a powerful argument for a politics and pedagogy of engagement and solidarity.

Preface

In 1979 my colleagues and I at the Ontario Institute for Studies in Education (OISE, a graduate school of the University of Toronto) began what we clearly understood as a legitimation exercise. A number of us were developing teaching and research rooted in specific commitments to enhancing the degree of justice and compassion present in our community. What gave our work a measure of coherence was the view that education might be understood as a practice of cultural production whose effects influenced not only the distribution of material goods and available opportunity structures but as well, the social imaginary through which people defined both what was possible and desirable. As university faculty we were able to follow our own individual and collective interests with minimal constraint. However, students with similar commitments felt the absence of an institutional "home"; a community of interest with which they could identify and in which intrainstitutional support practices (speaker series, study groups, newsletters, bulletin board space) could be mobilized. It was in response to this need that we established the Critical Pedagogy and Cultural Studies Forum at OISE. Animating communication and collaboration among a growing number of faculty and students, together with our colleagues in the OISE Center for Women's Studies in Education we participated in creating an institutional legitimacy for the broad spectrum of academic work including feminist studies, critical studies, antiracist education and radical pedagogy.

In the context of this legitimation effort a number of us started publicly using the term "critical pedagogy." Not only did the term begin to appear on and in OISE posters, bulletin boards, and catalogs, but some faculty began publishing books and articles using this terminology (see, for example, David Livingstone et al., *Critical Pedagogy and Cultural Power* South Hadley: Bergin and Garvey, 1987). In this respect we joined a growing number of educators across North America who were also seeking ways of naming and legitimating their efforts to define complementary possibilities for progressive practice. In retrospect, in relation to its time and context this strategy was useful. Much exciting work has taken place in the institutional spaces created by such efforts. However a decade later, critical pedagogy is in danger of terminal ossification.

It is no surprise that with the institutionalization of critical pedagogy have come efforts to fix its terms of reference. Supporters and detractors alike have attempted to render critical pedagogy into a category whose boundaries are fixed and clearly distinguishable. The interest seems to be in mapping this term within the terrain of educational studies where one can identify competing and complementary frameworks. At times, such maps help to clarify similarities and differences among efforts to think through the effects and prospects for various forms of educational practice. However, the practice of ideational cartography also creates the conditions of possibility for the exercise of a form of disciplinary power. Given that conceptual maps must illuminate difference, unfixed and shifting practices must be tied down, contained, and distorted so as to fit the requirements of the very concept of a map itself. In the case of critical pedagogy this has resulted in what seems to me a deleterious attempt to reify its assumptions, commitments, and practices. This is well illustrated by continuing efforts to locate critical pedagogy as encrusted in the work of Paulo Freire; necessarily incorporating his categories and assumptions. Also unhelpful in my view have been the efforts, both serious and ironic, to define a set of "founding fathers" for critical pedagogy as if an authentic version could somehow be found in a patriarchical vanishing point.

In conversation with those seeking a clearer sense of "what's to be done," I have continually tried to subvert the establishment of an orthodox notion of critical pedagogy. For me critical pedagogy is a useful term only to the extent it helps bring together people who share enough in the way of political commitments and educational perspectives to be able to learn together, refine our vision, and support our diverse efforts as educators. The utility of the term "critical pedagogy" is its reference to an ongoing project and certainly not a prescriptive set of practices. When it no longer performs this function, it would be better abandoned.

When I am asked "So what is critical pedagogy anyway?" or "Am I doing critical pedagogy yet?" I try to respond in a way that clarifies how it might be possible to move—tentatively, and with a degree of humility in regard to one's own ignorance—between notions of politics and practice.

Taking up this challenge has involved not only trying to refine and make more explicit the political vision that structures my work but as well, it has become the occasion of a constant reconsideration of many basic pedagogical questions. These questions have included: how is experience to be understood? What information and experience do I have access to that is important and possibly helpful to others? In what way does the form and substance of the knowledge engaged in teaching situations enable/constrain personal and social possibilities? How do I understand learning and the relationship teaching has to it? What is my view of a "person"? How do emotions, desires, and psychic investments influence teaching situations? How do the oppressive forms of power in my community manifest themselves in classrooms, and how do I situate myself in relation to such forms? And finally, how do I define my responsibilities as a teacher—to what should my students be held accountable, to what should I be held accountable?

This book is an interim report on my attempt to wrestle with such questions. Eight essays are divided equally between two sections of text. Six of these are previously unpublished. The four essays in Part I attempt to draw together a rather general but comprehensive statement of my efforts to define an educational practice consistent with what I understand to be "a project of possibility." The first two chapters develop the substance of this political vision in detail. Chapter 3 offers some ideas about how such a project might be extended beyond schooling while Chapter 4 discusses key aspects of pedagogy that influence how it will be manifest as a form of political practice. Part II provides four essays that display an attempt to work out some of the pedagogical problems associated with specific aspects of my teaching, research, and curriculum writing over the last ten years. Chapter 5 discusses the problem of teaching "theory" in a graduate school classroom. Using *The Merchant of Venice* and *The Heart of Darkness* as examples, Chapter 6 addresses questions pertaining to the use of "controversial texts" in programs of literary study. A previous version of this chapter was published in the *Journal of Urban and Cultural Studies.* Chapter 7, written with Don Dippo, draws on a long-term research and curriculum writing project in the area of work education to illustrate "what schools can do." This chapter, too, previously appeared in a slightly different form in the *Journal of Education.* Finally, I conclude in Chapter 8 with some initial thoughts on how a critical pedagogy of remembrance might be conceived. This final chapter marks the beginning of a new long-term effort to rethink the way in which education practices are implicated in the production of social memories and historical sensibilities. Klaus Staeck has generously given permission to reproduce his poster *Fremdarbeiter* in the context of this chapter.

This book was written with the help of many people. It would not have been completed without the constant discussion, critique, and encouragement of Wendy Simon, who contributed in more ways than she knows. Henry Giroux has been (as we say in Hebrew) my *haver;* brother and comrade, he has had with me a twelve-year-long discussion that has contributed immensely to the development of my thought and practice. Henry also provided a detailed critique of a draft version of the manuscript. Philip Corrigan made a major contribution to the book. The years he spent at OISE were of considerable importance in helping me clarify the political vision presented in Part I. I still miss our table at the Duke of York. In addition, Bob Morgan, Shehla Burney, Don Dippo, Rodrigo Vera, Magda Lewis, Ursula Kelly, Bluma Litner, Amy Rossiter, Anne Louise Brookes, and Ann Dean contributed much to the constant re-thinking of my project. This book in no small way is also the product of the ongoing discussion and critique provided, during the last three years, by a remarkable group of students at OISE. They have supported and challenged me throughout our nonstop work together. In particular, I wish to acknowledge and thank Arleen Schenke, Alastair Pennycook, Bonny Peirce, Helen Harper, and Alice Pitt, who have made major contributions to the development of this text. My work has also been considerably enhanced by discussions with Naomi Norquay, Judith Robertson, Helen Simson, Sharon Rosenberg, Michael Bach, Handel Wright, Joe Binger, Suzanne Carroll, Pat Riviere, and Jerome Meharchand.

I hope my words will not be read as those of "a critical theorist" or "critical pedagogue," imprisoning them within the barbed wire of academic fashion. Such constructions create ideological warrants for professorial authority that continue to reproduce the oppressive structures of university life. The question really is simple. Does the partial perspective presented here help in fashioning educational practices that enable people to alter the terms on which their lives are lived in favor of a life-sustaining, just, and compassionate community?

I

Engaging the Project

1

On Disruptive Daydreams

The future will of course have to be struggled for. It cannot be willed into place. But nonetheless we still have to dream and to know in what direction to desire.

Dick Hebdige, "Some Sons and Their Fathers"[1]

The desire to bring about a freer, less alienating society has inspired many actions, but the ability to imagine such a society to begin with, and then to see how it can emerge out of the present, must be there first. It is this that gives meaning to the slogan scribbled on Paris walls by the revolutionaries in May 1968—*Prenez vos rêves pour la realité.*—Take your dreams for reality.

Susan Crean and Marcel Rioux, *Two Nations*[2]

Wishes do nothing. In wishing there is not yet the dimension of activity. The wishful dream with no possibility for action is self-consuming. It is an impoverished dream, merely a diversion that provides a "temporary release from routine and character [but] never threatens to unravel them because it never occupies their home ground of everyday vision, community, and work."[3]

But hope, hope is something else.[4] Hope is the acknowledgment of more openness in a situation than the situation easily reveals; openness above all to possibilities for human attachments, expressions, and assertions. The hopeful person does not merely envisage this possibility as a wish; the hopeful person acts upon it now by loosening and refusing the hold that taken-for-granted realities and routines have over imagination.

Thus hope is different from the wish in that it is a predisposition to action rather than merely a foretaste of pleasure. It grows from commitment to responsibility and not from a passive yearning for ultimate peace and resolution. As a particular crystallization of desire, hope is constituted in the need to imagine an alternative human world and to imagine it in a way that enables one to act in the present as if this alternative had already begun to emerge.

Yet it seems lives are often filled more with wishes than with hope. Although hope has become an urgent necessity, few can sustain the dream of a better future beyond the fervent wish. The unprecedented threat to the life-sustaining biosphere, massive global armament, constant widespread economic and social dislocations, and mediated displays of pain, hunger, and cruelty are more than enough to try one's sanity. To make matters worse, political cynicism has become prevalent, while despair increases over the very possibility of finding the communality needed to address the problems of collective survival.

What could it mean to hope under such conditions? What hopeful imagination might inform the struggle for a better future and assist one to act as if a vision of that which is not yet has already begun to emerge? It is with such questions that I begin; tentatively, constantly astonished by my ignorance and partiality, but with just enough courage and chutzpah to think my words might be helpful. Trying to write beyond the assignment of language to a medium of personal expression, I have been cognizant that writing "does not translate a reality outside itself but, more precisely, allows the emergence of a new reality."[5] Neither research report nor policy analysis, my writing avoids detailed critique of existing forms of pedagogy. Yet I have maintained a critical intent. As an effort to think through an integrated conception of theory and practice that departs from much that is conventional in North American education, this text is meant to serve a communicative *and* critical function. Thus I have attempted, in departing from the taken-for-granted language of practice, to mark—through a different lexicon and syntax—all-too-familiar and unchallenged aspects of educational thought.

But my aspirations really do run along different lines. Critique is not the project. Rather, this book is an attempt to encourage and articulate a framework that might aid in constructing educational practices that both express and engender hope. My intent is to help to construct a pedagogy of possibility, one that works for the reconstruction of social imagination in the service of human freedom. My "point of practice" for this effort is schooling. Schools indeed, are just one historically constituted form of education among many. Thus, while I begin my argument in the context of schooling, I will argue for the extension of the notion of a pedagogy of possibility to a wide variety of sites of cultural practice.

In beginning with schooling, I begin in what to me is a familiar place.

Most of my work in education has been with students and teachers in schools; they have struggled to find innovative and progressive forms of pedagogy, and it is for and with them that I am attempting to offer a critical yet constructive way of reconstituting educational practice. So it is that I do mean my words for others. Yet how I mean them is of crucial significance. While I will be putting questions of social transformation on the agenda, I do so with the insistence that there be no more attempts at totalizing revolutions. Whether in efforts to impose a regional educational policy or a comprehensive national social and economic order, the finitude of "knowledge from above" is inadequate to the task of hope.[6] This is as much a self-reflexive statement as it is a perspective on the practice of others. In my twenty years of teaching within a school of education, I have come to understand the politics of my *material* location. That is, I and my words are often consigned to that very category, "knowledge from above." This is a distressing committal, constructed within a historically constituted division of labor, which, among other things, has been based on what has become a pernicious division between the expert and the ignorant. To transform this relation will require structural changes; an assertion that does not at all diminish the work of those in both schools and universities who have been striving to reconstitute what such a relation might mean.[7] But for me now, about to offer some thoughts on the relation between pedagogy and social transformation, how might I ameliorate the effects of such a consignment?

I want to attempt such a transfiguration, however partial, by here, early in this text, putting myself into the picture. I do this not as a confession of assumptions nor an attempt to initiate the critical reflexivity that autobiographical writing can valuably produce,[8] but in an effort to fully make present the situated, embodied character of what I have written, even when such writing is at times, abstract and impersonal. In other words, I wish to emphasize how what I have to say is partial in order to stress the seriousness with which I desire my writing to be relationally engaged.

But, for such a purpose, what might it mean to put myself into the picture? An Askenazi Jew, white, male, 48-year-old, heterosexual, able-bodied, university professor and parent, born in New York, working and living in southern Ontario for the last twenty years—certainly such reductive categories will not do. In fact, these categories only open up questions about the politics of my location rather than definitively answer them. More must be said, but without effacing what these categories do signal, the privilege and partiality of my position within the various interlocking relations of power that etch what Philip Corrigan[9] has defined as "the figure in dominance"; the one who has been setting the terms of North American life for the last 300 years.

What else must be said is complex, and I can only barely outline here what I hope is drawn more fully throughout this book. As best as I can tell, much of what I have written stands at the intersection of four lived experiences: (1) my commitment and investment in addressing my work from within a continuing attempt to understand what it means for me to be a Jew; (2) the pervasive contradiction of living every day in a society that, though founded on the aspirations of freedom and democracy, continues to reproduce forms of dominance and injustice; (3) the success and failures I have had in my own teaching as I tried to find ways of helping people address how possibility can be expanded in their lives and in the community in which we jointly live, and (4) the need to answer the friends, students, and colleagues who keep challenging me with the question of the practical significance of my theoretical commitments, particularly in regard to their meaning for educational practice. By no means a seamless web, these experiences have been knotted together in such a way that they rub against the grain of my participation in existing relations of domination. Such rubbing cannot, of course, eliminate this participation, but it can highlight the rough spots, the points of my own contradictions. If I can then see these, I know where there is work yet to be done; if you can see them, perhaps they will help in getting the measure of the limitations of what I have to say and how we might yet struggle toward the future together.

Henry Giroux[10] has argued that there are three basic concerns that any discussion of schooling must address if it is to constitute a "language of possibility." First, it must articulate a moral vision and social ethics that provide a referent for justifying a particular form of pedagogical practice. Second, it must specify a conceptualization that integrates issues of power, politics, and possibility in such a way as to clarify how schools may contribute to the social imagination of particular communities. Third, it must develop a conception of pedagogy that considers the relation between knowing and the production of subjectivity in a way that acknowledges the complexities of both the production of identities, competencies, and desires and the possibilities for a progressive agenda for learning within schools.

The organization of Part I of this book follows from a recognition of the importance of these three basic concerns. In the remainder of these introductory remarks, I begin by briefly outlining how the substance of schooling might be recast in a way that opens up the work of teaching to the problem of reconstituting a progressive moral project for education within aspirations for a broadly based social transformation. Following this, I then offer a social vision on which a pedagogy of possibility might be founded (Chapter 2); show how schools, along with other sites of cultural production, may be understood as integral to the struggle to establish such a vision (Chapter 3); and specify how a practice of pedagogy might be conceptualized that would help establish concrete forms of hopeful practice (Chapter 4). In doing so, I want to stress that the theory I offer is not a universalist abstraction but rather a discursive practice whose political value and interpretive authority is subject to the particular circumstances that will give these ideas their limit and cogency.[11]

DISRUPTIVE DAYDREAMS AND EDUCATIONAL PRACTICE

> Like we were twenty years ago, girls today are dreaming; they dream of a very easy life, a husband, children, a good job. It's so unrealistic that we thought something had to be done.
>
> Marguerite Seguin Desnoyers

> A cheerful and confident child, Cameron enjoys being part of the group. Although he has a tendency to daydream, he is most often attentive at lesson time. At times, he needs to be reminded to concentrate on the task at hand, as he tends to daydream.
>
> Senior kindergarten report card of Cameron Leigh

> Dreams come in the day as well as at night. And both kinds of dreaming are motivated by wishes they seek to fulfill. But daydreams differ from nightdreams; for the daydreaming "I" persists throughout, consciously, privately, envisaging the circumstances and images of a desired, better life. The content of the daydream is not, like that of the nightdream, a journey back into repressed experiences and their associations. It is concerned with as far as possible an unrestricted journey forward, so that instead of reconstituting that which is no longer conscious, the images of that which is not yet can be phantasied into life and into the world.
>
> Ernst Bloch, *A Philosophy of the Future*[12]

The three quotations above express markedly different perspectives on the value of daydreams. For Ernst Bloch, daydreams exist as both a critique and a projected transformation of the existing social and material world. Bloch views daydreams as a radical questioning and a fleeting resonance of freedom; articulating the embodiment of alternative identities and a horizon of possibility. He asserted that daydreams, as "images of that which is not yet . . . phantasied into life and into the world," are a form of anticipatory consciousness, a preemptive transcendence of necessity.

Yet for many teachers daydreams are not something that deserve special celebration. Is there a way in which Bloch's sense of the importance of daydreams can contribute to the reconstruction of what might be considered a progressive pedagogy? First of all, it is important to acknowledge that it is not very surprising that educators often suggest that the daydreams of youth must be suppressed or displaced. As guardians of the future, teachers commonly view youthful daydreams as superficial, unrealistic, and a waste of time; manufactured "illusions" that seem to suppress an ability for students to "understand things as they really are." In this view, daydreams are more often understood as wishful rather than hopeful, degenerating into an ever frustrated yearning that, convinced of its own futility, becomes a reverie of escape rather than a vehicle of transformation.[13]

Furthermore, those of us struggling to help transform oppressive and exploitative social relations may find ourselves appalled and depressed by the frequent narrowness of the forms of "better life" expressed in daydreams. At times we fail to remember that such dreams do not simply appear, but rather are the representational effects of the lives of people situated in social relations that complexly structure both desires and ways of making sense. Thus daydreams constituted on the grounds of oppressive social relations often seem to stand as the wish to reverse the positions of oppression rather than transform oppressive relationships. From this perspective the radical potential Bloch saw in phantasies of anticipation seems naively romantic.[14]

Yet in order to grasp the sense in which Bloch celebrated daydreams, perhaps one should not focus initially on the specific content of dreams. For it is not just the "unreality" or "politically regressive" character of youthful fantasies that worry us, but as well the circumstance and implication of their appearance. The "wild dreams" of sexuality, fashion, politics, language, art, and modes of everyday survival can be tolerated (even in their concrete manifestations) as long as they are contained (dreamt and then forgotten) beyond the borders of time and space allotted to "responsible preparation for adult life and the real world." However, when the dreams of youth refuse containment to certain hours of the day, days of the week, and times of the year, they become a threat and are seen as "desire gone amok." In other words, the preference is for daydreams to be something akin to conservation areas and nature reserves that preserve what is wild from everything else, which must be sacrificed to necessity.[15]

What is disrupted by such spillage of desire beyond proscribed borders of time and space are the processes of inscription of the social order upon the person, processes often characterized as the "function" of such institutions of daily life as schools, families, and work places.[16] In other words, disrupted is the very idea of "maturity" as the eventual attainment of an identity and character inscribed by the requirements of taken-for-granted, given social forms. Such disruptive daydreaming takes on an even more decisively radical potential[17] when it displaces desire onto images and activities that refuse the closure of the possibilities provided by existing forms of authority and relations of power. Within this disruptive dream, what is refused is the specification of what and how things are to be done and what one's responsibilities are within existing social arrangements and taken-for-granted assumptions and epistemologies. Indeed such dreaming can at times provide a glimpse of the common needs that are systematically denied by the forms that demand our loyalty and allegiance.[18]

It is here, then, within this conception of disruptive daydreaming, that perhaps we can begin to grasp what Bloch meant when he said that it is with dreams that we enter the "empire of hope." For disruptive daydreams are ironically hopeful in their refusal of necessity, or rather in their understanding of and refusal of that which is constituted as necessity. Indeed, such a refusal can be seen as the *beginning* of hope. In this sense disruptive daydreams are fragments of existence within which the necessity of the given historical forms of our daily lives are refused as we embody momentarily alternative identities.

In my view, conceptualizing daydreams in this way provides an initial sense of what the project of a truly progressive education could be. Thus I begin, with the assertion that education and disruptive daydreaming share a common project: the production of hopeful images. That is, the production of "images of that which is not yet" that provoke people to consider, and inform them in considering, what would have to be done for things to be otherwise. Agreement on such a basic assertion should not be too difficult to obtain. In these still modern times there remains a forward-pressing ethos of betterment that, while shaken and no longer a guarantee, has not been abandoned. Indeed, unless postmodern cynicism has totally overtaken the polis or the spirit of *Koheleth* [Ecclesiastes][19] has enveloped our hearts and minds, communities still must allocate a portion of their efforts toward developing a hopeful perspective on the future. For without a perspective on the future, conceivable as a desired and possible future, there can be neither human venture nor possibility.

Community efforts at developing hopeful perspectives are commonly located within a variety of sites and forms of education. Schools, as one of the possible sites of education within a community, are clearly implicated in such efforts. In this respect any school curriculum and its supporting pedagogy presuppose some process within which possible visions of one's relation to a future social and material world can be organized and legitimated. Here, then, I come to the key questions. What will be the substance of this process, and how is it going to be determined? Who is going to organize for whom and how, a schooling practice in the name of what version of one's relation to a social and material future?

These are not just practical problems but as well moral and political ones, and they are posed within a field of already-existing social forms and moralities. Indeed, the analysis of such forms and moralities as provided within state schooling is no cause for optimism. As Corrigan[20] has succinctly argued, state forms such as schooling normalize through a process that differentiates those who "get it right" from those who do not. This produces, on terms set by a limited range of state-legitimated forms, an internal homogenization of those who "succeed." Understanding schooling within such a frame means grasping the ways (complex and contradictory) in which forms of power and legitimation in schools structure a field of possibilities and regulate actual behaviors, including thought, speech, image, style, and action. In this process of regulation, particular identities, knowledge, interests, forms of sociality, needs, modes of embodiment, and expressivity are normalized and privileged. Those who either fail or refuse to acquire and display the required capacities are marked and mapped as simultaneously different and disadvantaged, executing a scarring and placing of bodies (frequently as acts of classism, racism, and sexism) in reconstituted relations of social inequality.

This by now is a well-told story for those of us who have been reading, for the last two decades, the literature on the sociology of education. The moral is, as long as schools require the standardization (for evaluation and grading purposes) of forms of knowledge and the proper manner of their expression, they will continue to function as sorting machines caught up in forms of regulation that reproduce existing relations of inequality and serve the interests of a white patriarchial capitalism. In this light, schools seem about the last place where one might realistically consider a pedagogy of possibility.

While I do not wish to contest the outlines of this rather bleak picture nor diminish the need for structural change, this view of schools cedes too much. The current hegemony over how schooling is to be done remains a project, not an accomplishment. Within the spaces that do exist in certain schools, courses of study, and classrooms, this hegemony has been and is being contested by students, teachers, and parents who remain genuinely hopeful that pedagogies which support social transformation can be realized. This book is dedicated to the recognition and good use of such places. It is also predicated on the need for and the possibility of "a long revolution" through questions of pedagogy, questions of what and how we teach in relation to how people learn and the limits and consequences (that we are now relearning) of what can be known by whom. I have grown deeply pessimistic about change at *solely* the level of policy and school organization. It is time to return to the core, approaching the problem from inside out, revising our pedagogies and then insisting on the changes needed to expand them, constructing administratively what is demanded educationally.

In the next three chapters I undertake to clarify the framework of a critical pedagogy that has been evolving within the interconnection of my ethical and political commitments and the teaching, curriculum writing, and research that have comprised my professional responsibilities over the last twenty years. This has entailed a movement away from a pedagogy based on generalized truth claims set in opposition to ruling hegemonies as well as pedagogical forms reliant on teaching how to "deconstruct" the ideological character of school knowledge and modes of knowing in everyday life. As will become evident, I am striving to clarify the outlines of an educational practice based on the partial, situated, embodied (and therefore responsible) character of knowing and the hopeful ethos of a critical, responsive imagination. For me, this project begins with a value-based social analysis and a particular ethically informed perspective on the future, issues which are the starting place for any discussion of a progressive pedagogy. For this reason I shall first turn to a consideration of what notion of "moral practice" might provide the justification for what I am calling a "pedagogy of possibility."

NOTES

1. Dick Hebdige, "Some Sons and Their Fathers," *Border/lines*, no. 11, Spring 1988, p. 35.

2. Susan Crean and Marcel Rioux, *Two Nations* (Toronto: James Lorimer, 1983), p. 6.

3. Roberto Mangabeira Unger, *Passion* (New York: Free Press, 1984), p. 112.

4. My understanding of "hope" is derived from the writings of Ernst Bloch. See particularly *The Principle of Hope*, vol. 1 (Cambridge, Mass.: MIT Press, 1986); Roberto Mangabeira Unger, *Passion: An Essay on Personality* (New York: Free Press, 1984), pp. 244–47); and David Hartman, *A Living Covenant: The Innovative Spirit in Traditional Judaism* (New York: Free Press, 1985).

5. Trinh Minh-ha, *Woman Native Other* (Bloomington: Indiana University Press, 1989), p. 22.

6. What is being called into question here is the dream of a social and educational science that will provide state authorities with information and procedures with which to direct the current of human affairs. In reference to the specific focus at hand, I think those of us attempting to create a critical pedagogy, while at the same time making its practical referents clear, must refuse to constitute it as a "method" that can be packaged and distributed.

7. See, for example, Wilfrid Carr and Stephen Kemmis, *Becoming Critical* (Philadelphia: Falmer, 1986).

8. A rich presentation of the intersection of the politics of location with the practice of social analysis, initiating important questions of research ethics, can be found in Valerie Walkerdine, "Video Re-Play," in Victor Burgin, Cora Kaplan, and James Donald, eds., *Formations of Fantasy* (London: Methuen, 1986).

9. Philip Corrigan "In/forming Schooling," in David Livingstone et al. *Critical Pedagogy and Cultural Power* (Toronto: Garamond, 1987), pp. 17–40; Philip Corrigan "Race/Ethnicity/Gender/Culture: Embodying Differences Educationally," in Jon Young, ed., *Breaking the Mosaic* (Toronto: Garamond, 1987).

10. Henry A. Giroux, *Schooling and the Struggle for Public Life: Critical Pedagogy in the Modern Age* (Minneapolis: University of Minnesota Press, 1988).

11. Bruce Robbins, "The Politics of Theory," *Social Text*, no. 18, Winter 1987–88, pp. 3–18.

12. Marguerite Seguin Desnoys spoke as head of the organizing committee of the International Conference on the Status of Girls in Montreal, 1985; she is quoted in the *Toronto Globe and Mail,* October 30, 1985, p. A18. The Ernst Bloch quotation is from *A Philosophy of the Future* (New York: Herder and Herder), p. 86.

13. Roberto Mangabeira Unger, *Passion,* p. 245.

14. Frigga Haug, "Daydreams," *New Left Review,* no. 162, March–April 1987, pp. 51–66.

15. Ernst Bloch, *The Principle of Hope,* vol. 1, pp. 77–113; Gary Peller, in "Reason and the Mob: The Politics of Representation," *Tikkun* 2, no. 3 (July–August 1987): 28–32.

16. Such processes are an attempt to found a social identity on a regulated unity by forms of normalization. Amid such practices dreaming can be a mode of testing the possibility of denied selves, capacities, and identities. See Roger White and David Brockington, *Tales out of School: Consumers' Views of British Education* (London: Routledge and Kegan Paul, 1983); Valerie Walkerdine, "On the Regulation of Speaking and Silence: Subjectivity, Class and Gender" in Carolyn Steedman, Cathy Urwin and Valerie Walkerdine, eds., *Language, Gender and Childhood* (London: Routledge and Kegan Paul, 1985).

17. But for an important critique of that potential, see Barbara Ehrenreich's *Hearts of Men: American Dreams and the Flight from Commitment* (New York: Anchor Press, 1983).

18. Ella Rowe, "Desire and Popular Culture: The Ego Ideal and Its Influence in the Production of Subjectivity," unpublished paper, Ontario Institute for Studies in Education; Stanley Aronowitz, "On Narcissism," in *The Crisis in Historical Materialism,* 1st ed. (New York: Praeger, 1981).

19. The spirit of *Koheleth* suggests the eternal fleetingness of all things and the inevitable motification of nature to which all human projects are subject. This renders effort as vanity since ultimately, "there is no profit under the sun." See, for example, Ecclesiastes 1:1–12 *The Holy Scriptures: According to the Masoretic Text,* vol. 2, p. 1968 (Philadelphia: Jewish Publication Society, 1955).

20. Philip Corrigan, *Social Forms/Human Capacities: Essays in Authority and Difference* (London: Routledge, 1990).

2

The Horizon of Possibility

A language of possibility does not have to dissolve into a reified utopi-
anism, instead it can be developed as a precondition for nourishing
convictions that summon up the courage to imagine a different and
more just world and to struggle for it.

Henry Giroux, "Rethinking the Boundaries of Educational
Discourse: Modernism, Postmodernism, and Feminism"[1]

The idiom of possibility stands empty. Accused of meaningless rhetoric,
it can only be rescued from the dismissal of convention and cynicism by
developing its substance, sketching both its form and therefore its limits.
This is not a task to be completed by one person. As I attempt to clarify
for myself the question of what might be an adequate notion of education as a moral practice, I am at the same time seeking to join with others
in what must be a collective and democratic venture.

During the 1980s, both in Canada and the United States, there was a
revival of the question of whether "creation theory" ought to be introduced into curricula concerning the genesis of human life. This revival
included a renewed interest in Jerome Lawrence and Robert Lee's well-
known drama *Inherit the Wind*. Written as a play (also produced twice as
a film, first with Spencer Tracy and Fredric March and more recently
with Kirk Douglas and Jason Robards), *Inherit the Wind* is loosely based
on the famous Scopes trial, which took place in Tennessee in July of
1925. In the play a teacher, Bert Cates, who has introduced the theories
of Charles Darwin to his class, is accused of breaking a state law forbid-

ding the teaching of evolution. Early in the play his girlfriend, Rachel, daughter of the local minister, expresses her ambivalent loyalty to Bert. Addressing a reporter sent by a metropolitan newspaper that is supporting Bert's defense, she says:

You make it sound as if Bert is a hero. I'd like to think that, but I can't. A schoolteacher is a public servant: I think he [*sic*] should do what the law and the school board want him to. If the superintendent says, "Miss Brown, you're to teach from Whitley's *Second Reader,*" I don't feel I have to give him an argument.[2]

Here Rachel enunciates a version of teacher responsibility, one that requires the acceptance, as given, of existing forms of bureaucratic rationality. It is a response that defines one point of an antithetical relation considerably sharpened in the first film version of the play. In a scene between Cates and his lawyer, Henry Drummond, Cates is expressing second thoughts over his decision to introduce theories of evolution to his students. After several moments of discussion Drummond issues a scene-concluding persuasive rejoinder, rhetorically asking Cates, "Are you a civil servant or a servant of the truth?"

Drummond's question to Cates is not a bad place to begin an attempt to define a desirable moral practice and its associated sense of teacher responsibility. Drummond repositions the issue of teacher responsibility in a discourse that poses the question of the relation of teaching practice to proposed notions of a desirable future human community. More concretely, implied in Drummond's ironic query is the underlying assertion that a desirable future community requires that a teacher be responsible to the truth, rather than a bureaucratic authority constituted as the arbiter of truth. While I find neither of these options satisfactory, at least Drummond's question helps define the problem. Without articulating a vision of how one's practices might relate to a vision for the future and without seriously taking up the question of how a pedagogy is constituted as a form of moral practice, any talk of teaching as a responsible and intellectual practice becomes an empty and abstract form.[3] The result would be a profession robbed of the light in which it would be capable of interpreting its practice as desirable. To avoid this desolate pragmatism, what is required is a purposeful vision that can provide the ethical grounds for the determination of pedagogical practice.

As I stressed in Chapter 1, I see education implicated in the production of "that which is not yet," presupposing a vision of the future in its introduction to, preparation for, and legitimation of particular forms of social life. In this sense a curriculum and the teaching practices that support it are a version of a dream of the future for ourselves, our children, and our communities. It is axiomatic that such dreams are never neutral. As teachers (particularly in state schools that serve a diversity of publics) we are always implicated in organizing the future for others and hence our actions always have a moral and political dimension.[4] But to make such statements is barely to begin the core of a discussion that puts on the agenda the warrant by which one's pedagogy is to be justified and sanctioned.[5] To suggest that education is a moral and political enterprise raises at least two central questions that must enter into deliberations as to how one should formulate one's responsibilities as a teacher. The first of these is what the moral basis of one's practice should be; that is, what are the desired versions of a future human community implied in the pedagogy in which one is implicated?[6] The second is, given our own moral commitments, how should we relate to other people who also have a stake and a claim in articulating future communal possibilities?

With these questions in mind, I now wish to return to Henry Drummond's rhetoric and consider the options for teaching he provides: that one is either a civil servant or a servant of the truth. The stance of a civil servant clearly has its defenders. This position suggests that teachers should define their practice in relation to "the truth" as arbitrated by others, specifically, legally constituted authorities. Required is the recognition that one's responsibility is to support the organization of which one is a part, suppressing personal views, interests, and preferences. The moral basis for practice within this stance becomes the ideal of organizational discipline. Discipline becomes a virtue and defines, in Max Weber's words, the honor of the civil servant.

The honor of the civil servant is vested in his [sic] ability to execute conscientiously the order of superior authorities, exactly as if the order agreed with his own conviction. This holds even if the order seems wrong to him and if, despite the civil servant's remonstrances, the authority insists on the order. This kind of behavior means for a civil servant "moral discipline and self denial in the highest sense."[7]

I am not quoting Weber here in any descriptive sense, asserting that all teachers function as civil servants. Rather, I am simply recognizing that even though teaching is an indeterminate and contingent task and can never be reduced to a bureaucratic set of rules, there is often considerable pressure on teachers to define the moral basis of their practice as fulfilling the mandate and guidelines of school authorities. While this may be a viable pragmatic response to the necessity of keeping one's job, and understandable as a response to inadequate school management or working conditions, I do not think it can stand as a moral basis of teaching practice. One reason is that it releases a teacher from pedagogical responsibility, transferring it to the "authorities." This transfer places teachers so that they can claim not to be in a position (nor is it their position) to judge the moral adequacy of their own practice. An extremely dangerous position, whose logic leads to Auschwitz, it is dependent on a scientism that constitutes teaching within methodologies that rob the educative relation of its complexity.[8]

But now I come to the second part of Drummond's question. I have deep reservations about teaching in the name of the truth. If the truth that is being referred to here is a transcendent one, a story that loses track of its mediations and thus the very possibility that someone might be held responsible for its determinations,[9] then I wish to part company with those who claim it as a ground for their practice. I do not think it possible to organize a set of teaching responsibilities and practices on a principle that stands outside human history (i.e., within a neutral universe of reason beyond the particularities of time and space).[10] This is not meant simply as a corrective to some philosophical mistake. As Gary Peller[11] states,

To some . . . the assertion that there is no neutral, authoritative, and apolitical interpretation of social life available sounds like a message of hopelessness and nihilism . . . this reaction is rooted in a conviction that the only kind of knowledge worth having is a kind of knowledge that can be elevated above social life and social history, that can be immunized from bias or change.

[Rather] the message of social construction and social contingency is one of hope. It is hopeful because it also suggests that there is no objective necessity or rational principle to justify the way things are, to legitimate the hierarchies and status quo distribution of wealth, power, prestige, and freedom.

As Donna Haraway asserts, this must not be taken as an immaculate relativism, "a way of being nowhere while claiming to be everywhere equally."[12] Nor should the introduction of this radical epistemological contingency be understood as ushering in an era of pluralism that absorbs all argument, rendering questions of responsibility and critical inquiry irrelevant.[13] While I am suggesting that the objectivity of knowing must be reconstructed to emphasize the partial, embodied, and therefore limited character of knowledge claims,[14] more is at stake than a self-critical partiality. What must be stressed is that this position *initiates* rather than closes off the problem of responsibility. That is, it requires that one hold open for assessment those practices which generate one's claim to knowledge. Thus while there may be no epistemological limit, no finally decidable relationship between perception and reality, I concur with Richard Kearney that we must affirm ethical limits. As Kearney emphasizes, "we reach a point in the endless spiral of undecidability where each one of us is obliged to make an ethical and political decision, to say *here I stand*. (Or, at the level of collective responsibility, *here we stand*.)"[15] In a prospective human community whose project is to secure fundamental human dignity (a project I will discuss more fully in a moment), this means working from an ethical imagination constituted within the fullness of a relation to another as an other. In this relation another is not reducible to our ability to know her or him. Rather, it requires a particular disposition, rendered in biblical text as "panim-el-panim," meeting the other "face-to-face." Without surrendering the obligation to hold the other accountable for diminishing the possibility of human dignity, the disposition of "face-to-face" requires an ethical response on our part to confront practices that diminish the dignity of the particularity of the other.

Given such a position, what is required is a political project from which one is able to assess and pursue knowledge forms in relation to their power to contest axes of material and symbolic violence. Power is not just abusive through the application of force nor within sets of relations that mystify, distort, and make false. Perhaps the more dangerous (more invisible) impact of power is its positive relation to truth; that is, in the "truth effects" it produces.[16] This is a matter of which sets of practices make or produce social facts; which technology of meaning-making practices establishes the existence of particular notions of what is true and right. Whether in education, work, sexuality, religious life, or in the provision of food and shelter, one must examine the extent to which dominant knowledge forms and ways of knowing are productive of the exploitation and the constriction of human capacities.

Here I am getting closer to the crux of the matter. No longer persuaded by innocent objectivities, as Dick Hebdige says, we still have to know "in what direction to desire." This, of course, is a question of value. In addressing this question, I begin with the rather basic assertion that educational practice should participate in a social transformation that is aimed at securing fundamental human dignity and radically reducing the limits on expression and achievement imposed by physical and symbolic violence. What constitutes human dignity is of course a long-debated question within social philosophy and political theory. My purpose here will not be to review and discuss this debate but rather to sketch the ways in which I as an educator am trying to come to grips with the necessity for me to respond to this question. This, then, is not an abstract philosophical question but one required by a practice that claims to be a critical pedagogy. How, then, can this be made more concrete?

I am working from the assumption that education is but one initiative in relation to the process of self-formation, the means through which people attempt to constitute themselves as subjects of their own experience. Recognizing both the discrete and interactive importance of sites such as one's family, various forms of popular media, the courts, formal and informal youth groups, sports organizations, and religious institutions, for teachers the question remains one of what relation can and should education have to the struggles of young people as they attempt to develop a sense of agency in their lives. In relation to the sites just mentioned, schools are similar in that they are places where a sense of what may be possible and desirable for both oneself and others is informed and contested. This includes a mobile and at times contradictory understanding of one's identity, place, and worth. This process is provoked through practices that organize and disorganize, regulate, and legitimate the truth value of knowledge claims, socially valued ways of knowing and communicating, what counts as "reasonable" objects and expressions of interest, and acceptable and desirable forms of embodiment. As a teacher, one is implicated in such practices, and thus, in principle, what one does matters a great deal. Thus the importance of the question, on what set of premises should I make pedagogical decisions?

The basic premise on which most North American education is currently based takes as the focus of educational practice the person as an autonomous being with multiple potential. The task of education is to help that person realize as much of his or her potential as possible. This is often romantically sloganized as helping one "be all that one can be."[17] This approach, which I will here label "self-realization," claims justification in the enhancement of human dignity and an aspiration to social pluralism. One of the most sophisticated and interesting expositions of the complexities of this position is outlined by Israel Scheffler.[18] Developed in the context of Harvard's Project on Human Potential, Scheffler presents an approach that does not assume that human potential is fixed nor that every potential one has is desirable in relation to community values. Nor does he assume that all potentials are compatible with one another, a view that alleviates the necessity of prioritization. Further, Scheffler views the concept of potential itself as multiple and constituted by the capacity, propensity, and capability for acquisition of particular knowledge and skills; each of which can be enhanced by changes in both individuals and the learning situations they are part of.

Yet I find this position unsatisfactory as a basic premise for pedagogical practice, unable to address what I consider crucial issues for the enhancement of human dignity and the reduction of physical and symbolic violence. The problem is in the way the self-realization approach structures a concept of possibility. As a normative framework, self-realization presumes a person in a social environment confronted with individual choice regarding her or his life opportunities. This choice is assumed to be an open structure of possibility through which one makes what one wants of oneself, assuming the necessary knowledge and skills for independent action have been acquired. When forms of discrimination are seen to unjustly limit one's options, then community representatives are required to intervene to equalize the opportunity to choose and act, ensuring the "possibility" that is inherent in the project of self-realization can be pursued. Here then, possibility is defined in relation to the choices an individual can make from within a given opportunity structure.

As I will try to show, my definition of possibility differs in that I see it as constituted within a structured field of normalized forms for the realization of communication and action.[19] What is highlighted here, but minimized within the self-realization position, is the structured character of private choice. Any minimization of this structuring process suppresses the ways in which a person's "opportunity set" is itself given in reference to regulated social forms. This means that if education is to be a resource for a process through which individuals attempt to become subjects of their own experience, pedagogical practice must find ways of addressing not only the enhancement of an individual's potential for the acquisition of skills and knowledge but as well the development of resources within which people can begin to challenge and transform those relations which structure the available opportunities from which to choose.

This point is perhaps best made by sketching out an alternative position. In doing so, I will retain a partial position and reflect my location within various tensions that constitute the terrain of my life. These range from embracing the promise of possibility inherent in modernism, the rejection of totalizing narratives for defining an emancipatory project, a devotion and commitment to a form of Jewish covenantial ethics, and a recognition of the "return of the real" in the ecological crisis that now confronts us all. As fragmented as this terrain is, I have taken Michael Walzer's advice that "it is better to tell stories than remain silent even though there is no definitive and best story . . . no last story that once told, would leave all future storytellers without employment."[20]

POSSIBILITY DEFINED AND PURSUED

> Advice given to youth by Canadian Olympic Canoeist: "Define your dream and go for it. If you really try, you can be anything you want . . . Canada's a land of true possibility."[21]

In schools, at home, and through the media such advice is given day after day, week after week. This message is not only intended to provide hope but to confirm a pride in our country's modernity; as a place where one's fate is no longer to be determined by such ascriptive characteristics as one's class, sex, race, ethnicity, or region of origin. Though it expresses one sense of what might be meant by a just society, as a message of hope the statement bears a false promise, capable of creating wishes and not the radical action that hope must engender.

Hope requires something more. It requires understanding how the prospect of possibility is situated within the everyday forms and relations that define its terms. To avoid being reduced to rhetoric, the question of possibility must be approached concretely and historically, as a notion derived from what Philip Corrigan[22] has called particular constellations of "human capacities/social forms." More explicitly, possibility is defined as the ways of speaking, writing, imaging, acting and embodying which, as a result of a particular constellation of capacities/forms, are materially possible and receive "coercive encouragement" as a result of being marked as neither deviant, pathological, inappropriate, unacceptable, or abnormal.

To develop an understanding of what is involved here, I want to begin with a quote from Raymond Williams.

We are born into a social situation, into social relationships, into a family, all of which have formed what we can later abstract as ourselves, as individuals. Much of this formation occurs before we can be conscious of any individuality. Indeed the consciousness of individuality is often the consciousness of all those elements of our formation, yet this can never be complete. The alignments are so deep. They are our normal ways of living in the world, our normal ways of seeing the world. Of course we may become intellectually aware that they are not normal in the sense that they are universal. We come to recognize that other people live differently, were born into different social relationships, see the world differently. Yet still, at certain deep levels . . . our actual alignment is so inseparable from the constitution of our own individuality that to separate them is quite artificial.[23]

What Williams is pointing at is the normalization of certain ways of doing things that become the taken for granted, "goes-without-saying" options for constituting daily life. But more than this, he is emphasizing that what is drawn from experience is a particular version of identity and possibility which itself constitutes what a person considers viable choices within the spheres of everyday life. In his extensive elaboration of these issues Corrigan discusses how such forms of regulation may be understood to be a central dimension of social forms. For Corrigan, social forms can be defined as "the expected set of [connected] ways in which actions have to be done to be properly accomplished."[24] Such forms set limits on the range of ways practices might acceptably be done and thus convey a sense of value or "rightness" about particular ways of doing things. In their "coercive encouragement" such forms display a dual sense of power in that they both inhibit and enable different sets of practices. Thus such forms are what constitute the concrete realities within and against which people organize and order the way they live their lives.

As a simple example, consider the institutional practice of schooling itself as a social form. The delimiting features of regulated time, space, and text that constitute state-provided schooling are but one in a range of possible ways in which a person might come to learn about the world and develop proficiencies for acting within it. Furthermore, within the space of schooling there exists a variety of locations (classrooms, halls, playgrounds, lunchrooms) with their own sets of constitutive forms for carrying out ways of communicating and acting. Of course not everyone will communicate or act within the set of options these forms specify as acceptable. Such "deviations" by themselves, whether as challenge, withdrawal, or lack of capability, do not undermine the form; judged as deviations they only reproduce it. Further parallel examples could be given in reference to a variety of spheres of everyday life. For example, "the heterosexual family" designates forms that specify acceptable ways of expressing intimacy and conjugality. "The business world" often refers to forms for accomplishing productive work and daily renewal of life set within the terms supplied by the logic of capitalism and a hierarchical exchange relation between a purchaser and supplier of labor.

What such examples stress is that it makes little sense to consider the notion of social forms abstractly, outside the context of history. Any discussion of social forms must take into account that some forms have come to constitute the legitimate, the "usual," the standard, the normal—marginalizing other forms in and through their difference. There is a rich and expanding literature that is providing a picture of how, within concrete historical circumstances, specific social forms have gained and maintained a dominance through legal, moral, and economic regulatory practices.[25] Such historical studies are important in continuing to emphasize that existing, taken-for-granted "ways of life" are value-laden human constructions and thus open to critique and revision.

But it is not a detailed discussion of social forms that I want to introduce here. Rather, for my purposes, what I mean to emphasize about social forms is the way they set the terms of the expression of human capacities. That is, the range of capacities that are affirmed, encouraged, and supported in any given concrete context is dependent on the substance and organization of the practices that define a social form. This observation is the key to a restructuring of the concept of possibility. In this light, possibility refers not to what an individual may choose to do but rather those options available in a situation when one simultaneously takes into account both the "coercive encouragement" of particular forms and the limited range of capacities those forms encourage. This means that there can be no "fully realized" person beyond and outside the history within which the forms of everyday life have been constructed. Hence the reason for stressing the phrase "social forms/human capacities." This expression is intended to be understood as an indissoluble relation, a particular dynamic constellation of enablement and constraint that, in any given configuration, defines the terms of what will count as possibility in a situation.

Thought of in this way, the prospect of possibility (and how it informs who and what we are) is inevitably caught up in a central historical contradiction. This is a contradiction between the openness of human capacities that we promote in a free society and the social forms that are present and set the terms on which much of life is to be lived.[26] Set within the frame of freedom as a desirable social good, such a contradiction appears inevitable. However, what is important to recognize is that its specific terms are, in principle, indeterminate. In other words, there is "flex" in this relation. Thus the degree and character of the contradiction between human capacities and social forms is dependent upon which range of forms have been regulated into dominance and how this has been done; further, it is dependent on how that dominance works to diminish and distort the expression and development of human capacities. The issue is not that social forms per se are a problem; abstractly understood, they are not only inevitable but also enabling. Rather, what is at issue is that any given constellation of forms and capacities can be interrogated as to the particular economic and cultural interests it supports and social relations it challenges or reproduces, dimensions that will have a determinate impact on the range of expression of capacities that can be expanded within set limits.

Thus the way one approaches the existence of this contradiction defines for me the frame within which pedagogy as a moral practice can be understood. Taking the stance that human dignity is enhanced under the banner of freedom, I have been trying to develop a pedagogy that would support the endeavor of creating specific social forms that encourage and help make possible the realization of an expanded set of differentiated human capacities rather than denying, diluting, or distorting those capacities. This would be a practice devoted to enhancing possibility through enabling ways of understanding and acting that encourage the transformation of particular relations between social forms and human capacities and hence the expansion of the range of possible social identities people may become. This then is what I refer to as a "project of possibility," using "project" in the particular sense in which it was discussed by Sartre:[27] as an activity determined by both real and present conditions *and* certain conditions still to come, which it is trying to bring into being.

It is in this context that education is, for me, a basic resource for the task of self-constitution. It is also in this context that pedagogy becomes implicated in questions of which knowledge and modes of knowing and learning would be of the most worth in enabling the enhancement of human freedom as the understanding *and* the transformation of necessity. Within such a political imagination, freedom is not a state of being but an openness to a process of possibility. As a practice, freedom is not a passive state but an activity, a method, a mode of living as questioning and changing. Freedom does not lie in discovering or being able to determine who one is, but in rebelling against those ways in which we are already defined, categorized, and classified.[28] Yet this principle cannot be posed as the ultimate good. Dignity and minimization of violence are not guaranteed by the expansion of human capacities. Thus, for me, a pedagogy of possibility as a satisfactory moral practice must include the facility to interrogate both social forms and their possible transformations as to their compatibility with three additional basic principles: [1] securing human diversity, [2] securing compassionate justice, and [3] securing the renewal of life.

POSSIBILITY CONSTRAINED

While my intent in this chapter is to outline my position regarding a possible basis for pedagogy as a moral practice, what I shall not do is present a detailed history and justification of issues surrounding the question of what constitutes an adequate moral vision. However, there are basic tensions recognized in social theory that are inescapable for anyone trying to think through the relation of their practice to a future desirable human community. These tensions have as the root problem the question of the degree to which the freedom of human possibility need be constrained in order to secure and address other dimensions of human dignity. Rather than argue the connection between human dignity and these additional dimensions, I will simply assert it, providing instead a fairly short discussion of each. I recognize that in particular circumstances each of these dimensions might be in tension both with one another and with the premise of the expansion of human possibility. I present no final vision for the resolution of these tensions. The task of struggling toward the future is accomplished through practices that make such tensions concrete and realizing a democratic process for resolving on a contingent basis, what is to be done.

Securing Diversity

In his book *Fragile Freedoms*, Thomas Berger expresses the sentiment I consider inherent in the desire to secure diversity. Diversity is not proposed as a solution to the problem of securing reciprocal equity within a social contract but as a fundamental condition of human dignity. Berger writes:

Under the Charter of Rights, Acadians throughout the Atlantic Provinces, together with French-Canadian minorities in every province, have the right, where numbers warrant, to have their children receive their primary and secondary school instruction in French, out of public funds. This latter provision should not be regarded as a concession made to a minority who have refused to be otherwise appeased. Rather, it should be looked upon as a manifestation of the central idea of Canada, a means whereby we acknowledge the virtues of diversity within our own nation and in the larger world. . . . It is not just a question of minority rights, it is as well a question of the health of the body politic. . . . Everywhere, and within every nation-state, there are peoples who will not be assimilated, and whose fierce wish to retain their common identity is intensifying as industry, technology and communications forge a larger and larger mass culture, extruding diversity. Diversity in Canada may help to ensure the permanence of diversity in the world.[29]

Yet this sentiment has encased within it many conceptual and practical problems, chief among them what will be meant by the form and substance of the notion of diversity. Consider the issue of substance. In securing diversity, what range of communication and action is to be considered? The possible list is clearly extensive and includes modes of speech and writing, ways of forming images, styles of dress, modes of embodiment, forms of friendship, expressions of talent, forms of relations between men and women, ways of interacting with one's environment, ways of utilizing space, orientations to the concept of time, modes of worship, and so on. In taking diversity seriously, one has to come to terms with the implications of such a list posing questions as to the desirability of constraints on any of its categories or on the forms of expression within any given category. Thus in the context of a highly interdependent, technological society one might wish to regulate boundaries as to how people set themselves in relation to time.[30] As another example, one may consider constraining, as incompatible with human dignity, particular modes of relationship between men and women, such as the assumption of male property rights over female bodies.

The form constituted for securing diversity is also a problematic issue. One conventional concept for doing so is the notion of "pluralism." To speak of pluralism abstractly not only begs the question of substance (pluralism of what?) but as well the set of relations within which it is to be defined. Thus for example, pluralism within the logic of capitalism could mean you are on your own to tend your garden, and I am on my own to tend mine. Meanwhile, we will both attempt to sell our produce within a "free market" of both large and small producers. Missing in this notion of pluralism is the importance of a concern for the plight of others and whether independence, as opposed to cooperative efforts, might be more conducive to supporting human dignity.[31] The same question of the set of relations within which pluralism is to be constituted can be further illustrated with another example. A common assumption about pluralism is that it refers to the securing of cultural diversity. How then should one think about what is being secured? Rather than a static construction (as is assumed by certain forms of anthropology and sociology),[32] culture is increasingly being taken as open-ended and consisting of a dialogue among subformations whose dynamics and power relations shift the "whole" as people within a "culture" respond to one another and those "outside" the formation. This view emphasizes that cultures are always in a constant process of transformation, redefinition, and reconceptualization. Yet in formalizing pluralism, there is an administrative tendency to essentialize and encrust certain phenomenological features of a culture as the key expressions through which cultural borders are defined and diversity secured.[33] How will such features get named, and who will be involved in this process? In such a procedure what is to be meant by cultural diversity? Furthermore, in a society of regulating social forms, where difference equals disadvantage, how will pluralism avoid becoming just another name for apartheid? What set of social relations will be able to secure difference without manufacturing disadvantage in the process?

Despite these complexities, diversity remains of prime importance both for the attempt to reduce the violence inherent in certain paternalistic administrative forms and in ensuring the extension of the equality of possibility. In my own work in thinking about diversity, I have come to place increasing importance on how one's body is constituted in social space and what certain relations and spaces do to our bodies. This has meant placing considerable pedagogical importance on ways of enhancing the diversity of modes of communication and physical embodiment in classroom settings. Such diversity can be seen as a set of productive tensions from which students and teachers may engage in a perhaps unresolvable, but nevertheless educationally productive process.[34] Here diversity exists as an opportunity for one to learn something one does not know. To listen to voices "from the margins" or "across the border."[35] This is not a matter of establishing tolerance but of trying to establish a unity that in the words of Holly Near "doesn't always mean agreement (and) doesn't ever mean the same."[36]

Compassionate Justice

Justice is a word that cannot be uttered as a facile gesture. The concept has occupied too many people for too many centuries. It has mingled with legal and theological argument, and it has mingled with human blood. It should be sticky on my tongue, yet I cannot fail to speak of it. I tend to approach justice from the side of compassion, not from the side of the law. Thus the importance of Abraham Joshua Heschel's remark that "justice exists in relation to a person, and is something done by a person. An act of injustice is condemned, not because the law is broken, but because a person has been hurt."[37] This position entails a view of justice as the negation of evil or suffering and is based on the presupposition that one is responsible for securing just action because someone has suffered, is suffering, or may be in risk of suffering. The fact that contingency and possibility of human suffering are intrinsic to human life does not at all absolve one from the requirement of pursuing justice.

However, like the sentiment of diversity, compassionate justice is not without its problematic character. Should all claims to suffering count equally? When striking Ontario physicians claimed to be suffering from a law that prevented them from billing above regulated fees, how was such a claim to be taken in relation to a single parent who would not be able to afford the care her sick child required if the law was repealed? This example emphasizes that questions of justice cannot be addressed outside the way I enter and respond to relations of power and oppression. In other words, for me, ethics are not acted out in the spirit of human isolation but rather mirror the responsibilities of relationship rather than the obligations encumbered within an autonomous self-sufficient moral reason.[38] This statement is based on the assumption that for diversity and dignity to flourish within an ethos of care and cooperation, everyone must be able to live under social and political conditions that enable us to assume the obligations of our mutuality. Securing compassionate justice is, then, not to be reduced to charitable donations (as important as ensuring basic existence is!) but requires both actions and understandings that will help people address the relations of power that limit the expression of agency and possibility in their lives. Thus it is from within this posture of compassionate justice that both Sharon Welch and Henry Giroux have stressed the importance of both present and past suffering as "dangerous memories" that may connect us to the future and one another in a reaffirmation of practical solidarity with all struggles against injustice.[39] It is the resolve to bring about a messianic time when we can dream without oppression as the material grounds for our dreams.

Renewal of Life

Until the last twenty years, eurocentric political theory and social philosophy has been silent on the question of either a desirable or necessary relationship with our environment, the biosphere which sustains all human life. Clearly this is in sharp contrast with other sources of moral practice, which have provided rather explicit orientations.[40] Clearly, redressing this silence has become a matter of survival.[41] If we admit that human dignity cannot be secured without a reverence for life and a commitment to its renewal, we can hardly, in 1992, ignore this issue as a basis for an adequate pedagogical practice.

What seems crucial to the emergent position I am trying to sketch out in this chapter is the recognition of the potential tension such a requirement introduces. Ted Benton has characterized the introduction of arguments regarding natural limits imposed on emancipatory projects as epistemic conservatism.[42] Readers familiar with the history of justification for the structures and practices of sexism, racism, and classism will recognize how arguments regarding the natural biological limits of certain members of the species rendered certain proposals for social transformation as both foolish and naive. Clearly, Freud would not have been impressed with the theologically driven sentiments expressed above in relation to the notion of compassionate justice.[43] As Benton makes clear, "where emancipatory thought parts company with epistemic conservatism is in its insistence that the structures of constraints which frustrate human potential are neither universal nor necessary . . . (thus providing) reasonable grounds for hope." Clearly then, the position I have outlined to this point has to confront the question of what I shall call "the return of the real," the need for social constructionists to recognize a purpose-independent reality of structures and forces that limit the expression of human possibility. This does not imply an unchangeable concept of nature, but it does recognize the interdependence of human life within a living planet as source of both constraint and indeterminacy of human plans.

I cannot present plans for the resolution of such tensions. Indeed, the need to work through such resolutions if not abstractly, at least in relation to particular forms of critical practice, is only now being recognized. At the very least, it places a necessary constraint on a project of possibility that prevents its reduction to an expressive individual aggrandizement without any sense of self-modulation. But at the same time, it can also turn one's attention to what must be understood and done to transform existing forms of consumer capitalism, whose very disregard for issues of the renewal of life require both critique and challenge.

FROM THE PERSPECTIVE OF POSSIBILITY

I have thus attempted to define the basis for what I see as a pedagogy of possibility, one committed to the expansion of the range of human capacities contained within the requirements of securing diversity, compassionate justice, and the renewal of life. This position is the guiding telos for what is to come in the remaining chapters of this book. In this sense, the chapters extend and make concrete these ideas while making no attempt at a further systematization of an abstract moral philosophy. In this section, I shall begin the process of concretization by illustrating how certain aspects of the position I have just drawn can inform deliberations regarding educational policy and teaching practice. The examples provided are in no way comprehensive; they are simply indicative of implications which follow from my project.

If the expansion of the range of possibilities available to people is taken as the starting premise of an educational agenda, then it is possible to examine different attempts to resolve the contradiction between capacities and forms that often are associated with particular institutional practices. As I stated earlier, this contradiction is defined through the openness of expression of capacities encouraged in a "free society" and the normative, regulating force of those social forms which define the terrain on which everyday life is lived. Historically, one dominant mode of managing this contradiction was to declare the openness of human capacities as greater for some than others. Thus the contradiction could be governed by the restriction of certain groups of people, on the basis of their gender or assumed "racial" characteristics, to a limited range of possibilities circumscribed by particular forms of curriculum and teaching. While the modern liberal state no longer condones such practices, the mode of this resolution is still employed when students are subjected to forms of categorization based on their performance within the opportunity set provided by a restricted set of educational practices. Such categorizations (in Ontario, "The Basic Level Student," "The General Level Student"), which carry assumptions about the limitations of student capacities, are then used as a prescriptive basis for the provision of a particular regulating form of pedagogy. Current efforts, at least in my home province, to redress the injustice of such practices through a process of "destreaming" are only now beginning to be explored.

But there has been another strategy for dealing with the capacities/forms contradiction that must also be brought into view. This is the attempt to define a particular moral hegemony on the basis of the requirements of existing socially constructed forms. Here the tactic is to subject capacities to the limits such forms require. One particularly pernicious attempt to manage the contradiction in this manner has been the suggestion that since "youth who embrace 'traditional values' make better high school students," school reforms should address "character development."[44] What "character development" means here is a particular narrowing of human capacities to those which will properly fit existing forms of schooling. For support, this position calls on studies that examine the relation between student values and high school success seeking to identify those human capacities that best fit the existing education practices. The results of such studies are then read as identifying the desired norm—the desired sense of identity, values, and sensibility—that students must "develop" to solve the school achievement problem. Those who fail to exhibit or "develop" such capacities are seen as deficient, lacking in appropriate character, and simply of lesser worth.

Taken to its logical conclusion, the identification of such deficient human character has created "moral panics" and perceived threats to nation and community.[45] Existing or traditional social forms are rendered natural or God-given and celebrated as the epiphany of a moral order rendering all versions of human possibility not in accord with the requirement of such forms as defective.[46] Thus in the light of a project of possibility such suggestions are quite readily rejected.

Another restriction of diverse human capacities justified on the basis of a moral (and practical) hegemony of existing social forms can be found in the way some educators cede the substance of educational policy to the presumed demands of the marketplace. As educators we are (in part) concerned with pedagogies that attempt to influence the ways in which youth will survive economically and socially after their required period of schooling. However, in relation to a project of possibility it is problematic to adopt constellations of curriculum, teaching, and evaluation practices that support the formation of identities solely in terms of labor market requirements. At a concrete level this practice can be found in many work education programs whose purpose is to enable the learner to become a successful producer of a valuable service through the acquisition of specific attitudes, knowledge, and skills.

But this view fails to acknowledge the concrete ways in which markets are always organized and regulated, systematically restricting the expression of human capacities. To grasp what is at issue here one must ask who controls, on what terms, and in what interests the following dimensions of market structure: work opportunities and job requirements, wage and pricing policies, investment capital, and profit margins. The resolution of such issues has particular warping and limiting effects on what is to be seen as viable forms of productive work, which itself has a regulative relation to what is seen as valuable and acceptable commodity forms of labor. The market must always be understood as a barrier to the possible, not only its facilitating condition. What "doesn't go" cannot simply be chalked up to "a lack of market acumen," "illiteracy," "immaturity," or "an unrealistic view of the world," but rather to a particular valuing that closes off the possible. Thus the problem in using existing market values for particular human capacities as the basis for justifying one's choice of the social forms through which educational practices are realized. Besides, there are other alternatives, practices committed to enhancing the ability of students to increase their effective participation in determining the practices that define their working lives.[47]

In contradistinction to resolutions of restriction, a project of possibility requires both the expansion of forms to accommodate capacities and the expansion of capacities to make the realization of new forms possible. This calls for a form of empowerment that allows one to treat character and community as more than just fate. Indeed, to open *both* character and community to revision counts for much in determining what one can hope for in life. Yet as I have also stressed, such a horizon of possibility can and should be constrained within an ethical imagination that privileges diversity, compassionate justice, and securing of the conditions for the renewal of human life. There is no formula with which to make this project pedagogically concrete (yet there is much more to discuss about the practical character of such a pedagogy; see Chapter 4). Nor I do wish to develop here a set of guidelines for and/or exemplars of such deliberations. What I do wish to stress, however, is that a project of possibility has a double ethical address: the person *and* the familial and communal forms within which people live. In this framework, one's pedagogy is not to be decided through a conventional form of deliberation whose purpose is to determine the relative balance of personal freedom and communal restraint encouraged within a given constellation of practices. Rather, one's task is to develop a pedagogy capable of narrating stories of possibility. Rooted in an ethical vision of securing human dignity, such stories would make visible that constellation of capacities/forms which is not yet and would remember (on personal and collective terms) that one's commitment to such a vision has not yet been fulfilled.[48]

This, then, is my disruptive daydream, my sense of that which is not yet in our lives but could be. Much of this book is devoted to ways in which we can grasp this as a hopeful and not merely a wishful dream. I will argue that such a project *can* inform our efforts in schools. In suggesting this, I am in no way minimizing previous critiques that have described the conservative and constricting character of many existing forms of schooling. But what I am attempting here is the provision of a "contravision" to that one-dimensional view of schooling as a socializing institution whose aim is to regulate a sense of human possibility in support of the interests of the ruling bloc constituted within privileged positions of gender, class, race, ethnic, regional and sexual relations.

Thus the project of possibility requires the situated refusal of the present as definitive of that which is possible. In this respect it connects with the tradition of the "radical No."[49] This is the refusal to acquiesce; to fit ourselves within the existing practices through which we understand and rule ourselves and one another. It is the origin of a practical, ethical, and political imagination requiring a vision of history that is developed not from the view of the "given present" but rather from "the present as revolutionary possibility."[50]

The basis for hope does not consist either in telling our versions of "true stories" or in simply finding our place within some tradition or ethical code. Hope is made practical because "we can identify and change those procedures or forms through which our stories become true, because we can question and modify those systems which make (only) particular kinds of action possible, and because there is no 'authentic' self-relation we must conform to."[51]

NOTES

1. Henry A. Giroux. "Rethinking the Boundaries of Educational Discourse: Modernism, Postmodernism, and Feminism." *College Literature*, Double Issue 17 (2/3) (1990). p. 41.

2. Jerome Lawrence and Robert E. Lee, *Inherit the Wind* (New York: Bantam, 1975), p. 30.

3. Henry Giroux, *Schooling and the Struggle for Public Life* (Minneapolis: University of Minnesota Press, 1988; see particularly chaps. 3 and 4).

4. How these issues can be taken up within an agenda of cultural politics is discussed in Chapter 3. For an initial formulation see Roger I. Simon, "Empowerment as a Pedagogy of Possibility," *Language Arts* 64, no. 4 (1987): pp. 370–82.

5. Here I am trying to introduce the concept of education as a moral practice. This is not to be confused with or collapsed into conventional notions of moral education often understood as the quest to educate the individual to be a responsible moral agent. It is not that this later question is irrelevant, but rather that it should not be confused with the questions raised by a consideration of education as a moral practice.

6. This formulation opens up some basic questions I can at this point only acknowledge. In placing the question of the moral basis of one's practice within a consideration of the desired version of a future human community, I am treading on difficult ground. Such communitarian referents for a moral warrant have become conventional fare since Émile Durkheim. The problem arises, of course, when one finds oneself in a community whose desired version of a future contravenes one's own sense of what is morally desirable. For important cautions and disagreements regarding the social order as a locus of morality see Zygmunt Bauman, *Modernity and the Holocaust* (Ithaca: Cornell University Press, 1989); Renato Rosaldo, *Culture and Truth: The Remaking of Social Analysis* (Boston: Beacon Press, 1989); and Iris Marion Young, "The Idea of Community and the Politics of Difference," in Linda Nicholson, ed., *Feminism/Postmodernism* (New York: Routledge, 1990).

7. H. H. Gerth and C. Wright Mills, eds., *From Max Weber* (London: Routledge and Kegan Paul, 1970), p. 95.

8. Such scientism has been documented as a form of teacher deskilling. See, for example, Michael Apple, *Teachers and Texts* (New York: Routledge, 1986), esp. Chapter 7; R. W. Connell, *Teachers' Work* (Boston and London: Allen and Unwin, 1985); and Thomas Popkewitz, ed., *Critical Studies in Teacher Education: Its Folklore, Theory and Practice* (London: Falmer Press, 1987), esp. Chapter 5; and Kathleen Densmore, "Professionalism, Proletarianization and Teacher Work."

9. Donna Haraway, "Situated Knowledges: the Science Question in Feminism and the Privilege of Partial Perspective," *Feminist Studies* 14, no. 3 (1988): pp. 575–99.

10. For variants of this position, see Jean-François Lyotard, *The Postmodern Condition: A Report on Knowledge* (Minneapolis: University of Minnesota Press, 1984); Linda J. Nicholson, ed., *Feminism/Postmodernism* (New York: Routledge, 1990); and Stanley Aronowitz and Henry A. Giroux, *Postmodern Education: Politics, Culture and Social Criticism* (Minneapolis: University of Minnesota Press, 1990).

11. Gary Peller, "Reason and the Mob: The Politics of Representation," *Tikkun* 2, no. 3 (July–August 1987): 28–31, 92–95.

12. Haraway, "Situated Knowledges," p. 584.

13. Hal Foster, "Against Pluralism," in *Recodings: Art, Spectacle, Cultural Politics* (Seattle: Bay Press, 1985).

14. Partial knowledge is located temporally and spatially. "Truth . . . is bound to a temporal nucleus which is lodged in both the known and the knower" (Walter Benjamin, as cited in Susan Buck-Morss, *The Dialectics of Seeing: Walter Benjamin and the Arcades Project* [Cambridge: MIT Press, 1989]).

15. Richard Kearney, *The Wake of Imagination* (Minneapolis: University of Minnesota Press, 1988), p. 361. But more extensively, see his "Conclusion: After Imagination?" (pp. 359–97) and the extended footnote on pp. 451–52.

16. Michel Foucault, "Truth and Power," in *Power/Knowledge: Selected Interviews and Other Writings, 1972–1977* (New York: Pantheon Books, 1980).

17. It is interesting to note that this was also the recruitment slogan for the Canadian Armed Forces in the late 1980s.

18. Israel Scheffler, *Of Human Potential: An Essay in the Philosophy of Education* (Boston: Routledge and Kegan Paul, 1985).

19. The notion that agency is linked to processes of structuration is developed in the work of Giddens and Foucault. See Anthony Giddens, *Central Problems in Social Theory: Action, Structure and Contradiction in Social Analysis* (London: MacMillan, 1979); and Michel Foucault, "The Subject and Power," in H. Dreyfus and P. Rabinow, *Michel Foucault: Beyond Structuralism and Hermeneutics* (Brighton, Sussex: Harvester Press, 1982).

20. Michael Walzer, *Interpretation and Social Criticism* (Cambridge: Harvard University Press, 1987), p. 65.

21. "Sunday Morning Magazine," CBC, Summer 1988.

22. Philip Corrigan, "Social Forms/Human Capacities: Further Remarks on Authority and Difference," in *Social Forms/Human Capacities: Essays on Authority and Difference* (London: Routledge, 1990).

23. Raymond Williams, *Resources for Hope* (London: Verso, 1989), pp. 85–86.

24. Corrigan, "Social Forms," p. 199.

25. Studies with particular reference to education include Bruce Curtis, *Building the Educational State in Canada West* (Philadelphia: Falmer, 1988); Kari Dehli, "Women and Class: The Social Organization of Mothers' Relations to Schools" (Ph.D. diss., University of Toronto, 1988); John Willinsky, *The Triumph of Literature/The Fate of Literacy* (New York: Teacher's College Press, 1991); Ivor Goodson, ed., *International Perspectives in Curriculum History* (London: Croom Helm, 1987); and Thomas Popkewitz, ed., *The Formation of School Subjects: The Struggle for Creating an American Institution* (New York: Falmer, 1987).

26. A full discussion of this contradiction would require a discussion of its historical character, particularly in relation to the past and current realities of North American society. This would include a discussion of the growth of modern liberalism and its connection with self-realization as a telos of society, the constitution of North America as a "new world" of possibility, and the rise of capitalism as the "ultimate" realization of desirable vehicle of possibility.

27. Jean-Paul Sartre, *Search for a Method* (New York: Knopf, 1963).

28. For an extended discussion of this theme in the work of Foucault, see John

Rajchman, *Michel Foucault: The Freedom of Philosophy* (New York: Columbia University Press, 1985).

29. Thomas Berger, *Fragile Freedoms: Human Rights and Dissent in Canada* (Toronto: Clarke, Irwin, 1981), pp. 24–25.

30. Philip Corrigan, "In/Forming Schooling," in David Livingstone et al., *Critical Pedagogy and Cultural Power* (Toronto: Garamond Press, 1987).

31. Frank Cunningham, *Democratic Theory and Socialism* (Cambridge: University of Cambridge Press, 1987).

32. For critiques of such ossification see James Clifford, *The Predicament of Culture: Twentieth-Century Ethnography, Literature and Art* (Cambridge: Harvard University Press, 1988), and Renato Rosaldo, *Culture and Truth*.

33. For a discussion of the implications of this process, see Roger I. Simon, "Being Ethnic/Doing Ethnicity," in Jon Young, ed., *Breaking the Mosaic: Race and Ethnicity in Education* (Toronto: Garamond Press, 1987).

34. Madga Lewis and Roger I. Simon, "A Discourse Not Intended for Her: Learning and Teaching within Patriarchy," *Harvard Educational Review* 56, no. 4 (November 1986): pp. 457–72.

35. Henry A. Giroux, "Border Pedagogy in the Age of Postmodernism," in Stanley Aronowitz and Henry A. Giroux, *Postmodern Education*, pp. 114–35.

36. Holly Near, "Unity," on *Speed of Light* (Redwood Records, 1982).

37. Abraham J. Heschel, *The Prophets* (Philadelphia: Jewish Publication Society, 1962).

38. David Hartman, *A Living Covenant: The Innovative Spirit in Traditional Judaism* (New York: Free Press, 1985), p. 101.

39. Sharon Welch, *Communities of Resistance and Solidarity* (New York: Orbis Press, 1985); and Henry Giroux, *Schooling and the Struggle for Public Life*, pp. 91–98.

40. Most salient for North Americans are the teachings of elders from among the people of the First Nations of the Americas. For example, well known is warning given by Chief Seathl to U.S. government officials more than 100 years ago: "What befalls the earth, befalls the children of the earth."

41. Anita Gordon and David Suzuki, *It's a Matter of Survival* (Toronto: Stoddart, 1990).

42. Ted Benton, "Marxism and Natural Limits: An Ecological Critique and Reconstruction," *New Left Review*, no. 178, November–December 1989, pp. 51–86. The quotation below from p. 57.

43. See Sigmund Freud, *Civilization and Its Discontents* (London: Hogarth Press), p. 264.

44. Alan Ginsburg and Sandra Hanson, *Gaining Ground: Values and High School Success*, Final Report to the U.S. Department of Education Washington, D.C.: Government Printing Office, 1985), as abstracted in *Report on Education Research*, vol. 18, 1986 (an independent newsletter published by Capitol Publishers, Arlington, VA): p. 2.

45. For example, see Anna Davin, "Imperialism and Motherhood," *History Workshop Journal*, no. 5 (Spring 1978): pp. 9–65; and Michael Rosenthal, *The Character Factory: Baden-Powell's Boy Scouts and the Imperatives of Empire* (New York: Pantheon, 1984).

46. I am not here rejecting tradition as a basis on which to construct a particu-

lar constellation of forms and capacities but rather the creation of a process within which all other forms of expressivity and action become rendered defective or immoral. I elaborate on the importance of tradition to the radical reconstruction of possibility in Chapter 8.

47. For a form of work education that does not deny the value of developing competencies but refuses to reduce pedagogical practice to a form of socialization to work based of the requirements of labor markets, see Roger I. Simon, Don Dippo, and Arleen Schenke, *Learning Work: A Critical Pedagogy of Work Education* (Amherst, Mass.: Bergin and Garvey, 1991).

48. Kearney, *The Wake of Imagination*, pp. 394–96.

49. I am thinking here of that No uttered by such diverse people as Henry David Thoreau, Emma Goldman, Mahatma Gandhi, Rosa Parks, and J. S. Woodsworth.

50. "The failure to distinguish between the present-as-given from the present as revolutionary possibility robbed historical practices of politics" (Susan Buck-Morss, "Benjamin's Revolutionary Pedagogy," *New Left Review*, no. 128, p. 59).

51. John Rajchman, *Michel Foucault*, p. 122.

3

Teachers as Cultural Workers

The work of formulating a pedagogy of possibility is not easily done alone. When teachers gather to turn their energies and attention to the specific task of constructing educational practices that might help students challenge and assess existing social conventions, modes of thought, and relations of power, there are a number of conversational incursions that are at times used to deflect and deflate such crucial work. Two such subversions concern me here. The first, usually spoken in a tone of doubt and frustration, sounds something like this: "Perhaps we're just wasting our time; maybe progressive change isn't possible; after all, don't schools simply reflect the society they're part of?" In contrast, the second interjection is usually spoken with more assertive assurance: "Look, despite our intentions, I think we're just tinkering with the system. To be practical and critical at the same time requires too much compromise. Besides, do you really think our isolated efforts will have any impact on the way most teaching is done? Focusing our energies so locally, on the details of pedagogical practice, is simply a form of co-optation, a way of marginalizing dissent and allowing us to simply be marginal."

These positions are constituted within particular assumptions concerning the ways in which one is to represent both schools and schooling and the work of teaching within them. They are worth considering in that they pose a basic challenge to the viability of one of the key subtexts of this book, the importance of a turn toward pedagogy as a vital mode of engaging in the task of social transformation. The first position, the doubt that any meaningful educational change in schools is possible because "schools reflect society" is the weaker of the two arguments. Myopically ahistorical, this stance simply glosses and hides too much. As numerous histories of schooling and curriculum have shown,[1] schools have long been one of the central sites in which various groups have attempted to constitute notions of cultural authority and regulate the way people understand themselves, their relationship with others, and their shared social and physical environments. These histories convey clearly that to reduce schools to mere "reflections," is to suppress the constructed and often contested character of school organization and practice.

Any "turn toward pedagogy," conceived as a challenge to existing conventions of schooling must be understood as entering into a continuing legacy of historical contestation. What was and still is at issue is how to respond to such value-based questions as what range of purposes schools should serve, what knowledge is of most worth, who should get access to what forms of knowledge, what it means to know something, what notions of authority should structure teaching and learning, and so on. This means that any construction of a pedagogy of possibility that takes its insurgent character seriously must be able to locate itself within an understanding of how such a practice enters the discursive tradition I shall be calling "cultural politics." In fact, it is through this path (i.e., pedagogy's connection to cultural politics) that I wish to address the second argument, the view that a turn toward pedagogy is a diffusion of energy better placed in the service of more macro level analyses and struggles.

The path of pedagogy, of course, cannot and should not ignore the realities of policy formation in state-controlled schooling. The central questions of who (and on what basis) is given legitimacy to decide for whom, what forms of schooling and standards of competence are in the best interests of a community remain central concerns for critique and analysis. Recent Canadian and American commentaries have continued to point to the hegemonic vision and logic of corporate capitalism and individual consumerism as the still-dominant justifying framework within which such decisions are being made.[2] As these commentaries make clear, educational policies are being justified in relation to the interrelated goals of maintaining an internationally competitive economy, reducing the constant dollar value of government budget allocations to education, promoting economic and cultural partnerships between public schools and private corporations, narrowing the competency standards to which students and teachers will be held accountable, and, to ensure those narrowed competencies, deskilling teachers within the search for prescriptive content and methods. My intention is not a facile dismissal of these directives. There is certainly a lack of and need for public debate and scrutiny regarding such policies. That these directives have become the presumed and undebated framework for much North American educational policy is in no small measure due to the realities of conventional forms of political power. That is, the content of educational policy is indeed influenced by who gets to participate (and in what way) in the current structures of educational decision making and bureaucratic organization. For this reason, the attempt to define new, workable structures for determining forms of schooling in specific communities remains an important challenge for those of us committed to both the further democratization of education and the transformation of the social interests it is capable of serving.[3]

As important as this task is, however, by itself it remains insufficient. Hope for a different future, for an expanded set of possibilities for conceiving what contribution schooling might make to citizens and their communities requires more than just a change in who makes decisions. What is required is some attention to what one might call the "social imaginary," the way of naming, ordering and representing social and physical reality whose effects simultaneously enable and constrain a set of options for practical action in the world. This notion necessitates taking up the question of power beyond its conception as something that can be possessed and used to physically or juridically constrain or coerce the actions of others. It requires a notion of power that emphasizes its productive effects, underscoring the way it works, not just on people, but through them. In this view, power inheres in the forms of knowledge and desire that guide the possibility of conduct and order possible outcomes of certain forms of action.[4] In other words, productive power enables and regulates possibility through structuring of the field of action of others.

Integrally connected to the notion of productive power are the practices of semiotic production, a realm I argue that is central to the concerns of pedagogy. In introducing the term "semiotic production," I am attempting to signal the centrality of those practices implicated in the formation and regulation of meaning and imagination. Such practices include not only the creation of particular modes of symbolic and textual expression, but as well, the ways that such significations are placed within systems of distribution and display. As practices of power, such practices are provocations of processes that constitute knowledge, significance, and desire. For this reason, the production of various forms of image, text, gesture, and talk—as well as their ordered presentation and efforts to influence their mediation—have to be understood as integral to the possibility of either the reproduction or transformation of any social order. In other words, cultural practices matter, and the modes and conditions of their production deserve close attention.

To fully grasp the relation between culture and power requires the recognition that particular modes of semiotic production are not arbitrary but rather are historically and economically constituted by the social forms within which we live our lives. For example, in both art and education—two major sites of "cultural work"—dominant modes of semiotic production often attempt to normalize "truthful" or "useful" textual practices and image repertoires as well as what counts as their adequate display and mediation. Such normalizations are efforts to regulate particular ways of seeing the world and defining "common sense." Thought of in these terms, practices that articulate particular modes of semiotic production are simultaneously educational and political in that they attempt to inform a sense of what is significant and "true" as well as what is desirable and possible.

As educators, our work is explicitly located within the realm of semiotic production. Our attempts to engage students are constructed within specific modes that we hope will provoke particular forms of communication, comprehension, and interest. How we provoke this engagement, within which productive regimes and with what corresponding strategies and questions, defines much of our pedagogical practice. Of course, semiotic production is an activity that takes place in many locations throughout the social fabric of daily life. Schools are just one of the many sites where attempts to exercise productive power are realized. This is an obvious circumscription on the importance of school-based pedagogy. But as well, taken up not as limit but as possibility, this recognition of the multiplicity of points through which power is exercised can be the basis for a radical hope in relation to efforts at progressive practice. As I shall argue, this means that one does not have to wait for state-, board-, or even schoolwide reform to grasp the potentiality of one's local efforts.

TOWARD ARTICULATION

My argument, as a teacher, is addressed to colleagues who wish to understand and enhance the value of their critical pedagogical work, while facing fully the realization that reform at the level of alternative, counterdiscursive curriculum and teaching will not by itself change the structures that determine the terrain on which our lives are now currently lived. It is an argument addressed to those who can no longer be content to accept, in the face of this contradictory awareness, that one's pedagogical efforts are worthwhile if they can modestly make a small difference in the lives of a few students. To such teachers I now pose these questions: On what basis might we connect our efforts to practice a pedagogy of possibility with the work of others in locations of cultural production different from schooling? Grasping the connection between our work and those of others in a variety of diverse sites where notions of knowledge, truth, and desire are being produced, what might this mean in relation to possibilities for future cooperation and alliance? Viewed from the context of these questions, this chapter is a deliberately exploratory essay. It is intended as a discursive intervention whose goal is to constitute, organize, and articulate a new set of relations between education and other practices of semiotic production. As such, it is an attempt to lay the ground[5] for a practical "articulation"[6] among various groups of "cultural workers" (among which I include teachers) which, as a contingent and specific assemblage, can contest dominant forms of cultural production across a spectrum of sites where people shape their identity and their relations with the world.

In trying to make apparent a particular articulation across a range of practices called "cultural work," I am attempting to make visible a new arrangement, a particular linkage or connection among people whose primary work commitments are within a variety of sites of semiotic production. The articulation at issue here is the question of the possible terms of reference on which different groups of cultural workers might see their efforts as mutually supporting. Such terms require both a practical framework within which one can envision how one's work might complement the practice of others as well as a political vision, informed by a social imaginary and ethical sensibility, which posits a "unity" within which differences may be explored, understood, and refined. The remainder of this chapter is an attempt to explore who might be understood as educators and/or cultural workers and how they might see their own unique practices connected with other attempts to redefine the hegemony that constitutes our daily life options. Within this discussion the concept of "semiosis" will emerge as central to clarifying the possibilities of such an articulation. This concept, which involves the sense-making practices through which meaning is produced in the context of historically and concretely defined engagements with written, visual, and/or aural forms, provides a substantive basis for considerations of both the politics and learning supported by particular practices of representation and the structures within which we encourage people to engage them.

SCHOOLS AS POLITICAL-CULTURAL TECHNOLOGIES

Clarifying how and why teachers' work in schools might be linked both pedagogically and politically with cultural work in other sites requires retheorizing the political-educative function of schooling. Asserting that schools and the work of teaching within them are inseparable from "politics" is deceptively simple. It is important that the particular notion of "politics" embraced by this statement be made explicit. Schooling and teaching may be said to be "political" in a variety of ways. First, and perhaps most common, is the recognition that curriculum policies, teaching conditions, and pedagogical practices are all informed by the conventional "politics" of provincial or state governments and locally elected school boards. Second is the recognition that schooling is implicated in the differential allocation of knowledge and symbolic rewards among different groups of people in such a way that patterns of social inequalities seem to be maintained through the participation (or lack of it) of members from these different groups. In this sense, schooling is taken to be implicated in the maintenance of relations of dominance and are thus seen to have "political effects." But there is yet a third way to understand schooling practices as political; this is through the recognition that schools (and the particular forms of pedagogy they contain), as sites of semiotic production, are inevitably caught up in the inseparable relation between culture and power referred to above.

The notion of "politics" implied here refers to the value-based determination of the field of material, social, and symbolic resources that both set limits and enable particular possibilities across a full range of daily activities. These activities include work, transportation, the provision and maintenance of shelter, the provision and preparation of food, participation in expressive and pleasurable forms of sexuality, rituals and relationships that nourish spiritual needs, and meaningful and pleasurable engagement in or with such expressive forms as sport, cinema, music, literature, art, and broadcast media. While schools and teaching may do little to directly affect the material and social resources that structure such possibilities, they do participate in something quite vital to how this notion of politics is to be done. Organized within particular modes of semiotic production, schooling attempts to participate in the formation of discursive regimes that both frame what might count as a material or social resource and produce, organize, and regulate notions of the possible, sensible, and legitimate actions open to us. As such, schools constitute sites of *cultural politics* organized through modes of semiotic production that employ various cultural technologies for representing, displaying, and facilitating the mediation of knowledge claims about the world and ourselves.

Thought of in this way, schools are tantamount to "dream machines," sets of social, textual, and visual practices intended to provoke the production of meanings and desires that can affect people's sense of their future identities and possibilities. The productive apparatus at issue here is the sets of organizational, curricular, and teaching practices that attempt to frame the ways in which meaning is produced, identities shaped, and values challenged or preserved. It is such practices that I will be calling "cultural technologies," deliberate attempts to structure the processes of semiosis, that is, the way signs are mediated as people attempt to attribute meaning to aspects of their own and others' existence. I will be arguing that viewing schools as cultural technologies has important implications for rethinking how teachers might connect their efforts to other forms of cultural work. However, I will first consider more fully what is implied by gathering the practices of school and classroom organization, curriculum, and teaching under the notion of "cultural technologies."

ON TECHNOLOGY

It is not without some hesitation that I have chosen to use the term "technology" in relation to schooling practice. The use of this word is potentially misleading; after all, the attempt to devise strategies of instructional technologies constituted as "teaching machines" (both prior and subsequent to the introduction of computers into classrooms) is now a significant part of the continuing history of educational practice. For this reason, I must emphasize at the outset that I am not implying that teachers should be understood as technicians or that teaching can be reduced to a series of technical operations. I wish to locate myself differently. The notion of technology has another historical referent, one made manifest in a particular strain of philosophy and political theory,[7] and it is this intertextual connotative reference that I wish to preserve. Thus I wish to use the term with particular specificity and care.

Most commonly, "technology" refers to a means to an end; a means usually associated with manufacturing and the scientific utilization of equipment, tools, and machines. While my concern here is with the practices of semiotic *production* (and I do want to claim that such practices are both enabled and circumscribed by a particular sense of the notion of "technology"), I am in no way suggesting that the concept of semiotic production be understood as a mechanistic process. In order to develop a different notion of technology, I wish to distance myself from those positions which draw a strong dichotomous contrast between technology and art.[8]

In my view, any attempt to characterize technology through its oppositional difference from art is misleading in that it reduces technology to a question of prescripted method and instrumentality. Rather, I wish to focus on a characteristic that art and technology share, given that both can be understood as forms of practice constituted within particular ways of knowing and making. This is notion of *poiesis*, what Heidegger describes as "a bringing forth into presence."[9] In the context of *poiesis*, technology is implicated in the occasioning or the setting of something on its way to arrival, a mode of organizing and regulating a particular way of bringing something out. In this sense, technology sets on its way a revealing of that which was previously not present. In the process of being revealed, technology constitutes the regime of knowledge and truth within which productive processes will be determined. Particular notions of technology (such as modern positivist technology) will have particular *poietic* modes, particular copenetrations of making and knowing. As one commits to and invests in them, such modes become the frames within which a particular ordering of the real is required and particular forms of productive work are structured and governed.

Thus as a generic concept, "technology" implies the specification of a mode of production; a way of organizing and regulating the bringing forth into presence of something previously without presence. This means that "technology" must always be understood in its plurality, as variegated fields of different forms of power/knowledge. In reference to any specific technology we must ask: How is this technology constituted within particular discursive regimes? How do these regimes order the world into its components and relationships and establish particular knowledges and truths so as to make specifiable particular operations for constituting that which is to be revealed? This ordering of the real, this constituting of particular forms of knowledge and truth (this social, epistemic notion of technology) is prior to its manifestation in any particular material form. In other words, as Deleuze suggests, "technology is social before it is technical."[10] Technology, then, is no mere means. Concretized as a set of regulated procedures, mechanisms, and techniques, the notion of technology is expanded to include the production of that which is knowable in relation to material, social, and spiritual forms; notions of the knowable that assume a practical, pragmatic character in their very articulation of cultural power.

CULTURAL TECHNOLOGIES AND PEDAGOGY

But what of the notion of a *cultural*[11] technology? Is there some specific distinction implied by the referent cultural that might help in grasping a previously unarticulated relation between schools and other sites of semiotic production? For me, cultural technologies reference sets of intentional institutional arrangements and practices within which various forms of images, sound, text, and talk are constructed, presented, *and* engaged. Such technologies are implicated in the production of the range of meanings that give people a sense of who they are and what their futures might be about. In other words, I have been emphasizing their implication in the formation and regulation of identities and desires. In addition to schools (and other specifically educational sites such as literacy programs, ESL classes, union-sponsored seminars, and adult continuing education courses), examples of sites where cultural technologies become manifest include the cinema, theater, television, advertising, architecture, public health forums, print journalism, popular music, story-telling festivals, and religious study and ritual.[12] This illustrative list is not meant to be inclusive. Its diversity is deliberate. My intent is to argue the importance of "cultural technologies" as a concept that provides an expanded range of relevance for the notion of pedagogy, allowing us to better understand how the work that goes on in schools (and other sites conventionally understood as 'educational') may be "articulated" with other forms of cultural work in order to open the possibilities specified and normalized within our social imagination.

What must be emphasized about a cultural technology, what gives it a particular specificity, is its status as an apparatus of semiosis. In other words, a cultural technology attempts to put into effect an organized and regulated process of the production of meaning. As an "apparatus" it is a productive contrivance that is at once both material and abstract. It is material in its concrete embodiment of particular forms of distribution and display of symbolic inscriptions that may take the form of visual or textual information, questions and/or instructions. It is abstract in its specification of a set of signifying practices that attempt to structure and govern the framing of that which is to be known through the practices of language, image, gesture, and action. I am particularly emphasizing here that cultural technologies *attempt* to organize and regulate the production of meaning. This stress on intention and not effect is quite deliberate. While employed as an endeavor to constitute the work of semiosis, cultural technologies cannot inscribe or guarantee meaning. The character of semiosis as a potentially open-ended and indeterminate process prohibits any simple reduction of meaning to representation. Thus from the perspective of cultural technologies, it is a vast oversimplification to posit such sites as schools, cinema, architecture, and forms of religious worship as prescripted arrangements that, through their symbolic representations, serve and accomplish a particular set of social interests.

This, of course, is not to suggest that the substance and organization of representations (whether textual, auditory, or visual) are irrelevant. Rather than determining particular meaning effects, cultural technologies frame ("put on the way") acts of both representation and comprehension and recognition. That is, cultural technologies tend toward the enabling/constraining of the production of meaning integral to both the realization and engagement of representations. In doing so, they rely on discursive formations that at least partially situate both those people who construct representations and those who engage them.[13] In other words, cultural technologies assemble positions[14] from which people construct visual, written, aural, or gestural forms of "textuality" and address others through such textualities. But as well, such technologies also assemble positions from which people may attempt to grasp and hence mediate the symbolic fields that surround them.

While it is important not to cede to cultural technologies an overdetermination of effects, as practices of symbolization and communication organized within discursive regimes, such technologies often become an essential part of the social organization of relations of power. Hence, it is important to grasp that such assemblies are rarely neutral and in reality, never simply address "people" as generalized abstractions. Particular modes of representation and comprehension and their resultant meanings are subject to both normalization and standardization within specific social forms. Authorized cultural technologies can be understood as sets of institutionalized practices that produce a limited set of ways of communicating with others. The normalization and standardization of such practices in particular contexts produce what are taken as the proper ways communication should be done (see chap. 2, particularly pages 20–22). Such modes of regulation attempt to define the range of the "customary, accepted, normalized and expected" and in the process delimit particular expressive capacities as marginal, false or perverse.[15] This indeed is a moralizing project whose politics need always to be named: who is organizing what for whom, in whose interest, and in the name of what vision of the future. Forgetting such questions places the discussion of semiosis at a level of unlocated abstraction that suppresses the recognition of relations of difference and power that cultural technologies often mobilize.

As important as it is to consider how cultural technologies are employed in the social organization of power, it is crucial that as educators we recognize that people do not live their lives within unified discursive fields. That is, the texture of daily life makes available a multiplicity of locations within which specific forms of sociality with different degrees of affective significance are constituted through various cultural technologies. Thus, in the span of a day I might play my tape of Otis Redding singing "Try a Little Tenderness," listen to a feminist radio program on a public access radio station, teach a class in which we discuss how different forms of masculinity are produced both in schools and sports, discuss the relationship between Abraham, Sarah, and Hagar in my Torah discussion group, participate in a demonstration protesting the portrayal of African history in a historical exhibit at a local museum, attend a weight-control clinic, shop at the Eaton Center, leaf through a copy of *Playboy* at the barber shop,[16] play a game of softball and then have a drink with "the guys," go to a local theater to see Clint Eastwood do his version of "the sensitive male" in *Heartbreak Ridge*, listen to a recording of Act 2 of *La Traviata* with my wife, watch "The Bill Cosby Show" episode I taped on my VCR, and then flake out at 2:00 A.M. watching Arnold Schwarzenegger in *The Terminator* on the videotape my son rented earlier in the day.

My point here is that the meanings I produce in the course of my day's activity of comprehension and communication are potentially multiple and contradictory and vary in their affective significance. What I understand to be an appropriate semiotic and pragmatic relationship to nature, my body, other men, women, my work and the work of others, my wife, my children, Bill Cosby, Arnold Schwarzenegger, and Torah—all these semiotic and pragmatic relationships are multiply determined not just in relation to one apparatus of meaning production but through the socially constituted mediation of several. I am not by any means suggesting that the production of meaning in sites such as schools, television, cinema, popular music, magazine publishing, religion, and radio represent an unconstrained semiosis. This, of course, is not the case. Certainly the forms of capital and interest that control which representations are produced and distributed are central to the real relations of power in any community (succinctly put by the phrase "the freedom of the press is defined by those who own the presses").[17] However, neither is it the case that each site is empty of counterdiscursive possibilities. That is, particular articulations of symbolic productions in schools, magazines, information radio, religious study groups, popular music, film, and health clinics (just to name a few) can and do provide a framework within which the modes of representation and comprehension that underpin existing forms of dominance (e.g., people over nature, men over women, capital over labor, Canada over the First Nations of America, whites over "people of color") can be modified, challenged, refused, and replaced. Furthermore, the existence of such counterdiscursive practices across sites of semiotic production[18] is a vital ingredient in helping to coalesce particular groups of people into expressions of identity and solidarity required for specific struggles for equality of possibility.[19]

In emphasizing the productive capacity of cultural technologies, I am stressing that such arrangements need not be seen as simply vehicles of socialization, intended to adapt people to the requirements of existing social forms. While there is no question that some cultural technologies can be and are used within such efforts, it is important to appreciate that others are fundamental for challenging normalized horizons and expanding the possibilities we have for reconstituting our sense of what our futures might be. This must be taken seriously by those of us who are attempting to work with and within such technologies; redefining them in attempts to raise new questions about which social practices constitute relations of justice and compassion and how the social imaginary might be expanded against the grain of the constricting visions of currently normalized notions of gender, productive labor, sexuality, and physical health. This applies not only to us as teachers but as well to all others whose work constructs a particular provocation of semiosis; for example, film makers, writers, actors and directors, storytellers, architects, public health nurses, and religious leaders.[20]

Here, then, is the justification for introducing the notion of cultural technology into the conversation concerning the potential for a pedagogy of possibility. The articulation needed to place education within the heterogeneous space of cultural studies produces a new resonance among all its regions and components. This resonance is the question of pedagogy. It signals a shift from an exclusive concern with the substance and method of representation to questions such as which representations are engaged by whom, how, why, and with what consequences. Except in respect to skills training, occasions of pedagogy are occasions for the provocation of semiosis. Such pedagogies reference the hopes and intentions that the meanings, produced within the relations within which people construct, present, and engage representations (e.g., classes, viewings, performances, occupancies, religious services) will at least be informed by the positions made available within particular discursive regimes. In this sense, without reducing all aspects of cultural practice to modes of education, all cultural work needs to address the concerns of pedagogy. Thus I am suggesting that within a new articulation of cultural work, we can collaboratively address common questions in reference to our semiotic provocations. These include questions such as: What knowledges and perspectives are needed by whom and why? How can taken-for-granted meanings be challenged? What practices elicit an investment of old desires and mobilization of new ones? How can commitments and passions be aroused and sustained? How can these effects be realized within an open process of learning and, where appropriate, how can the process of semiosis be extended dialogically and dynamically through time? And finally, what is the moral and ethical framework within which all of these questions are to be addressed?

CULTURAL WORK AND PROGRESSIVE PEDAGOGIES

Teachers and other cultural workers share the intention of organizing a symbolic practice that provokes semiosis. A *critical* symbolic practice would embody a pedagogical project aimed at enabling ways of thinking and structures of feeling that open and sustain actions that express an ethically informed expansion of human possibility (the substance of which I discussed in detail in Chapter 2). Yet within this counterdiscursive orientation one must consider specific issues in relation to both substance and form of the provocation intended. As cultural workers with progressive pretentions, what is our view of learning and its relation to questions of power? What is the pedagogical relation we desire between ourselves and those who engage our work? With what intent do we offer and encourage our own modes of knowing and their resultant claims, our own structures of feelings and their ethical sensibilities?

In my view, a progressive pedagogy cannot proceed from the intention of getting those people who participate in our classrooms, watch our films, read our books and magazines, listen to our radio programs and music, occupy our buildings and urban spaces, and attend our congregational activities to think and act as we do. From a critical pedagogical perspective, occasions of organized symbolic production are not meant as imprinting exercises. If we assume people always come to an engagement with symbolic productions already knowing and with concerns and questions important to their lives, the task for the progressive cultural worker is to engage such people so as to provoke their inquiry into and challenge of their existing views of "the way things are and should be." This will mean offering questions, analyses, visions, and practical options that people can pursue in their attempts to participate in the determination of various aspects of their lives. While the image of learning within a critical pedagogy may be characterized as occurring within a structured provocation and challenge, it must remain open and indeterminate. Required is practice rooted in a ethical-political vision that attempts to take people beyond the world they already know but in a way that does not insist on a fixed set of altered meanings.

Such a view by no means characterizes the span of what has been previously been called "progressive" cultural practice. To illustrate what is at issue here, I wish to turn to a brief discussion of the reexamination that has been taking place with respect to the practice of documentary photography.[21] As a cultural technology[22] used to support efforts at social reform, documentary photography is an excellent place to begin a display of the value of a multiple site inquiry into the political/pedagogical problems inherent in cultural work.

Since the invention of photography, one dominant use of the photograph has been that of a tool of persuasion.[23] This use has been predicated on the notion that a photograph is a transparent display of things as they are, epistemologically indexical in relation to "reality." Conceived as a technology of truth telling, as a neutral witness with a requisite objectivity, the photograph has often been situated outside politics though used for political purposes. Much of the history of "documentary photography" has been the history of the deployment of the photographic image in efforts to educate and provoke the conditions necessary for either the confirmation or reform of particular social policies. From the early work of Jacob Riis and Lewis Hine, who captured the impoverished lives of immigrants in New York City at the turn of the century, to such documentarians of the grinding poverty of the 1930s depression as Walker Evans and Dorothea Lange, to the contemporary "accidental" work of John Filo, who recorded the death of Jeffrey Miller in 1970 at Kent State University, to the "AIDS portraits" of Rosalind Soloman, "taken" images have been placed within sets of discursive practices with the express purpose of guaranteeing their truth.

Along with the solidification of this notion of "documentary" practice during the last hundred years, has been the simultaneous emergence of a counterpractice. Begun in the early work of post–World War I movements like Dada, surrealism, and constructivism, artists working with photography developed new practices based on a recognition of the constructed nature of the relation between the photographic image and truth. More recently, developments in feminist and postmodern theory have continued, elaborated, and shifted this critique, a critique vital for continuing ability to help us see how it is that photography has been and is being used as an element of productivist power articulated by cultural technologies seeking to secure consent to specific ways of naming the world.[24] However, as important as these critiques are, as a teacher, what excites me most are the cultural practices that take such critiques as their point of departure.

At issue in such practices is an attempt to rethink and reconstruct the pedagogical relation between image and viewer. Accompanying the centering of the *representational* (as opposed to the transparent) character of the photograph has been a rejection of a photographic practice that seeks to educate by revelation, literally a process of exposing and providing the truth to the viewer. Education by revelation is not an inappropriate framework within which to group various versions of contemporary "progressive" curricula and teaching practice. Needed are alternative views of how to employ image and text in the context of one's teaching. For this reason, I think it important to study the practices of other cultural workers who are trying to formulate modes of practice that embody a different politics of learning. For this reason I would like to briefly discuss one aspect of the work of Connie Hatch, particularly as described by Abigail Solomon-Godeau.[25]

Without placing and marking her work within a genre or movement, suffice it to say that I am interested in Hatch's work because it attempts to reemploy the photographic image within a practice that makes its representational character clear. Furthermore, within this practice, Hatch's photographs are not allowed to guarantee a discursive truth but rather seek to initiate a process within which the viewer grasps a view of herself amid the contradictions structured by the social relations of class and gender. Illustrative of such a practice is Hatch's slide/audio trilogy *Serving the Status Quo: From Stories We Tell Ourselves, Stories We Tell Each Other.* As Solomon-Godeau describes it:

In this trilogy four people—a working-class couple in the suburbs of Burleson, Texas; a young lesbian New Music composer who supports herself as a computer technician; and a fortyish waitress in an exclusive San Francisco women's club—talk about their lives and their work. As we listen to their self-narratives, the black and white slides click by, dissolving into one another, presenting us with pictures of the subjects at work, at home, at leisure.

Hatch is well aware of Walter Benjamin's famous dictum: "To supply a productive apparatus without—to the utmost extent possible—changing it would still be a highly censurable course even if the material with which it is supplied seemed to be of a revolutionary nature."[26] Her work is so interesting precisely because Hatch understands how the political is intertwined with the mode—and hence the pedagogical relation— through which she offers her work to her viewers. For example, in Part 1 of the trilogy, "Work/Possessions: One Family," "stories" of Chris and Faye Edwards (the couple from Burleson, Texas) are visually and aurally presented in such a way as to make apparent the difficulties the couple have in sustaining their family life and consumption patterns within the class and gendered character of their labor. Such is the site of embodied contradiction and the loss of narrative coherence. Here Hatch works to provoke the viewer into a reflexive apprehension of the "stories" through which Chris and Faye are represented. What becomes manifest is not a truth unknown to the Edwards and revealed to the viewer. Rather, the contradictions, if recognized, make apparent the viewer's own complicity in relations that continue to reproduce the entanglement of powerlessness and desire. Hatch tries to accomplish this pedagogical provocation through a continuous counterpoint of image and speech— both clearly constituted as self-conscious self-presentations but most importantly, juxtaposed and sequenced to continuously disrupt any possibility that the lives of Chris and Faye can be subsumed within any simple notion of a narrative coherence.

Hatch's work contests the basic trope of the reformist documentary: the depiction of the subject—and the subject's circumstances—as spectacle usually deployed to a different audience and a different class. It is also intended to contest the immobilizing effect produced by presenting the visual "fact" of individual victimization as a metonyn for the (invisible) conditions that produced it, the slippage from the political to the anecdotal or emblematic.[27] As constructions, her images are "misread" as posed falsifications. Rather, it would be more to the point to see them as problematic truth claims that must be investigated. In other words, Hatch's pedagogical work leads not to silence but to questions, questions supportive of that continuous reflexive integration of thought, desire, and action sometimes referred to as "praxis." Rejected by this pedagogy is action constituted within the terror of political correctness or a mindless disembodiment of revolutionary discipline.

While all three parts of Hatch's trilogy are worth studying in depth, that is not my intent here. Rather, it has been to point to a pedagogical reconstruction that illustrates the potential for an articulation of interests between teachers and other cultural workers. There is much to learn from one another as we go about the specifics of our work. There are possibilities for an alliance. An alliance would mean that we could on occasion cooperatively share and interrogate our strategies and insights and perhaps begin developing a clearer sense of how to interweave our provocations. The task is nothing less than developing a critical cultural work that challenges a citizenry to a renewal of the prospect for our collective future.

NOTES

1. See, for example, Bruce Curtis, *Building the Educational State: Canada West, 1836–1871* (London, Ontario: Althouse Press, 1988); Ivor Goodson, ed., *School Subjects and Curriculum Change* (London: Falmer Press, 1987); Ivor Goodson, ed., *The Making of Curriculum* (London: Falmer Press, 1988); and Thomas S. Popkewitz, ed., *The Formation of the School Subjects: The Struggle for Creating an American Institution* (Philadelphia: Falmer Press, 1987).

2. Ken Osbourne, *Educating Citizens: A Democratic Socialist Agenda for Canadian Education* (Toronto: Our Schools/Our Selves Educational Foundation, 1988); Michael Apple, *Teachers and Texts: A Political Economy of Class and Gender Relations in Education* (New York: Routledge and Kegan Paul, 1986).

3. As experiments in Canada, Britain, and the United States have shown, "community control" of schooling is not an unproblematic concept. What is a school community? Who is a legitimate community member? How will political representation be established? These questions and more make any easy reference to democratization shallow rhetoric. It is not my purpose to explore these issues in this book; however, for an introduction to some of the important issues regarding the democratization of school policy decision making, see Clive Haber and Roland Meighan, eds., *The Democratic School: Educational Management and the Practice of Democracy* (Ticknall, Derbyshire: Education Now Publishing Cooperative, 1989).

4. This definition of power is substantially developed in Michel Foucault, "The Subject and Power," *Critical Inquiry* 8, no. 4 (1982): pp. 777–95.

5. It is important to stress that an articulation between teachers and other cultural workers cannot be achieved by this writing. This writing can help by preparing the ground, making the possibility visible. However, the substance of articulation can only happen through direct, politically understood practice.

6. Ernesto Laclau and Chantel Mouffe, *Hegemony and Socialist Strategy: Towards a Radical Democratic Politics* (London: Verso, 1985); and Ernesto Laclau, *Strategies*, 1, no. 1 (1989).

7. In developing the following discussion of technology, I have drawn from the work of Martin Heidegger, "The Question Concerning Technology," in *Basic Writings*, David Farrell Krell, ed. (New York: Harper and Row, 1977); George Grant, *Empire and Technology: Perspectives on North America* (Toronto: House of Anansi, 1969); Michel Foucault, *Discipline and Punish* (New York: Vintage Books, 1979), and *History of Sexuality*, vol. 1 (New York: Vintage Books, 1980); and Teresa de Lauretis, *Alice Doesn't: Feminism, Semiotics and Cinema* (Bloomington: Indiana University Press, 1984). My work here should not be misconstrued as simply an adoption of the positions worked out in these various (and in some ways contradictory) texts. Borrowing up to a point from Heidegger and Grant, but leaning more toward Foucault and ultimately de Lauretis, in the following pages I have tried to build a discussion that clarifies what is at issue for teachers and other cultural workers in the concept of "cultural technologies."

8. See, for example, Michael Goldhaber, *Reinventing Technology: Policies for Democratic Values* (New York: Routledge and Kegan Paul, 1986).

9. In his characterization of modern, materialist technology, Heidegger relates but ultimately contrasts *poiesis* and technology. While referring to Heidegger, I am breaking with his analysis. This is a decidedly Nietzschean move and influenced by my reading of Foucault. For those interested in Foucault's relationship to the work of Heidegger, see Gilles Deleuze, *Foucault* (Minneapolis: University of Minnesota Press, 1988), pp. 94–123.

10. Gilles Deleuze, *Foucault,* p. 40.

11. Both Foucault and de Lauretis employ the phrase "social technologies." Indeed, de Lauretis takes up cinema as a specifically social technology. I view their use of the referent "social" as specific to the intent of clarifying how sites of production of images and texts are historically and socially constituted and form regimes of power whose effects may be traced to the reproduction of specific relations of dominance such as patriarchical definitions of gender identity, homophobic definitions of normalized forms of sexuality, and Eurocentric colonialist ideologies. While acknowledging the importance of such effects, in choosing to emphasize the term "cultural," I am attempting to foreground something else. Because my point of departure for this analysis is the question of how, as teachers, we might re-vision the character of our work and its possible effects, I am attempting to emphasize modes of textual and image production in such a manner as to open up a way of seeing how all technologies of the symbolic are implicated in questions of pedagogy. Thus I recognize that the technologies I am referring to in this chapter are both social (constituted socially and have social effects) *and* cultural (in that they organize and regulate symbolic productive processes through which meanings are absorbed, recognized, understood, accepted, challenged, distorted, taken further, dismissed, and so on).

12. In arguing that schools, cinema, theater, and the like are arrangements that manifest cultural technologies, I am simply pointing to a range of generalized forms within which one might find a historically situated variety of technologies. Thus it is crucial to recognize that in principle, there is more than one specific way of "doing" education, cinema, theater, broadcast television, architecture, and so on. Yet none of the instances of these generalized forms can exist without the specification of some particular version of a cultural technology that defines how the "work" constitutive of these forms will be done. Furthermore, in particular conjunctures of time and space, certain technologies will have gained or been regulated into dominance rendering both the methods and effects of such technologies as natural and normal while marginalizing other practices as "experimental," "peripheral," or "perverse."

13. Note that in sites such as schools most contemporary pedagogies would have both students and teachers making representations and engaging with them. Of course, engaging in representations is just as much an act of meaning production as is the writing, drawing, acting, photography, and so on that are the concrete means for making representations.

14. I intend the term "subject position" to reference the simultaneous agentic moment of participation in the work of semiosis and the subjection within discursive regimes that constrain and enable practices of representation, comprehension and recognition. See Julian Henriques, Wendy Hollway, Cathy Urwin,

Couze Venn, and Valerie Walkerdine, *Changing the Subject: Psychology, Social Regulation and Subjectivity* (London: Methuen, 1984).

15. Consider what this implies about schooling. If we examine the history of public schooling, it is quite evident that state schools were originally established by some people for the children of others as public institutions with a clear agenda of moral regulation. Established were sets of practices which articulated an entire apparatus of cultural production. Such practices included the regulated distribution of teaching and learning to particular times and places, the specification of controls that would determine who would participate in such an apparatus, the specification of images and texts to be used, and methods of organizing student learning thought to optimize acquisition, the specification of knowledges and meanings students and teachers would be accountable for producing, and so on. In other words, schools have been sites within which legitimated authorities have attempted to "regulate into dominance" particular ways of meaning.

16. I have been warned by some friends to remove this reference to "leafing through *Playboy*" because of its potential to be read as "politically incorrect" behavior. Yet to do so would be to assume that "leafing through *Playboy*" requires a semiosis that submits unequivocally to a discursive regime in which women are constituted as the object of men's pleasure. While the intelligibility of the magazine requires positioning oneself within that discourse, to deny the complexities of complicity and assume that one has significantly invested in such a position (and that other frameworks for reading have not been generated in my access to other discourses) would be to fall into the trap of reading off the use of a popular cultural commodity from a consideration of its content. See Henry Giroux and Roger I. Simon, "Popular Culture as a Pedagogy of Pleasure and Meaning," in Henry A. Giroux and Roger I. Simon, eds., *Popular Culture, Schooling and Everyday Life* (Granby, Mass: Bergin and Garvey, 1989).

17. While noting that various cultural technologies may interpenetrate, how this interpenetration is organized and regulated is quite important to grasp. Note that copyright laws are now affecting the interpenetration of film and television within schools by limiting access to such resources for use in the classroom.

18. Counterdiscursive strategies are not dependent on institutionalized forms of symbolic production. The symbolic substance and value of commodities are always susceptible to the creative symbolizations grounded in the informal, organic relations of local communities.

19. Jacqueline Bobo, *"The Color Purple:* Black Women as Cultural Readers," in E. Deidre Pribram, ed., *Female Spectators: Looking at Film and Television* (London: Verso, 1988), pp. 90–109; Barbara Harlow, *Resistance Literature* (New York: Methuen, 1987).

20. I make this argument without in any way implying the *reduction* of art to either education or politics.

21. An important version of such a reexamination can be found in Martha Rosler, "In, Around and Afterthoughts (On Documentary Photography)," in *Three Works* (Halifax: Press of the Nova Scotia College of Art and Design, 1981).

22. As Solomon-Godeau suggests, "As part of a larger system of visual communication, as both a conduit and agent of ideology, purveyor of empirical evidence and visual "truths," documentary photography can be analyzed as a sign

system possessed of its own accretion of visual and signifying codes determining reception and instrumentality."

23. The history of photography may be characterized along the twin axes of what Solomon-Godeau calls the index and the icon, the index representing the display of truth and objectivity and the icon representing the display of subjectivity, art, and beauty (Abigail Solomon-Godeau, *Photography at the Dock: Essays on Photographic History, Institutions and Practices* [Minneapolis: University of Minnesota Press, 1991]).

24. See, for example, the Solomon-Godeau discussion of the constructed character of the well-known U.S. Farm Security Administration sharecropper photographs (Solomon-Godeau, *Photography at the Dock,* pp. 176–80).

25. See particularly Solomon-Godeau's essay "Reconstructing Documentary: Connie Hatch's Representational Resistance," in Solomon-Godeau, *Photography at the Dock,* pp. 184–217.

26. Walter Benjamin, "The Author as Producer," in *Reflections: Essays, Aphorisms, Autobiographical Writings* (New York: Harcourt Brace Jovanovich, 1978), p. 228.

27. See the essay "Who Is Speaking Thus?" in Abigail Solomon-Godeau, *Photography at the Dock,* pp. 178–79.

4

Pedagogy as Political Practice

This chapter is about desire, perhaps yours, most certainly mine. It is about the desire to awake or incite a particular passion in those with whom we teach,[1] a passion that invests with a particular urgency, the challenge to taken-for-granted social truths and the struggle for a more just and compassionate moral order capable of sustaining the diversity of life which inhabits our planet. Furthermore, it is about the problems of not only mobilizing this desire but as well, developing the knowledge needed to direct and sustain it. Thus it is a chapter about the practical, political action called pedagogy. More specifically, it is about a particular school-based version of such pedagogical work. What I am about to do is raise several interconnected themes that, in my view, seem fundamental for thinking through what it might mean to construct a pedagogy of possibility in such settings. While my referent from here on will be the classroom, I hope the possible connections of these issues to other sites of cultural work will not be lost and may be posed as questions for subsequent collective discussion.

Perhaps I should begin this exposition of issues with a brief explanation for the use of the term "pedagogy," for certainly the word has its detractors.[2] One can hardly use the term in conversation in schools and living rooms without a degree of embarrassment at sounding like a pretentious academic. Most people want to know, and often with some degree of aggressiveness, "Isn't pedagogy just a highfalutin word for teaching?" Well, I must admit, I do use the term to some degree as a provocation; as an attempt to rupture everyday talk about classroom practice and introduce suppressed or forgotten issues back into the conversation. So if I can successfully evoke questions about the term, I then try to outline the distinction between pedagogy and teaching as follows. In staff rooms and classrooms, teaching manuals and curriculum guidelines, teaching is most commonly referred to as the strategies and techniques used in order to meet a set of predefined (often given) set of objectives. Not unsurprisingly, talk and writing about teaching are primarily carried out in the language of method for the purpose of proposing viable classroom suggestions. When such discussions take into account the constraining realities of curricular content, teaching resources, time restrictions, and student interests and learning characteristics, they are a vital source of shared ideas and can certainly be helpful in working out the details of what one actually does as a teacher.

But in my view, something is often missing from such discussions of teaching. In any discussion of practice, it must not be forgotten that education is implicated in the production, accessibility, and legitimization of the language and images that give our relations with our social and material world a particular intelligibility. This means that educational practice is a power relation that participates in both enabling and constraining what is understood as knowledge and truth. When we teach, we are always implicated in the construction of a horizon of possibility for ourselves, our students, and our communities. Remembering such a perspective in conversations about practice means finding a way of discussing practices that reference not only what we, as educators, might actually do but as well the social visions our practices support. To examine how practice relates to future visions of community life, an alternative is needed to the separation of "philosophy" and practice and the impoverishing reduction of the teacher's concern to questions of "what works."

The notion of pedagogy perhaps provides this alternative. As David Lusted suggests, "How one teaches is of . . . central interest, but through the prism of pedagogy, it becomes inseparable from what is being taught and, crucially, how one learns."[3] In the previous chapter, I characterized pedagogy as a provocation of semiosis, an attempt to constitute the work of meaning production on particular semiotic terms. What is emphasized in this view are the processes through which we are encouraged to know, to form a particular way of ordering and giving sense to the "booming, buzzing" significations that surround and engage us. In this sense, pedagogy is a practice within which one acts with the intent of provoking experience that will simultaneously organize and disorganize a variety of understandings of our natural and social world.

Seen in these terms, pedagogy is hardly innocent. Constituted within cultural technologies, pedagogies stress that the realities of what happens in classrooms organize and are organized by how a teacher's work within an institutional context specifies a particular version of what knowledge is of most worth, what it means to know something, and how we might construct representations of ourselves, others, and our physical and social environment. Such an emphasis on the power/ knowledge dimensions of pedagogy does not at all diminish its concern with what is to be done. As a complex and extensive term, the concern of pedagogy includes the integration in practice of particular curriculum content and design, classroom strategies and techniques, a time and space for the practice of those strategies and techniques, and evaluation purposes and methods. All of these aspects of educational practice come together in the realities of what happens in classrooms. In other words, talk about pedagogy is simultaneously talk about the details of what students and teachers might do together *and* the cultural politics such practices support. Thus to propose a pedagogy is to propose a political vision.[4]

As outlined in Chapter 2, affirming a commitment to a project of possibility requires the construction of an education rooted in a view of human freedom as the understanding of necessity *and* the transformation of necessity. Such a pedagogy will require forms of teaching and learning linked to the goal of educating students to take risks, to struggle with ongoing relations of power, to critically appropriate forms of knowledge that exist outside their immediate experience, and to envisage versions of a world that is "not yet"—in order to be able to alter the grounds upon which life is lived.[5] However, such statements, to the degree to which they remain unproblematic and disembodied from the work of teaching, only stand as hopeful abstractions. Thus the task must be to deepen the discussion of what is at stake when one attempts to determine what forms of practice would support a pedagogy of possibility. Without pretense to comprehensive coverage, the following discussion will address three themes of central concern to this endeavor: the requisite counterdiscursive quality of learning, the classroom relations that might support such learning, and the erotic character of pedagogical commitment.

PEDAGOGY AND COUNTERDISCOURSE

As one sets out to teach within the framework of a pedagogy of possibility, one of the first questions to be asked is what content and method are presupposed by such a viewpoint. Obviously, a teacher has to have some idea of the topics and issues to be addressed and the concrete ways students might collectively engage them. Thus pedagogy is never an abstraction; it always takes contingent shape. In the real world of teachers' work, one always proceeds from a "point of practice," from a specific time and place and within particular themes. Such themes are often broadly specified by institutional arrangements that have predetermined who is going to teach what to whom, for example, junior division language arts, grade nine science, senior level history, adult ESL. Themes are also specified by specific contextual concerns with application across a broad spectrum of topics such as gender equity and antiracist education. While certainly I do not wish to naturalize nor justify the fragmentation of teaching and learning that predominates across North America, it is important to recognize that such forms of organization do provide the substantive sphere within which most teachers are likely to assess the practicality of a pedagogy of possibility.[6] Accepting this as a starting point, a teacher might reasonably ask: How might I begin thinking about critical classroom practice, given the content focus within which my work is organized?

There are no abstract, decontextualized answers to the question of which practices constitute a pedagogy of possibility, no prescriptive curriculum and methodology within which to encapsulate its terms. Rather, those seeking to work within this pedagogical form must approach such a task strategically, locally and contextually formulating practice within an integrated moral and epistemological stance. One might begin with a critique of the explicit, implicit, excluded, and unarticulated notions of curriculum, assessing each for its implication in the unjust diminishing of human possibility.[7] Thus depending on one's point of practice, a pedagogy of possibility might be a practice that seeks to address issues such as the destructive effects of hegemonic language forms when they become the sole lingua franca of the classroom,[8] the canonical provision of notions of knowledge, truth, and beauty without regard to the grounds of their construction,[9] the violence perpetrated by an educational practice that inadequately addresses the reproduction of sexism and racism,[10] the scientism of science that constructs a powerful and excluding ideology regarding what it means to do science,[11] or the forms of work education that reduce valued labor to that which fits existing economic arrangements.[12]

To further develop an understanding of what is at stake in this strategic approach, it is essential to consider the relationship between pedagogy and experience. As a concept with multiple connotations, it is important to take some care in delimiting the particular notion of experience I have in mind here. I am drawing on a discussion by de Lauretis in stating that by experience,

I do not mean the mere registering of sensory data, or a purely mental relation to objects and events, or the acquisition of skills and competences by accumulation or repeated exposure. I use the term not in the individualistic, idiosyncratic sense of something belonging to one and exclusively her (or his) own even though others might have "similar" experiences.[13]

Instead, by "experience" I mean a process that constructs configurations of subjectivity, that is, the conscious and unconscious thoughts and feelings, images and memories that realize one's sense of self, others, and our material environment in such a way as to constitute possibilities of existence. Of course, possibilities of existence are not simply constituted in subjectivity, but neither can they be solely attributed to socioeconomic forces and their corresponding social organization of everyday life. For significant social transformation to occur, undoubtedly such forces will have to be addressed. However, for our work as teachers, it is pivotal to register that change also occurs through discourses and representations that actually and concretely affect the lives of people.[14]

This discursive construction of subjectivity is an unending process taking place, in often contradictory ways, in a multiplicity of sites and relations. In this view, subjectivity is an ongoing construction, the effect not of images or texts that simply impose particular ideas or values, but rather of the personal, subjective engagement of social reality within discursive regimes that lend significance (value, meaning, and affect) to the events and conditions of everyday life. As process, experience defines the multiple and at times contradictory dispositions to action that result from the semiotic interaction of outer world and inner world, the continuous reciprocally constitutive realization of ourselves and our apprehension of reality. In other words, how we know who we are, how we know our world are issues that have to be grasped in relation to the way people attempt to "grasp the real" within particular modes of knowing.[15]

As I began to outline in the previous chapter, I view the practice of pedagogy as an attempt to influence experience and its resulting forms of subjectivity. As a mode of organizing and regulating symbolic productive practices, pedagogy attempts to influence the way meanings are absorbed, recognized, understood, accepted, confirmed, and connected as well as challenged, distorted, taken further, or dismissed. Indeed, the practical work of pedagogy is always grounded in the discursive regimes that structure the particular forms of representation (written texts, television programs, music, films, personal stories, experiential simulations) to be engaged and the different modes of engagement deemed desirable. Hence the practice of pedagogy inescapably includes an epistemological dimension leading to a crucial point regarding the substance of a pedagogy of possibility. In choosing "texts" (either written, visual, auditory or experiential) and in encouraging and enabling ways that students might engage them, what must be considered is the political dimension of both the forms of representation chosen *and* the structures of meaning that particular modes of learning are intended to provoke in relationship with these forms.

Forms of apprehension of social reality can enhance or diminish human possibility. Without developing extensive examples here (but see Chapters 5, 7, and 8), what I am emphasizing is that teaching always includes questions of epistemology, which are also questions of politics. This is simply echoing a point that has been stressed within feminist theory for years. As Catharine MacKinnion says, "To feminism, the personal is epistemologically the political, and its epistemology *is* politics."[16] What she is signaling to those of us working toward transformation in the way we engage ourselves, others, and our material world is the importance of understanding and intervening in the formation of discourses through which reality is apprehended.

Thus a pedagogy of possibility might be thought of as a counterdiscursive activity that attempts to provoke a process through which people might engage in a transformative critique of their everyday lives. This means addressing the "naturalness" of dominant ways of seeing, saying, and doing by provoking a consideration of why things are the way they are, how they got to be that way, in what ways might change be desirable, and what it would take for things to be otherwise. The resources for such a critique are, at minimum, dual. They include *both* existing counterhegemonic discourses emergent within the contradictory ways that people have of making sense of their daily lives *and* the formalization of texts within counterdiscourses that suggest new ways of naming and knowing, desiring and defining how human possibility might be considered. A pedagogy of possibility would be responsible for ensuring its participants had access to both resources. How might a teacher address such a task practically? Where can counterdiscourses enter the classroom? Such questions raise three curricular emphases worthy of deliberation: the telling of new stories, the retelling of well-known ones, and the reflexive consideration of consciousness.

The stories we tell, the narratives that give coherence and meaning to our lives, set the terms within which we are able to formulate the possibilities of existence. This is particularly so when we understand that the history we engage, the science we study, the rules of grammar we are told we have to follow, mythologies we engage regarding desirable forms of masculinity and femininity, all these representations are narrative forms that circumscribe our lives and enable existing forms of productive and affiliative relations. While hegemonic narratives are always contestable from the viewpoint of those uncolonized moments within everyday life, from a pedagogical viewpoint it is crucial not to discount the importance of telling new stories "so as to inscribe into the picture of reality characters and events and resolutions that were previously invisible, untold, unspoken [and so unthinkable, unimaginable, 'impossible']."[17]

By no means, however, is such an effort unproblematic. For example, we might judge existing curricular materials to be implicated in the reproduction of unjust social relations (e.g., sexism, racism, classism, heterosexism) and that "new stories" are needed. But given that teaching is always constrained by time and space, what does this judgment imply? Does it lead to a legitimate form of exclusion of material? Who will be involved in making such choices? What process of deliberation will be used, and what forms of authority will be invoked? Another set of issues arises in recognizing that "new stories" are also available through popular narratives and memories that often critique dominant ideologies. How can one draw on such knowledge in one's pedagogy? Assuming this means working with knowledge embedded in the social forms and popular culture of students' everyday lives, what should be done to avoid making students who live outside dominant and ruling forms feel that they are being singled out as the marginal "other" when we take seriously the knowledge organized within the terms of their everyday lives? Furthermore, many popular knowledge forms are forms of violence. Should such forms simply be excluded? If not, how should one address memories and subjugated knowledge that apparently support racist or sexist relations? What of experiential knowledge that appears to us irrational or simply wrong? How do we address it?

Another curricular strategy teachers might employ in attempting to put counterdiscursive forms on offer is the retelling or rereading of well-known stories. This strategy is an attempt to rub familiar narratives against the grain. This often includes filling in the gaps in historical accounts in order to express the violence that is the forgotten legacy of our Enlightenment heritage and producing new meanings in relation to old stories, thereby provoking a shift in the ground of reading the social and natural. Here too there are problematic issues to consider. Given that meaning can never be secured by pedagogical practice, it is important to deliberate when it is appropriate to engage a rereading of what might be understood as reactionary material.

But in addition to telling new stories and retelling old ones, there is a moment within which counterdiscourse must turn reflexive and be employed in efforts to comprehend and critique one's own embeddedness in histories, memories, and social relations that are the ground for one's understanding of the social world and one's actions within it. This means that both student and teacher experience will become "official" curriculum content. Especially in the context of North American adaptations of Freirian pedagogy, such an assumption has become almost a commonplace of critical pedagogy.[18] While articulating such experience can be both empowering and a form of critique against oppressive forms of cultural authority, experience is not an unproblematic notion of knowledge formation since it moves always in relation to the discursive regimes employed in the production of subjectivity. Thus, the teacher is confronted with the difficult question of what to do after personal stories are told. How can one avoid the conservatism inherent in simply celebrating personal experience and confirming that which people already know? In other words, how can we acknowledge previous experience as legitimate content and challenge it at the same time? How do we encourage student "voices" while simultaneously encouraging the interrogation of such voices?

As important as the concept of counterdiscourse is for a pedagogy of possibility, it cannot be stressed enough that the provision of such forms is not sufficient. Different pedagogies will have different notions of a moral space in which such counterdiscursive efforts attempt to enter. German National Socialism in the 1930s included both a counterdiscourse and a pedagogy of possibility that I would vigorously want to contest. That is why it has been necessary for me to continue to clarify how my teaching practice is to be grounded in a particular social analysis. Yet this can never become an orthodoxy without recognition of its own partiality. As we do our pedagogies, the moral vision they imply must be clarified and subjected to constant critique. Such visions need to be democratically struggled for and never omnipotently imposed. Indeed, I would suggest that part of the responsibility of a pedagogy of possibility is to make visible and problematic its own production as both content and teaching-learning strategies. In this context, students could be helped to first understand the questions and issues that have motivated the curriculum which is giving structure to learning and then consider and challenge the relation between the details of classroom practice and the social vision they are intended to support.

The point I have been trying to stress is that the task of a pedagogy of possibility is the provision and enabling of new (counter)discourses, which, in their implication with the ongoing construction of subjectivity, may lead to the predisposition to new actions, actions which in turn may lead to new questions and re-formations of the material and social world. In other words, a pedagogy of possibility, if successful, will challenge its participants with processes of reorientation, redefinition and revisioning.[19] This challenge to go beyond one's existing knowledge and identities constitutes no small degree of risk; risk of failure, loss of coherence,[20] rupture of existing relations with family and friends, social ridicule, colonization within new ideologies, and a feeling of disempowerment as old certainties are abandoned. Clearly then, one cannot undertake such a pedagogy without some attention as to how such risks can be both recognized and attenuated.

COMMUNITIES OF SOLIDARITY

The jeopardy emergent in a pedagogy of possibility underscores the point that pedagogical practice is always social. It attempts to enter a particular social space dialectically, comprehending and transforming the communicative contours that structure the relations within which teaching and learning take place. Given the potential personal and interpersonal risk associated with a pedagogy of possibility, how a teacher takes into account the social relations of one's classroom is an issue of no small importance. One place to begin discussion of this issue is to consider the dimensions of a social form supportive of critical re-visioning and transformative action. I will speculate on three of these dimensions before providing a more global characterization of such a form. It is important to stress that at this point I am seeking to outline possible normative characteristics of classroom relationships before discussing some of the substantial constraints on their realization.

Communicative Openness

In her recent book *Talking Back,* bell hooks writes "the academic setting, the academic discourse I [we] work in, is not a known site for truthtelling."[21] The truth she is referring to here is that forged in the struggle to break the hegemonic discourse that continues to rationalize and reproduce practices of domination. Yet, for a pedagogy of possibility to exist in schools, such truths must be told. Whether it is in the form of new stories or the retelling of old ones, counterdiscursive ways of speaking and writing will form much of the substance of classroom communication. Whether located in personal narratives or the abstractions of theoretical writing, teachers and students will sooner or later face unfamiliar and, at times, disconcerting modes of address and ways of naming the world. Indeed, part of the notion of pedagogical practice is to help students understand such discourses and begin using them as frameworks for reconstituting their horizon of possibility. That there is both threat and anxiety in the process must be both recognized and respected. Thus it is by no means trivial to stress the need for a basic sense of trust and respect in such classrooms.

As I have learned, the practices of patience and mutual recognition are crucial. As students strive to make sense of new discourses and contradictory experiences, while beginning to write and speak in perhaps unfamiliar ways, they justifiably have a need to assert both their agendas and contributions into the public space and time of the classroom. This in turn raises a host of issues as to how that space and time will be shared, which issues will be sustained and which dropped, what modes of speaking and writing will receive recognition, and so on. Students (and the teacher) may find themselves in disagreement not only over how texts should be read but in ways that seem to challenge the wisdom of "personal" experience. These, of course, are processes of learning, which if truncated often short-circuit what might be collectively accomplished. Hence reciprocal support and a sense of collaborative struggle is almost a condition without which a pedagogy of possibility cannot proceed. Yet, without forsaking the importance of the classroom as a public sphere of collaboration and encounter, a sensitivity to the risks of critical re-visioning would also seem to require the opportunity for more private communications within which people can express the doubts, fears, and stories they cannot or are not yet willing to share publicly. I do not wish to belabor the obvious here, but simply to underscore that without such a dimension of communicative openness critical teaching becomes an impossibility.

Recognition of Partiality

Committed to a radical historical contingency for all knowledge claims including its own, a pedagogy of possibility cannot be allowed to degenerate into either a political epistemological dogmatism nor the cynical relativity that characterizes some forms of postmodern social constructivism. Rather, such a pedagogy calls on those who participate within it to be responsible and accountable for their truth claims. As Kathleen Weiler notes, this means abandoning a transcendental basis for our politics[22] and understanding that "the truth" is about specific and particular forms of embodiment and not a vision promising transcendence of all limits and responsibility.[23] This is an argument for the embodied, locatable, partial situatedness of knowledge, a position that demands a collective assessment of both the promise and limit of our claims about the world within the "webs of connections called solidarity in politics and shared conversations in epistemology."[24] This means that in the classroom people must find the opportunity for the legitimate expression of their own views while simultaneously subjecting such views to examination as to their partiality, embodiment, and constructedness within the differential positions offered by relations such as gender, race, class, age, and region. This indeed is a difficult challenge, requiring a collective process within which the emergence of conflict and difference should be expected. Within a pedagogy of possibility, cooperative learning is not to be reduced to a productive harmony. One must be ready to accept difference and disagreement as resources for learning without overromanticizing their realities. Diversity and dissent can destroy community as much as it can be a source of vitality particularly when teachers and students fail to see how difference is almost always constituted within relations of power. This, then, is where a responsible reflexivity must lead, to our own understanding of the relations of power in which we participate as we offer our knowledge claims to each other.[25] I will return below to the issue of the multiple forms of power that course through classroom relations, but for the moment I want to follow a different tack. I have asserted that a recognition of partiality demands a collective assessment of epistemological responsibility. This requires a consideration of the question "responsible to what?"

Sense of Collective Venture

Much of Western liberal education presumes a focus on personal development. Most often students enter educational settings either with individually set agendas or agendas assumed for them, but rarely with a sense of how in learning together they can participate in both an intellectual and political venture. However, if one proceeds from the position of the partiality and responsibility of all knowledge claims, the presumption of traditional Western education (founded on the practice of the dispensation of enlightenment) is radically called into question. Something new is required of the student, an assessment of epistemological responsibleness. This task, much like an environmental assessment, requires collaboration and a sense of collective venture. It means that the interested character of knowing be made topical and that students contend with questions of collective desire in relation to a socially organized horizon of possibility. In this sense new ways of knowing are mobilized to address the questions of locating limitations in people's lives, weighing the justice of such limitations, and considering how possibility can be expanded.

These three dimensions (communicative openness, recognition of partiality, sense of collective venture) are but three of the complex dimensions that would define a social form capable of sustaining a pedagogy of possibility. How might one characterize the general outlines of such a form? In response, I want to suggest the formation of a "community of solidarity" as the form of sociality ideally suited to support a pedagogy of possibility. Both solidarity and community are such overused slogans they are in danger of complete trivialization. What might their concatenation mean? First of all, as my comments above regarding the importance of conflict and difference indicate, a community of solidarity cannot be reduced to the occasion of agreement or unanimity of opinion. Sharon Welch[26] has offered the suggestion that solidarity could mean attempting to live one's own life as though the lives of others matter. But she also recognizes that taken to its extreme, this is impossible. In this sense solidarity would become an overwhelming burden, requiring that one either be a "*lamed-vavnik*"[27] or go insane. But perhaps one cannot travel too far from this extreme. In the context of working in heterogeneous groups crisscrossed with diverse relations of dominance, solidarity would—as Johann Metz[28] suggests—exclude any form of freedom and peace at the expense of the suppressed (and reproduced) history of suffering of other nations or groups. At the very least, this would require an attempt to divest forms of power that unjustly limit others and understand one's implication in the situation of the other (an analysis that would be infused with a comprehension of how power works to enable and disable). At the same time missing is a sense of project; absent is that which is not yet but which is striving to come into being. Perhaps, then, it is necessary to add something akin to Agnes Heller's notion of civic courage.[29] Thus in the spirit of a project of possibility I suggest that being in a community of solidarity means living for a particular definition of being human without a specification of its content or a guarantee of its historical possibility. This requires a form of courage to act to limit unjust restrictions even when by doing so you leave yourself vulnerable because the world hasn't changed yet. This notion echoes Moraga, Perez, Smith and Smith when they suggest "we don't have to be the same to have a movement, but we do have to admit our fear and pain and be accountable for our ignorance. In the end, finally, we must refuse to give up on each other."[30] In a classroom context, attempting to put a practical cast on what is obviously a utopian concept, a community of solidarity signals the struggle for a set of relations that strive for open communication among relations of power/difference while attempting to both recognize and define an interdependence within a particular moral universe.

It is crucial to emphasize that a community of solidarity can neither be demanded, imposed, nor constructed; it can only be achieved. It can only be an achievement born out of struggle for its existence. The core of this struggle is for the achievement of (to borrow a Hebrew concept) *hevrutah,* a sense of belonging to a moral culture that allows one to argue over its definition without feeling that an experience of collectivity has been dissolved. Social practices constituted within and through *hevrutah* do not demand solidarity but enable or evoke it. As Welch reminds us, the ability to love and to work for justice is something given through the power of community—the attempt to bring justice makes no sense as an abstract imperative outside a communal context.[31]

To this point a community of solidarity stands simply as a wish, a rhetorical abstraction with little sense of becoming hopeful without a clearsighted effort to address the constraints on its achievement. Indeed, such constraints are formidable. To attempt to understand their genesis requires rethinking what is at stake in classroom interactions. At one level, it is easily recognized that the way people interact in a learning context depends to a large extent on how the work of teaching and learning is organized. Thus the considerations of the use of space, the placement of furniture, the scheduling of discussion time, the tasks students will be required to address, the evaluation procedures to be used—all these factors, to the degree to which they organize the work of educational settings, will influence how people engage each other. But there is of course another dimension to the social relations of learning that is critical. All participants are always situated in the classroom within the wider relations of power that mark the communal social fabric. Through this lens, the myth of the classroom as an ivory tower fades away as relations of dominance inscribe themselves on both bodies and forms of embodiment. Thus factors of race, gender, class, sexual preference, ethnocultural group membership, and regional identifications combine in both complementary and contradictory ways to affect levels of participation, feelings of exclusion, chances for agreement, and possibilities of mutuality. This then specifies a second level of influence that leaves classroom relations doubly organized.

While teachers and students may feel they can have some direct control over how the organization of classroom work affects the prospect of a community of solidarity, it is quite another matter when it comes to social relations whose directions of force are secured across a multiplicity of social sites outside the classroom. Thus while one may strive to develop an organization of classroom work that is for example, nonclassist, nonsexist, or nonracist, this by no means will eliminate the effects of capitalism, patriarchy, and colonialism from the classroom. That one is constantly being positioned within such relations while striving to stand outside them is often a great source of frustration and despair for those of us "trying transformations"[32] in our everyday lives. In her discussion of feminist pedagogy, Linda Briskin cogently emphasizes this point.

A focus on nonsexism suggests that, through desire, individual teachers can liberate their own classrooms from gendered social realities. This attributes an extraordinary power to individual teachers and no doubt provokes guilt and self-doubt when teachers are unable to put such a nonsexist environment in place . . . (obscuring) the degree to which the classroom environment is shaped by the relations between students . . . (and) disguising the reality that educational institutions are part of a complex of institutions—the state, families and households, workplaces, etc.—which both reflect and reinforce the values and practices of patriarchal capitalism.[33]

This point perhaps underscores both the difficulty and urgency of the concept of a community of solidarity. To take such constraints on its realization into account would require not only converting one's efforts at nonclassism, nonracism, and nonsexism into active attempts to address structures of dominance through questions of how to extend practices in this regard beyond the classroom but it is decisive as well that we find means of addressing the oppressive ways such relations limit what learning can be in our own classrooms without falling into the trap of guilt that immobilizes all possibility of change.[34]

To pursue this matter a bit further, I want to briefly consider the impact of such issues on the notion of authority in the context of classroom relations. In the following section of this chapter, I will address the issue of the problematic character of authority as it inheres in the conventions of the work of teaching, but here I am concerned with how classroom authority is affected by relations of dominance organized outside the classroom. What is at issue for me here is how a person's "authoritativeness" is imputed or ascribed, that is, how is it that one's words are taken seriously, as those of a speaking and writing subject who knows. This is not just a matter of to whom do we attribute expertise but rather to whom do we cede trust for naming the responsible character of one's knowledge claims. It is widely felt that this issue is affected by one's position in relations such as race, gender, and class. That the truth has to be told by white, ruling-class men has characterized Western institutions of learning for centuries. However, in attempting to counter this historical hegemony of authoritativeness, there is a danger in running the problem back the other way. This happens when uninterrogatable authority is ascribed to classroom members by virtue of their positionality as a member of an oppressed group. This essentialization of experience within a form of relationship called identity politics needs careful scrutiny. While important arguments have been and can be made for privileging previously subjugated knowledge and forms of knowing, such "truths" can never be immune to questions of discourse and responsibility. Thus, within a community of solidarity certain key questions will become crucial to consider. How do we situate ourselves in relation to others, and how do others situate us? What are the limits of this positionality, and can it be changed? Given that relationships are not stable unities, how can we shift among a variety of forms of mutuality and complementarity? How are we to maintain a community of solidarity when our "readings of the world" reveal contradictory and conflicting experiences and struggles?[35]

Those who work in schools will, of course, realize that none of the limitations on the achievement of a community of solidarity that I have discussed so far address the realities of the institutional constraints imposed on both teachers and students. Not only are classroom relations unisolatable from socially organized relations of dominance, they are integrally affected by structures of education that are themselves determined amid the realities of state regulation and shifting economies. Thus issues ranging from constraints on use of classroom material to forms of classification and grouping imposed at a district or school level to accountability requirements for both teachers and students all provide obvious problems for developing critical teaching and learning. In no way do I wish to diminish such issues. As Henry Giroux has written,

Unless teachers have the authority and power to organize and shape the conditions of their work so that they can teach collectively, produce alternative curricula, and engage in a form of emancipatory politics, any talk of developing and implementing progressive pedagogy ignores the reality of what goes on in the daily lives of teachers and is nonsensical.[36]

However, not only must such issues be addressed locally and contextually, but more is at issue than the fight for the necessary working conditions. Teachers embarking on such a pedagogy have to be prepared for a sizable investment of time and energy in an activity that will likely require battles for legitimization and be inherently conflictual. What, then, will enable teachers to sustain themselves in such work? What sorts of collegial association would help in this regard? How can support be given for one's "private" life, not only as a source of replenishment and renewal but in full recognition that love, justice, compassion, and joy are required in numerous places? Then again, there are questions of what constitutes an adequate preparation for the initiation of such forms of teaching. What new competencies must be learned? What new sources of information and opportunities for study should teachers be encouraged to seek? What other experiences besides teaching might contribute to such pedagogies?

Communities of solidarity are in themselves projects, something not yet but which could be through the struggle to define the conditions of possibility for their realization. In the face of the litany of problems and questions that require resolution before such a project can be fully realized, it should be remembered that such struggles are themselves pedagogical. This is to emphasize that pedagogy is not the achievement of univocality out of difference but rather a space within which meanings are posed and contested in the struggle to define the moral culture within which we will live our lives together. As Magda Lewis and I have written, pedagogical practice always implies

a struggle over assigned meaning, a struggle over discourse as the expression of both form and content, a struggle over interpretation of experience, and a struggle over "self." But it is this very struggle that forms the basis of a pedagogy that liberates knowledge and practice. It is a struggle that makes possible new knowledge that expands beyond individual experience and hence redefines our identities and the real possibilities we see in the daily conditions of our lives. The struggle is itself a condition basic to the realization of a process of pedagogy: it is a struggle that can never be won—or pedagogy stops. It is the struggle through which new knowledge, identities, and possibilities are introduced that may lead to the alteration simultaneously of circumstances and selves.[37]

EROS AND PEDAGOGY

Jane Gallop has given us a provocative warning regarding what some might judge as a masculinist desire to provoke desire in others. Exploring the concept of pedagogy in the works of the Marquis de Sade, she observes that

pederasty is undoubtedly a useful paradigm for classic Western pedagogy. A greater man penetrates a lesser man with his knowledge. . . . This structure and its sexual dynamic becomes explicit in Sade. The student is an innocent, empty receptacle, lacking his own desires, having desires "introduced" into him by the teacher. If the phallus is a sign of desire, then the student has no phallus of his own, no desires, is originally innocent. The loss of innocence, the loss of ignorance, the process of teaching, is the introduction of desire from without into the student, is the "introduction" of the teacher's desire. From the first dialogue of Sade's *Philosophy:* we will place in this pretty little head all the principles of the most unbridled libertinage, we will inflame it with our *fires* . . . we will inspire in it *our desires.*"[38]

This quotation from Gallop needs to be juxtaposed with the opening paragraph of this chapter, in which I "confess" my pedagogical desires to "awake or incite a particular passion in those with whom we teach." While a pedagogy of possibility makes no assumption of student innocence, nor does it presume an "empty receptacle" lacking in one's own desires, the parallel between Gallop's reading of Sade and the aspirations of a pedagogy that forswears disinterest is close enough to be discomforting. It must be asked what is emotionally at stake when I enter into a relationship with students with the desire to provoke a "particular passion" in them. Is there a particular eros that underlies my aspiration for a pedagogy of possibility?

I wish to come at this disquieting question sideways, drawing yet another literary analogy by considering the figure of Faust[39] as a pedagogue. As the prototypical "modern" professor, Faust was unhappily consigned to his study. He wanted the inclusion and vivification that engagement with community can provide. Making a pact with Mephisto (the devil, who was to be his teacher and guide) in exchange, for his soul, Faust sought the embrace of both worldly knowledge and passions. But in this embrace what Faust had to offer was his modernity, the desire to help by sweeping away the encrustations of an old order in preference for the new. Faust too had a desire to provoke a particular passion in others. Perhaps we too are being led by Mephisto if we assume that such passion proceeds from the corruption of intellectual innocence, that dissatisfaction with accepted knowledge begins the process of education. Through Gramscian eyes, what is at stake is a particular hegemonic relation imbued with the Mephistolean ethos that asserts, "I am the spirit that negates all." Indeed, Mephisto poses, through his relationship with Faust, the creative necessity for destruction. This too is discomforting. The notion of a pedagogy of possibility is partly premised on the idea of the destruction or negation of the world as "fact," on the necessity of showing that the apparent can no longer be taken for granted. There is an element here of what Walter Benjamin called the destructive character who

has the consciousness of historical man whose deepest emotion is an insuperable mistrust of the course of things and a readiness at all times to recognize that everything is wrong. . . . The destructive character [who] sees nothing permanent. But for this very reason he sees ways everywhere.[40]

Hence the concern previously registered that those who enter the discursive field of a pedagogy of possibility risk destruction of their ability to return to a safer, more certain place.

Mephisto's message to Faust was that he was not to blame himself for the casualties of his pedagogy, arguing that since destruction and negation are part of the natural order, the intellectual stands morally absolved of responsibility. As I have stressed, such a stance is directly challenged by a pedagogy of possibility founded on the situated, embodied character of knowledge. But such a stance does not resolve the questions posed by the erotic relation that underlies the Faustian embrace. As teachers with both vision and commitment, our relation to our students is part of a design we have on them. We do have images and ideas we think others should or could usefully take seriously.

The liberal, industrial West has developed a social division of labor that has produced a large class of relatively independent producers of culture and ideas. But ironically, the very division of labor that has allowed for the production of a lively and thriving critical culture has also locked it away from the world around it. As cultural workers we participate in restricted, institutionalized communities within which we try to find the time, resources, and support to produce pedagogies that (we argue) seek to open the range and depth of human desires and dreams. While these arguments are important to our own lived constellation of work/pleasure/play, there is no mistake that we also mean our ideas and images for others. I, as an academic in a graduate school of education certainly work within historically constituted relations that require that I have a stake in asserting the importance of my ideas for others, knowing full well the dangers of "false generosity."[41] In other words, recognizing an aspect of ourselves in Faust, but simultaneously moving to distance ourselves from its implications, what then is the alternative to an eros which expresses love through the negation of the lived grounds of the other, destroying what to some may be a peaceable kingdom as the only way to win love and express our own?

There is a Jewish story that tells how God, seeing that it was good, rejoiced in the completion of creation. This joyful pleasure was heightened in the figure of the human, made in the image of God. For not only had a pleasing form been molded from clay, but a particular passion had been provoked. Taking on God's attributes, the first humans professed and displayed a love of justice and compassion. Unfortunately, the creation was a bit imperfect, a little unstable; violence and deceit became endemic to our species. God was not just a little upset at this imperfection of his will to power. It was only at the time of Noah that God finally gave up on what Nietzsche later would describe as omnipotence, learning instead a new basis for relation with our species, a new eros founded on self-limitation and the mutual recognition of partners in creation. God didn't become less of teacher, nor was the passion to provoke a passion in others diminished, but the entire framework within which this was to be carried out shifted.

Jane Gallop's accusative warning is on the mark. For a pedagogy rooted in the recognition of partiality, no assumption of omnipotence will do. We know that when people ignore the intrinsic dignity of particularity, forgetting our own limitations and speaking as if we were the mouthpiece of the universal, we unleash new forces of barbarism destructive of human dignity.[42] While we still mean our pedagogies for others, this desire must find expression in the recognition of the particular dignity of others, not as objects, but as people with whom mutuality is possible. Such statements are of course not new, but perhaps what is, is the recognition of the urgency of the task and the difficulty of its realization.[43] What is *not* needed is the pretensions of empathy, the claim to share an understanding of the positions and feelings of others, but rather the recognition of the impossibility of such claims and hence the requirement that we listen and try to hear what is being said. This is another way of saying that the erotic character of a pedagogy of possibility cannot be founded on sincerity or intensity of professed commitments but rather on the fascination with the dignity and worth of those whom we teach. What this might mean is suggested in Martin Buber's distinction between a teacher's influence and interference.[44] Interference is defined as a "will to educate" with all its concomitant sets of expectations of what is required of students. Buber counterposes to this stance a response formed through what he calls "experiencing the other side." I wish to reformulate this not as an empathic response, but rather an attempt to hear first, how the response of the other is formed on a ground that is open to change within history and second, to reflexively consider the ground on which as teachers our own dispositions and feelings are formed, seeking transformations here too that will be driven by the collective venture of human possibility.

NOTES

1. Maxine Greene, "The Passion of the Possible: Choice, Multiplicity, and Commitment," *Journal of Moral Education* 19, no. 2 (May 1990): pp. 67–76.

2. Etymologically, pedagogy's referent is the "science of the child" and its associated applications to the practice of teaching. The term, however, has come to have a general reference across a wide range of cultural practices, is no longer limited to children, and cannot be reduced to scientific prescription.

3. David Lusted, "Why Pedagogy?" *Screen* 27, no. 5 (September–October 1986): p. 3.

4. This argument is also made in Roger Simon, "Empowerment as a Pedagogy of Possibility," *Language Arts* 64, no. 4 (April 1987): pp. 370–82.

5. Henry A. Giroux and Roger I. Simon, "Schooling, Popular Culture and a Pedagogy of Possibility," in Giroux and Simon, eds., *Popular Culture, Schooling and Everyday Life* (Toronto: OISE Press, 1989).

6. While this is clearly a reformist statement, I am not at all precluding the necessity of new courses, new curricula, and new institutional forms for any radical rethinking of North American education.

7. Deborah P. Britzman, "Who Has the Floor? Curriculum, Teaching, and the English Student's Struggle for Voice," *Curriculum Inquiry* 19, no. 2 (1989): pp. 143–62.

8. Catherine E. Walsh, *Pedagogy and the Struggle for Voice: Issues of Language, Power, and Schooling for Puerto Ricans* (Toronto: OISE Press, 1991).

9. Henry Gates, Jr., "The Master's Pieces: On Canon Formation and the Afro-American Tradition," *South Atlantic Quarterly* 89, no. 1 (Winter 1990): pp. 89–111.

10. Kathleen Weiler, *Women Teaching for Change: Gender, Class and Power* (South Hadley, Mass.: Bergin and Garvey, 1988).

11. Sandra Harding, *The Science Question in Feminism* (Ithaca, N.Y.: Cornell University Press, 1986).

12. Roger I. Simon, Don Dippo, and Arleen Schenke, *Learning Work: A Critical Pedagogy of Work Education* (Granby, Mass.: Bergin and Garvey, 1991).

13. Teresa de Lauretis, *Alice Doesn't: Feminism, Semiotics, Cinema* (Bloomington: Indiana University Press, 1984), p. 159.

14. See Teresa de Lauretis, "Feminist Studies/Critical Studies: Issues, Terms, and Contexts," in De Lauretis, ed., *Feminist Studies/Critical Studies* (Bloomington: Indiana University Press, 1986); Chris Weedon, *Feminist Practice and Poststructuralist Theory* (London: Blackwell, 1987).

15. "Different forms of consciousness are grounded, to be sure, in one's personal history; but that history—one's identity—is interpreted or reconstructed by each of us within the horizon of meanings and knowledge available in the culture at given historical moments, a horizon that also includes modes of political commitment and struggle. Self and identity, in other words, are always grasped and understood within particular discursive configurations. Consciousness, therefore, is never fixed, never attained once and for all, because discursive boundaries change with historical conditions" (Teresa de Lauretis, "Feminist Studies/Critical Studies: Issues, Terms and Contexts," in de Lauretis, ed., *Feminist Studies/Critical Studies*, p. 8).

16. Qtd. in de Lauretis, *Alice Doesn't*, p. 184.

17. Teresa de Lauretis, "Feminist Studies/Critical Studies: Issues, Terms and Contexts," in de Lauretis, ed., *Feminist Studies/Critical Studies*, p. 11.

18. Ira Shor, ed., *Freire for the Classroom: A Sourcebook for Liberatory Teaching* (Portsmouth, N.H.: Boynton/Cook, 1987).

19. Bluma Litner, *Exploring Critical Revision as a Process of Empowerment* (Ph.D. diss., University of Toronto, 1990).

20. Jane Flax, "Re-membering the Selves: Is the Repressed Gendered?" *Michigan Quarterly Review,* special issue, *Women and Memory,* 26, no. 1 (Winter 1987): pp. 92–110.

21. bell hooks, *Talking Back: Thinking Feminist, Thinking Black* (Toronto: Between the Lines Press, 1989): p. 29.

22. Kathleen Weiler, "Freire and a Feminist Pedagogy of Difference," unpublished manuscript (photocopy) (Department of Education, Tufts University, 1990).

23. Donna J. Haraway, "Situated Knowledge: The Science Question in Feminism and the Privilege of Partial Perspective," *Feminist Studies* 14, no. 3 (1988): 575–99. The quotation is from p. 584.

24. Donna Haraway, p. 12 draft version; see also Haraway's brilliant and detailed exposition of this position within the realm of scientific discourse in *Primate Visions: Gender, Race and Nature in the World of Modern Science* (New York: Routledge, 1989).

25. Elizabeth Ellsworth, "Why Doesn't This Feel Empowering? Working through the Repressive Myths of Critical Pedagogy," *Harvard Educational Review* 59, no. 3 (August 1989): pp. 297–324.

26. Sharon Welch, *Communities of Resistance and Solidarity: A Feminist Theology of Liberation* (New York: Orbis Books, 1985).

27. According to Jewish legend, a *lamed-vavnik* is one of the thirty-six righteous people on earth whose merit preserves the world from being destroyed.

28. Cited in Sharon Welch, *Communities of Resistance,* p. 58.

29. See Henry Giroux's brief reference to Heller's concept in his *Theory and Resistance in Education: A Pedagogy for the Opposition* (North Hadley, Mass.: Bergin and Garvey, 1983), pp. 201–2.

30. Cherrie Moraga, Julia Perez, Barbara Smith, and Beverly Smith, cited in Elly Bulkin, "Hard Ground: Jewish Identity, Racism and Anti-Semitism," in Elly Bulkin, Minnie Bruce Pratt, and Barbara Smith, eds., *Yours in Struggle: Three Feminist Perspectives on Anti-Semitism and Racism* (Brooklyn: Long Haul Press, 1984).

31. Sharon Welch, *Communities of Resistance;* see p. 67.

32. Susan Hardy Aiken, Karen Anderson, Myra Dinnerstein, Judy Lensink, and Patricia MacCorquodale, "Trying Transformations: Curriculum Integration and the Problem of Resistance," *Signs,* Winter 1987, pp. 255–75.

33. Linda Briskin, "Feminist Pedagogy: Teaching and Learning Liberation," *Feminist Perspectives,* no. 19, Canadian Research Institute for the Advancement of Women (Ottawa, August 1990), pp. 12–14.

34. Audre Lorde, "The Uses of Anger: Women Responding to Racism," in *Sister Outsider: Essays and Speeches* (New York: Crossing Press, 1984).

35. See Kathleen Weiler's cogent discussion of this in her *Women Teaching for Change: Gender, Class and Power* (South Hadley: Bergin and Garvey, 1988): pp. 125–145.

36. Henry Giroux, *Schooling and the Struggle for Democratic Public Life* (Minneapolis: University of Minnesota Press, 1988), p. 102.

37. Magda Lewis and Roger I. Simon, "A Discourse Not Intended for Her:

Learning and Teaching within Patriarchy," *Harvard Educational Review* 56, no. 4 (November 1986): p. 469.

38. Jane Gallop, "The Immoral Teachers," *Yale French Studies,* no. 63 (1982): p. 118.

39. There are, of course, numerous translations of this classic by Johann Wolfgang von Goethe. I will cite here a local favorite, *Goethe's Faust,* trans. Barker Fairley (Toronto: University of Toronto Press, 1970).

40. Walter Benjamin, "The Destructive Character," in *Reflections: Essays, Aphorisms, Autobiographical Writings* (New York: Harcourt Brace Jovanovich, 1978), p. 302.

41. Paulo Freire has warned us against those who dispense "false generosity." "Whatever the specialty that brings them into contact with the people, they are almost unshakably convinced that it is their mission to give the latter their knowledge and techniques. Their programs of action include their own objectives, their own convictions, and their own preoccupations. They do not listen to the people, but instead plan to teach them how to 'cast off the laziness which creates under development.' " (*The Pedagogy of the Oppressed* [New York: Herder and Herder, 1970], p. 153).

42. David Hartman, *A Living Covenant: The Innovative Spirit in Traditional Judaism* (New York: Free Press, 1985), p. 304.

43. Raymond Williams, "Resources for a Journey of Hope," in *Toward 2000* (London: Penguin Books, 1983).

44. Martin Buber, *Between Man and Man* (New York: Macmillan, 1965). See in particular chap. 3, "Education," esp. pp. 96–97.

II

Reinventing Practice

5

The Fear of Theory

It is necessary, says Freud, to interpret the phenomenon of doubt as an integral part of the message.

Jacques Lacan[1]

What is quite consistently made marginal for most people is any sense that they already know more than they think they know. The standardization of both kinds and forms of knowledge *and* the proper manner of their behavioural expression in educational practices and experiences is but the most visible instance of a quite general consequence of the regulation of social forms.

Philip Corrigan[2]

The countenance of fear and hope are turned toward the same horizon. Hope is directed toward the future through its goal of effecting practical changes in the world,[3] while fear anticipates an experience of negation or destruction. Those of us who teach, in sites ranging from elementary to graduate school, face numerous students whose entry into the classroom initiates the volatile mix of the expectant emotions of fear and hope. What is it in an educational encounter that provokes these emotions? How should we understand this provocation and what does this provocation tell us about the problems of formulating a pedagogy of possibility?

I wish to put aside at the outset that portion of student fear and hope instigated by the adventure of new social encounters, for example, the new class, the new teacher, the new school. Instead, my concern will be with the anticipatory relation that students have to the knowledge that is assumed to be on offer in a classroom or course. Specifically, I will be concerned with the particular textual forms and verbal practices that students and teachers often identify as "theory." This usually refers to a "scheme of ideas" that attempts to both describe and explain a particular set of events or practices.[4] It is important to note that "theory" in this sense applies to a broad range of possible curricular content that includes not only advanced disciplinary study but content such as elementary school science or social studies as well. Thus, I do mean to suggest a degree of generality in the following argument, an argument, however, I shall not pursue in the abstract. Rather, I wish to locate the discussion within my own practice teaching at the Ontario Institute for Studies in Education—the graduate school of education for the University of Toronto.

The large majority of students who enroll in the school in which I teach are or have been employed in some form of educational work. Many are practicing teachers who are attending graduate school in order to upgrade their qualifications and gain access to new ideas they hope will help improve educational practice. Others have worked in a variety of informal settings as diverse as labor unions, prisons, community-sponsored English language programs for new immigrants, women's organizations, and agencies attempting to empower people experiencing physical and mental disablement. Others seek knowledge they hope will aid them in the responsibilities they have for improving the quality of the educational programs offered within their organizations. Still others come seeking the knowledge and credentials that they hope will help them move into university settings where they might pursue the opportunities to conduct research and "advanced-level" teaching. These students then all come with complex sets of hopes for what their studies will accomplish. For many of the students with whom I am fortunate enough to work, these hopes are underscored by a commitment to a vision (articulated with varying degrees of explicitness) of what, as a social practice, education could and should be.

The most common and public ground on which I engage these hopeful students is the context of a course.[5] In the courses I teach I try to open up and think through questions of how education might be understood as a moral and political practice as well as a technical one. In this context I ask people to engage with a wide variety of often unfamiliar theoretical material and assess to what degree the viewpoints and concepts of this material might be useful in reformulating a form of practice consistent with the vision they want such practices to support. In doing so, I do not efface my own moral, political, and educational commitments but rather try to make public my efforts to make similar kinds of assessments.

While this ground is intended and often seen as a hope-engendering space, it is important for me to recognize that for many students it is simultaneously a space provocative of fear.[6] It is this provocation that I now wish to pursue in an attempt to trace its origins, effects, and implications. It is a provocation I am here calling "the fear of theory."

SOME PRELIMINARY QUALIFICATIONS

This discussion should not be construed as a complaint against "lazy students," nor should it be seen as a glib indictment of education as rife with anti-intellectualism. Indeed I am beginning this exploration with the presumption that expressions of the fear of theory are quite legitimate and worthy of intense scrutiny, that they can teach us something about pedagogical practice that we need to understand. I also want to note that the fear of theory is not something easily acknowledged, especially in the context of a graduate school. Those of us who study and work in universities are not supposed to admit to the experiences of anxiety, intimidation, and even cowardice when confronted with unfamiliar theoretical discourse. There are, of course, differences among people in regard to their willingness to make such an admission. In my experience, male students have a more difficult time naming the unease that may accompany confronting a theoretical text (no surprise!). In any case, my hope here is that "fear" will not seem too strong a word for the emotion that accompanies the anticipation that there is something in theory that is noxious. My guess is that the fear of theory is something most of us who have studied in schools have experienced (and still experience) and that the topic under discussion here will strike a cord of recognition among my readers.

I recognize that as a teacher who "assigns" theoretical material and "puts it up for discussion," I am complicitous in the production of fear. However, I also realize that the eliciting conditions for the production of this fear are not simply bound to the outlines of my pedagogy. In other words, the response to my pedagogy is also connected to its location in a particular institutional form; within trajectories of student ambition and hope; and within the intersecting relations of class, gender, race, ethnicity, region, and sexual orientation which articulate aspects of the ways in which being a student in a graduate school of education is lived.

It is also important not to be pedagogically naive about fear occasioned by the challenge of theoretical knowledge. To the degree that fear is either immobilizing or leads away from a fair engagement with a text it is, of course, destructively limiting. However, certain manifestations of fear might be taken as positive, as an indication that a particularly significant moment of learning may be at hand in which old investments are about to be questioned, modified, or possibly displaced. But even in this positive light—as I will argue below—such moments are pregnant with both the expansion of human possibility *and* the negation of knowledges and commitments that might be valuable resources for hope.

What I am suggesting and intending to display here is an attempt to think through the ways in which our teaching is implicated in the production of fear. The purpose of such an effort is to see what might be done (personally and institutionally) to re-vision our own educational practices in behalf of a project of possibility. Thus this chapter is in part a reflexive analysis fixed upon my own forms of "pedagogic action."[7] The danger in such a venture is one of self-rationalization. I may in the end wish to fix up my old boat while others may argue that its timbers are rotting and the entire voyage on which I am embarked is ill conceived. This of course is the risk of any reassessment of one's commitments and praxis.

MANIFESTATIONS OF FEAR

To provide a more visceral sense of what I am referring to, I want to briefly describe several manifestations of the fear of theory that I have noticed during my years of teaching. While the question of who it is that is most likely to exhibit such manifestations is extremely important, I am postponing a discussion of this issue until later in the chapter. At this point, I shall simply foreshadow the issue by acknowledging that the following evidence for a fear of theory is most often expressed by students who have had to struggle for acceptance and recognition within the dominant institutions that define the terrain of everyday life. These are students whose lives have been lived within the prescriptive and marginalizing effects of power inscribed in relations of class, gender, ethnicity, race, and sexual preference.

Perhaps the most pervasive manifestation of the fear of theory is silence, specifically, the silence of a student who is unable to speak or refuses to risk speaking in class when theory is being discussed. In this sense the request to "do theory" results in actively silencing students. While it is important not to reduce all silence to silencing,[8] there is no question that many students fear making a fool of themselves as they try to enter the realm of unfamiliar "theoretical discourse." This fear will of course be exacerbated if the teacher or other students are quick to point out the inadequacies of any given contribution to discussion. Furthermore, this fear of ridicule is double edged. The anticipation of ridicule not only induces a fear of being ridiculous but as well the apprehension that in one's very ridiculousness one is made even more unworthy than one suspects one already is.[9] This is sometimes expressed as a concern that one has nothing "worthwhile to say," that one is unable to be as insightful or clever as others and as a consequence may not be worthy of his or her place in the class. When such fears are continually elicited, many students judge the risk of speaking too great and simply remain quiet.

A second manifestation of the fear of theory is the expression of anger. As one might suspect, given the form of subjugation present in the experience of being silenced, there is often a close connection between fear and anger. This connection is powerfully presented in the Nietzschean concept of "ressentiment." This can be understood as a directing of one's rage and imagined forms of compensation toward the object assumed to be the source of humiliation and injury.[10] This means the fear of theory at times leaves scars, bodily marks of humiliation that occasion the "ressentiment" sometimes expressed publicly in the classroom but more often experienced late at night, in the safety of that hoped-for "room of one's own," as one wrestles with a text one is supposed to "master" for class the next day.

When "ressentiment" does surface in the classroom, it is often as an attack on what is posited as deliberately marginalizing obscurantist "jargon" and those responsible for propagating it. The texture of this attack is nicely nuanced by recalling that the term "jargon" was originally derived from the old French, where it referred to the warbling or chatter of birds. From this referent it was extended to refer to unintelligible talk or writing.[11] The fact that jargon is often related to speech designations like "babbling," "spouting off," "mouthing off," and "speaking gibberish" is a clear indication of the adversarial intent of the accusation of jargon. It is important to emphasize that this adversarial address is spoken from a position of marginalization and subjection, allowing "one to suppose that words are suspected by the dominated."[12] What they might be suspected of I will address more fully in the next sections of this chapter; however, a brief glimpse of the threat of theory might be useful at this point.

Raymond Williams makes an extremely important point in noting that "in branches of knowledge which bear on matters which already have a common general vocabulary the problem (of the adversarial usage of jargon) is even more acute, since the material reasons for specialized precision are less clear or absent."[13] This is clearly the case for education, as it is for psychology, sociology, and anthropology. While Williams acknowledges that "specialized vocabularies can be developed . . . to a fault" [mea culpa], he also emphasizes that "the use of a new term or definition is often the necessary form of a challenge to others' ways of thinking or of indication of new and alternative ways." Williams is pointing here to at least two potential sources that connect fear to anger. On the one hand, students both fear and resent the potential humiliation of being excluded from a discourse that is supposed to have some relevance to everyday lives. In other words, there is a "ressentiment" at being "made stupid." As one of my students once raged: "I am a successful teacher, a successful administrator, I got good grades in university, and I've done well in graduate school; I never was made to be stupid until I took your class." On the other hand, Williams is also pointing to the disruptive character of theoretical language; the fact that it may call into question the adequacy of one's taken-for-granted ways of communicating about daily realities. It is the issue of what is at stake in such a disruption that I will return to in a moment.

A third manifestation of the fear of theory is the mode of speech many students exhibit when engaging in theoretical discussion. I am referring here to a hesitant, at times apologetic, self-effacing tentativeness about the point one is trying to express. This signals the apprehension that "I've got it wrong" and more importantly that "I'm not capable of being smart in this context." While this is often a plausible interpretation of hesitant, self-qualifying speech, an important qualification must be added. Kathleen Jones has written:

The ideal of autonomy and participation in rational discourse excludes certain forms of expression, linked metaphorically and symbolically to "female" speech, from those which make authority coherent. For example, sociolinguists recently have argued that female patterns of speech reveal a different expressiveness than do male patterns. Rhythms, nuance, emphasis and assertiveness in tone and syntax appear to vary with gender. Nevertheless, we define the masculine mode of self-assured, self-assertive, unqualified declarativeness as the model of authoritative speech. "Female" hesitancy and other-oriented language patterns, considered as the marks of uncertainty or confusion, are derogated.[14]

Taking Jones's point into consideration means it is not possible to collapse a particular mode of speaking into a simple reflection of fear and inadequacy. Particular ways of speaking are presumed to indicate that you really know what you are talking about, and this presumption establishes norms for authoritative participation that mitigate against the inclusion of certain groups of people with different modes of relating and discussing. Thus hesitant, self-qualifying expressions may result from feeling that one not only has got it wrong, but one is unable to find the "correct" forms of expression to indicate that one has got it right. On the other hand, hesitancy may be motivated by an attempt to deliberately downplay one's assertiveness in an effort to draw more people into a discussion and develop cooperative modes of learning.

The final manifestation of fear of theory I shall mention here is less often expressed in a public forum and more often stated in private communication. This is direct admission (or confession?) of fear of being "found out." The range of concerns expressed in this form include many things that can be "found out": that one does not belong in this class;

that one does not belong in graduate school; that one is not as smart as others think; that one is not really an "intellectual"; that one is not as well read as one should be, and so on. All of these fears are at least in part directly connected to the potentially humiliating and displacing potential of theoretical discourse. It is to the consideration of why theory can get caught up in such relations of power that I now wish to turn.

THEORY AND POWER

Some commentators have linked the educator's flight from theory to the reduction of knowledge to narrow questions of technique. Giroux, for example, has asserted that the constricting effects of a culture of positivism have reduced interest to an exclusive concern with "what works."[15] While there is no doubt that the concerns of practice have been constituted within a hegemonic search for methods of instruction independent of questions of educational purpose and value, this is not the whole story. If it were, theory would simply be dismissed as an irrelevance, something that was opposed to instead of linked to practice. It would not be a provocation for fear and anger.

Thus we must turn to additional perspectives if we are to clarify what is at stake in the fear of theory. One such perspective that may be useful is the view that emphasizes the integral connection between knowledge forms and forms of power. Within this view, in order to trace the effects of theory, it is necessary both to historicize its production and contextualize its distribution. Within education, most discourse that stands for theory about educational practice has been produced within a division of labor between those who construct theory and those for whom it might have some pragmatic value. This is not a natural division, but one that has been shaped by the incorporation of educational research and teacher training into the institutional context of the university. This incorporation has a 100-year history in North America that is still very much in process. Within the university a particular set of epistemological assumptions about knowledge and truth have guided the task of constructing how we might best understand the issues of educational practice.

Furthermore, this division of labor is implicated in the common suspicion that theory has colonialist tendencies. That is, given that many educators meet theory on the grounds of university courses or school board–sponsored workshops, theoretical discourse often strikes people as something that is being done to them rather than a resource for their own practice. Thus when theory is taken up in the context of some pedagogic action, it is recognized as a form of symbolic violence to the extent to which it is understood as a preferential and absolute imposition of meaning. This recognition is particularly acute if such discourse is apprehended as knowledge that constitutes teachers and teaching practices as the objects of that knowledge. In such a case, a person's objectification within theory and the corresponding demand that one constitute oneself as a subject acting within the frame of reference of that theory, fully articulates the nexus of power/knowledge.[16]

But what is at stake in this recognition that pedagogical presentation of theory involves the mobilization of power/knowledge? To the extent that our pedagogy demands that students take the theory we offer seriously, it implies the potential negation of aspects of one's personal and professional identity and the corresponding investments one has in retaining those identity positions. Of course, not all theory demands an aspect of self-abandonment. Indeed, many educators seek theory as a source of legitimation for previously established assumptions and practices.[17] But I am concerned here with understanding the fear of theory, and in this respect I think it is important to recognize theory's disruptive potential. Professionally, one might face a call to abandon a particular mode of practice that appeared successful and through which others recognize one's competence. This was succinctly put by one of my students in a final course essay.

The course theorizes that to attempt projects of possibilities for our students, educators must first recognize that "schools cannot and should not be defined as a mode of moral regulation that seek to produce ways of seeing and being seen according to what those in power view as the appropriate and legitimate forms." This seems to presuppose that the hegemonic nature of educational institutions can be recognized and negotiated by educators within the system, and forced me to ask myself: can I do this? If I accept, as a moral project, a pedagogy of possibility for my students that encourages counterhegemonic perceptions, what models do I use? I have been a happy and successful member of educational institutions for thirty-four years. My subjectivities as student and teacher have been produced, organized, and legitimated in schools, and my forms of meaning and teaching practices have been consistent with the ideological principles of the dominant discourse. Can I achieve the critical distance to question what is appropriate and legitimate in such a way as to negotiate or resist in order to implement new practices in my own and my students' production of knowledge? Even if I theorize effectively, to what extent can I effectively implement new practices? To theorize is a set of semantic practices with which I am familiar; to implement change in my present methods of knowledge production is an affective *disruption*.

Beyond the disruption of professional identities are even deeper disruptions. These are the potential disruption to one's location in a set of class, gender, and ethnic relations. It implies the demand to give up (or, more minimally, compartmentalize) the knowledges and commitments that people have grown up with and which constitute important resources for coping with everyday life. The students who sense this form of disruption are obviously those whose lives have not been constituted in what Philip Corrigan has called "the figure in dominance" (see Chapter 1). The students in my classes who have spoken and written about this most clearly are ethnic, working-class women and men who are the first in their families to "make it out" and who sense that graduate study and the discourse of professional achievement is making them "Other" to the very groups to which a portion of one's fragmented self is tied. This process is illustrated in the story Valerie Walkerdine tells of her suppression of her own working-class knowledge.

There was a phrase [my mother] . . . used at home: it was kind of a game. . . . When she was doing domestic work, in order to find out how she was progressing . . . she would often call out . . . "what's the keleuraiteel?" She had told us that "keleuraiteel" was French for time and through this special phrase [my sister and I] learnt something and shared a kind of knowledge which was private, a game which served to bind together the participants. Later in my first French lesson . . . the teacher asked if anyone knew any French words. I called out I knew the French for time and the word was "keleuraiteel." Everyone laughed. I never again volunteered a piece of knowledge from home which, I learnt quickly, was, on every level and in every subject, the place of the wrong knowledge, the wrong culture. To leave this knowledge was then, in a very painful way, to split from home, a terrifying splitting which told me that the new knowledge could be mine, the glamour, the dream, so long as I rejected the old, rejected and left my home.[18]

Walkerdine emphasizes that such stories should not be taken as celebration of knowledges subordinated within the dominant institutions like schools and universities. Rather, she is stressing how our subjectivities are constituted within multiple and often contradictory discursive practices and how students are forced to confront new ways of naming and claiming their world in relation to the old ways they have invested in. The class is one occasion where this happens, and it is this occasion that is implicated in the fear of theory. We need to take a closer look at how this works.

THE SOCIAL FORMS OF EDUCATION

To begin the process of examining how a pedagogy that provokes a fear of theory is produced, I want to begin with a characterization of the classroom as a social form. Corrigan defines social forms as "the expected set of [connected] ways in which actions have to be done to be properly accomplished"; "signifying behaviors" that convey a sense of "value, evaluation, belief and commitment."[19] Constituted within specific discursive regimes and image repertoires, such forms set limits on the range of ways practices might acceptably be done. Applying this notion to education, we observe that the most common set of forms through which education takes place is "schooling." Furthermore, schooling itself is a particular configuration of settings whose practices are ordered and regulated within social forms. For example, in my institution the work of doing education is accomplished in settings such as a course and its manifestation as a series of weekly classroom meetings, individual discussions with students in faculty offices, thesis committee meetings, computer conferencing programs (within which students and faculty discuss various topics), and informal discussions among students (and sometimes faculty) in hallways, the cafeteria, and the local pub. Corrigan would name these various settings as a regulated repertoire of social forms, a social grammar of schooling or, in this case, for "doing OISE."

The regulated character of these settings is captured by the notion that they all contain "compulsions to behave" that are revealed either when they are refused or challenged or when someone is deemed unworthy to participate in them because she or he is unable to elicit practices consistent with the required form. Thus if a teacher asks for comments on an assigned reading and receives complete silence as a response, the ordered character of a particular classroom process is both disrupted and revealed. Likewise, the regulated character of the educational process is also revealed when a single mother, who is having a hard time raising her children and holding down a part-time job, who is taking several graduate courses and finds herself at two in the morning unable to grasp just what it is that Michel Foucault is saying, decides that perhaps graduate school is beyond her abilities.[20] Thus we cannot view the various institutional sites that make up its educational practice as neutral or natural. Rather, they are practices that demand both a subjection to a range of practices that define the way things are normally done and a particular process through which we come to recognize ourselves as subjects whose actions are informed by a taken for grantedness as to how such actions are to be done (the result being the pathologization of any deviation from the responsibilities defined by forms).[21]

It is important to grasp just what it is that such forms realize in what Corrigan calls their "coercive encouragement." Specific social forms render other ways of accomplishing something as old-fashioned, inefficient, inadequate, strange, wrong, and the like. In their concrete manifestation, forms provide models or standards for how things should be done, creating the basis for evaluating the adequacy of all other practices. This also provides the basis for identifying who and what range of practices is to be considered as appropriate and exemplary, articulating ideal types of embodiment and performance that other participants are encouraged to realize. Thus it is through these processes that forms effect a moral regu-

lation of social life, through the processes Corrigan terms "systematization," "standardization," and "normalization."

It is through these processes that the range of forms that define the
schooling offered by a specific institution regulates and limits not only
the ways that education takes place but as well, the terms on which students can demonstrate their capabilities and define themselves as competent. The implications of these processes of regulation are important to
grasp. Consider how language practices might be regulated within such
processes. Language is the medium through which education—that is,
schooling—is most often done. In graduate schools of education this is
almost exclusively so. What language is to be used and how it is to be
employed is a key element in defining the processes of systematization,
standardization, and normalization of any given site of educational practice. Thus in sites of education such as classrooms, doing education is
informed by a coercive encouragement of a specific way of speaking and
writing.

It must be remembered that the legitimacy and effectiveness of both
words and rhetorical forms do not come out of dictionaries or style manuals but rather the required and expected ways of expression in concrete
situations. Thus being in a graduate school and participating in a particular course will likely create a hierarchy of expressive genres that students are "coercively encouraged" to acquire. In this sense the language
of the classroom is never innocent, but structured by the social grammar
not only of schooling but as well, the societal forms through which a
public culture is expressed.

The hierarchy of expressive genres is embedded in the very material
organization of classroom activity and course structure. This can be
made clear in both explicit and tacit ways. For example, assigning grades
to particular student performances displays a model of what is to stand
as adequate use of unfamiliar concepts and language. The texts students
are asked to read and the language used in the class by the teacher organize a way of speaking and writing that renders other modes of expression less adequate. As well, students may quickly identify particular
class members who are considered exemplary in their perceptiveness
and expressive abilities.

These values, evaluations, beliefs, and commitments will of course
also be influenced by the embeddedness of a given course in the dominant forms of the educational institution of which it is a part. It is important to stress that while the individual teacher obviously is in a position
to affect the mode of social regulation under which a particular group of
students may come together to study and learn, this is only partially so.
For example, a teacher's attempt to encourage students to experiment
with different written rhetorical forms may be limited by students' prior
experience in other courses, the textual examples of academic work they

have read, and their own commitment to a particular previously learned version of what it means to display their competence. Also to the extent that a teacher and students serve as co-constituting authorities for legitimizing a particular form of schooling, a teacher's influence will be limited.

LANGUAGE PRACTICES AND STUDENT IDENTITIES

As this perspective on social forms indicates, the language practices in a classroom are in-formed by (and hence inform) the modes of regulation that constrain how a given instance of schooling is to be accomplished. But something more is at stake in the regulation of language practices than just a form of schooling. I wish to argue that the language practices through which the social forms of a classroom are accomplished effect a moral regulation that, for some students, is implicated in the malefic provocations of theoretical discourse. To argue this position requires considering the relationship between language practices and processes of identity formation. This position assumes that language is a primary medium through which the social organization of identity takes place (including what is competence and what is ignorance). I do not mean here language in the limited and abstracted sense of a formal system of semantics and syntactics. Rather, I am referring to an always already contextualized set of language practices organized and regulated within a particular set of social forms. It is these practices that encode different positions of subjectivity and semantic possibilities, a consequence at once both personal and political.

The implications of this view have been grasped, articulated, and extended by feminist theorists who have been trying to evolve a conceptually plausible and strategically practical understanding of the construction of gender identity. For example, Teresa de Lauretis, in reference to feminist writing as a distinctive set of language practices, makes it clear how language practices are to be understood as implicated in the social organization of identity.

There are discursive boundaries that distinguish feminist writing and speech from others. This includes not only specific terms, concepts and rhetorical strategies . . . but also shared assumptions, interpretive paths, inferences drawn from events and behaviors, and unstated premises. . . . These discursive boundaries—by which I do not mean simply constraints but also configurations—delineate possible meanings, or what I would rather call a horizon of meaning . . . at a given historical juncture. . . . [These are] patterns by which experiential and emotional contents, feelings, images, and memories are organized to form one's self-image, one's sense of self and others, and of our possibilities for existence.[22]

De Lauretis goes on to disclaim a form of language determinism, recognizing that "one's possibilities of existence are not simply the effect of one's subjective limits and discursive boundaries," but she also emphasizes that the limits on human possibility cannot "be simply attributed to an immutable deployment of socioeconomic forces that will be changed someday when the conditions are right." In other words, de Lauretis is emphasizing the educational and political potential of the discursive regimes and image repertoires within which we make sense of our experience.

Different forms of consciousness are grounded in one's personal history; but that history—one's identity—is interpreted or reconstructed by each of us within the horizon of meanings and knowledges available in the culture at given historical moments, a horizon that also includes modes of political commitment and struggle. Self and identity, in other words, are always grasped and understood within particular discursive configurations.[23]

To fully appreciate what is at play in references to de Lauretis's notion of "discursive configurations," it should be emphasized that she is not only referring to a particular constellation of words and concepts but as well to the particular evaluative tone or accent that a discursive regime imparts to particular signs. This underscores the notion of language's inherent "multiaccentuality,"[24] a concept that recognizes that though different classes and social groups may use the same signs, in doing so they will impart a particular range of reference and evaluative accents to particular usages. De Lauretis illustrates this in her statement that "the horizon of meaning or range of experiential contents conveyed by the single English word 'motherhood' has been significantly expanded and shifted by Adrienne Rich's *Of Woman Born*." What is significant for my argument here is de Lauretis's recognition that a particular discursive configuration—in its assertions, tone, and rhetoric—presupposes a horizon of competing, contrary utterances against which it asserts its own energies.[25]

WHAT'S ON OFFER IN THIS COURSE? THEORY AS DISCOURSE

The above formulations can now be utilized as a way of seeing just what is at issue when a new theoretical language is introduced into a course. What is on offer is access to a discourse and, through this discourse, the possibility of engaging the social world differently. In other words, when students are asked to engage with a theoretical position and hence are confronted with new and sometimes difficult speech and writing, they are being asked to at least temporarily take up a position within a mode of producing a range of textured significations. This regulated productivity defines a horizon of meanings and recognizable possibilities. But, and this is the crucial point, when such theory is offered or assumed to have some relevance to one's work as an educator and hence aspects of one's personal and/or professional identity, taking up a position within such a theoretical discourse is neither a neutral nor abstract exercise. In our insistence that theory matters, we recognize it has an integral connection to questions of practice. Given this connection, we cannot ignore the fact there are evaluative and affective dynamics in the way our students will consider theoretical discourse. This is underscored by Linda Alcoff's insight (in reference to feminist discourse but with obviously broader implications) that taking up a position within a new discursive perspective "does not necessitate a change in what are taken to be facts, although new facts may come into view from the new position, but it does necessitate a political change in perspective since the point of departure, the point from which all things are measured, has changed."[26]

It is in this sense that I am arguing that the systematized, standardized, and normalized practices of a particular course offer positions in language that have implications for affecting new identities and disorganizing old ones. This last point must be stressed, given the dialogic and often contradictory character of a discursive configuration (in the sense outlined above). Teaching practices that attempt to authorize a particular discourse not only organize particular ways of envisioning social existence and the practices of social reproduction but as well threaten to disorganize others. Of course, discursive positions offered or invited are not necessarily positions accepted. One may hear theoretical language both rejected and deformed. This accounts for the adversarial cries of "Jargon!" and the profusion of jokes students make about new theoretical language as they struggle to understand not just the "plain meaning of a text" but more centrally the implications of a new perspective for their view of themselves and their relationship to others.[27]

Thus theory in education is never simply an "academic question." Its potential consequences for the organization and disorganization of identities make a pedagogically motivated confrontation with theory a potentially threatening and noxious situation. In this sense, classroom language practices are not only a mode of social organization but, also potentially, a mode of disorganization.

In this perspective, the fear of theory is quite warranted and at least double. First of all, one may be excluded from access to a particular theoretical discourse. There are many possible sources to such an exclusion. Not the least of these is that the comprehension and assessment of a new discourse takes time. Students whose lives are lived amid the responsibilities of raising children, earning an income, food shopping, taking care of ailing parents, and so on—in other words, positioned within relations of class and gender to take on responsibilities because there is little choice—engage in a host of actions which sap their energies and leave little time for study.[28] Equally important, however, is the fact that the range of language practices seen as acceptable in a university setting often excludes those whose expressive patterns have been derogated as inadequate or unacceptable. Thus, a homogenization of textual forms in the range of reading material offered in a course will require a student population with a history of developed capabilities adequate to the language practices regulated into dominance.

If one cannot gain the required access within which a particular discourse becomes comprehendible[29] (something that may take a considerable effort to achieve), there are some potential unpalatable consequences. If one is in a course where others seem to embrace a discursive configuration that seems either nonsensical or unintelligible, what is risked is one's marginalization and the possibility that one will have to "live through" that course in a position of subordination.[30] Furthermore, if one has invested in the status and authority of the school one is attending, or the professor, and/or the course one is taking, and further has a desire to be acknowledged as competent and worthy in that context,[31] the inability to take up a position within a discourse can become a disconfirming experience. This is particularly so for those who have been marginalized from the dominant institutions of cultural definition. They may see their current failure to understand the significance of what others see as a failure of their own capacities, a moment of reproduction of subordination which, in its ideological character, is malicious. To the extent that such emotional dynamics are implicated in the fear of theory this explains the prevalence of such emotions among those who have felt themselves outside "the discourse that counts." While at OISE this has included teachers from working-class and "ethnic" backgrounds—many of them women—these are not the only positions of exclusion. The same bases for the fear of theory are often expressed by part-time evening students holding down full-time day employment as well as those educators whose training and professional lives have left them unfamiliar with anything other than a technicist discourse concerned with only instructional tactics.

However, the fear of theory is not just warranted by the potential subordination one might experience in a pedagogical confrontation with new discourse. As previously stated, fear may be warranted in terms of the potential values and desires a new discourse might be seen as contradicting or suppressing. Concretely, this might mean repressing desires and eliminating actions that would be seen as inappropriate and improper from the new discursive perspective. The potential tyranny one sometimes feels in the self-imposed demand to constitute not only one's practice but as well one's thoughts and feelings within a "politically correct" feminism or antiracism is illustrative of this issue. As important as such discourses are, they can have disabling consequences. Theory can indeed be the source of ambiguity and confusion as people wrestle with the implications of competing perspectives that have been in-formed within the very separate social forms of their existence.[32]

Within this view we now can begin to clearly see that the fear of theory is not something that is an individual attribution, located as an individual problem that must be therapeutically resolved by the student. Rather, we can see the fear of theory as a product of a particular conjunction of human capacities and histories and social forms. Furthermore, we can see that the fear of theory is a fear of the symbolic violence that can be inherent in institutional forms of pedagogic action, what Bourdieu and Passeron have called the imposition of a cultural arbitrary by an arbitrary power.[33]

Looking at the fear of theory in these terms, what can we learn? Of what importance are the issues raised to this point for a consideration of how a pedagogy consistent with a project of possibility might be constructed? A pedagogy that is constituted through a set of forms that restricts the exercise of human capacities so as to marginalize and exclude is a practice that in the frame of this book, must be rethought. Clearly, the goal must be a nonexclusionary, nonviolent pedagogy within which new and unfamiliar discourses can be addressed and assessed.

TOWARD PEDAGOGY

In my view, the pedagogical goal in relation to the fear of theory is not the individualist overcoming or repression of fear. I have tried to make clear that there is a legitimate warrant for such fears. Taking this warrant into account, I suggest our objectives must be an assessment of the objective basis for fear; a modification of pedagogic action to reduce its implication in the production of fear, joint action to reduce the social and institutional organization of fear, and the creation of a fair basis for evaluating[34] the practical and moral value of given theoretical discourse.

It has become commonplace to assert that learning is a process of coming to meaning. The above understanding of the fear of theory allows us to see that this process may at times become one of contestation, a struggle among competing or contradictory discursive configurations, each concealing a history of contending linguistic and nonlinguistic practices implicated in the reproduction of particular interests and values. It is important to consider how this struggle is lived in the process of learning and what implications it has for teaching with texts representative of a particular discourse.

An interesting approach to these questions is provided (in part) by

Shoshana Felman's important article in *Yale French Studies*.[35] In this article Felman argues that we can learn something important about pedagogy by considering psychoanalysis as a pedagogical experience.[36] In making her case, she draws on the writings of both Freud and Jacques Lacan. The argument is developed within a consideration of psychoanalysis as a means of accessing information previously unlearnable.

Of key importance to the questions at hand within this chapter is Felman's discussion of Lacan's understanding of ignorance. In Lacan's view, ignorance is not a simple lack of knowledge but rather something that has to be understood as an integral part of the structure of knowledge held by a person at a given point in time. Lacan's discussion implies that the material to which teaching should be directed is that which is not remembered or, more precisely, that which will not be remembered. Lacan is asserting here an active process of forgetting, an imperative to forget. Thus ignorance is understood "not as a passive state of absence—a simple lack of information" but rather "an active dynamic of negation, an active refusal of information."[37] This active refusal is an excluding from consciousness of whatever it does not want to know. In this light, teaching is to be directed not so much at the lack of knowledge as to resistances to knowledge, to what Lacan calls a "passion for ignorance," or the desire to ignore.

As I have already argued, the resistances and refusals provoked by a pedagogically motivated encounter with theoretical discourse can be linked to the fear of social subordination and a subjection to symbolic violence, as well as the disorganization and contradiction of conflicting commitments and desires. How might Lacan's notion of ignorance as an active refusal of information be conceptually and practically helpful in further understanding these negative provocations of theory?

Felman suggests that the nature of ignorance is *"less cognitive than performative* [my emphasis] . . . it is not a simple lack of information but the incapacity—or the refusal—to acknowledge one's own implication in the information." This is important because it brings to the surface the pedagogical implications of ignorance itself—the fact that it can teach us something. Thus Felman suggests "the pedagogical question crucial to Lacan's own teaching will be: Where does it resist? Where does a text precisely make no sense, that is, resist my interpretation? Where does what I see—and what I read—resist my understanding? Where is the ignorance—the resistance to knowledge—located? And what can I thus learn from the locus of that ignorance?"[38]

The key insight here is that resistance itself can be a crucial source of learning. A teaching that is directed by this insight will be one that does not pose as its objective the transmission of ready-made knowledge. Rather, it is aimed at the creation of new conditions, within which recovery of the knowledge needed to assess a new discourse is made possible.

What might this condition be, and what pedagogical actions might it require? Such a condition would first of all be one within which both teacher and students overtly acknowledge their objective situatedness in a set of relations fully implicated in the production of knowledge. For the fear of theory, this would mean understanding its locus in the constructed threat posed by the unintelligibility of a text and/or its potential for disruption of established commitments and desires. Thus, teachers would have to be prepared to examine together with their students how a particular configuration of pedagogic forms, group and institutional structures, and personal histories and capabilities may be forming a dynamic of threat and exclusion. In addition, however, what is also needed is a pedagogic process that allows students to interrogate the discursive grounds in which various aspects of one's self is positioned and therefore to understand how a new theoretical discourse might be "leaning against" old values and beliefs. This requirement is crucial for any aspiration we might have for working within a nonviolent process of teaching theory, a process in which we do not overtly or implicitly demand that students be dislodged from one "reality" only to be bound to another.

It is perhaps a cliché to state that such a pedagogy will need to be dialogic in form. While it is beyond the bounds of my intention here to fully develop the outline of such a pedagogy, it is possible to register a few relevant thoughts. First of all, in my view the concept of a dialogic pedagogy is perhaps one of the most confused and misdeveloped ideas in the literature on critical teaching. At a simplistic level it has been taken as a process within which a student "voice" is "taken seriously" and in this respect is counterposed to a transmission pedagogy. But this is both a vague and trivial statement. While most of those authors who discuss the concept draw on the work of Paulo Freire, is in and of itself an inadequate resource for the requirements of the dialogue.

What is crucial in Freire's work, as it is in many current attempts to formulate a feminist pedagogy, is the constant reminder that the dialogue in which students and teacher are to participate together is always grounded in the realities of the lived relations within which the participants find themselves. This means not just those constituting classroom dynamics but as well the relations that all participants are enmeshed in every aspect of their lives. Thus students who are coming to theory are not just there out of curiosity (although this, of course, is a wonderful basis for exploring new ideas) but as well will be required to put their own individual tone, their own signature on their understanding of a given discourse; including an assessment of the relevance of that discourse for the political struggles and practical requirements of teaching against the grain. This dialogue must in part be an assessment of any given mode of thought for affecting a transformation of people's action in the world.

But if my previous analysis has any cogency, we also can recognize that such dialogic grounds are not enough. If we listen as well to the voices of de Lauretis, Bakhtin, and Lacan, we can hear yet another insistence. This is the need for a dialogic process within which the struggle over the sign is given its due and recognized for the havoc it can create. Thus we need processes within which both teacher and students (as coparticipants) can explore what Felman has called that knowledge that resists knowing that it knows. Lacan perhaps provides the clue as to what this is about:

One always knows enough in order to occupy the minutes during which one exposes oneself in the position of the one who knows. . . .
This makes me think that there is no true teaching other than the teaching which succeeds in provoking in those who listen an insistence—this desire to know which can only emerge when they themselves have taken the measure of ignorance as such—of ignorance inasmuch as it is, as such fertile—in the one who teaches as well.[39]

What is to be recognized in a dialogic pedagogy is that both student and teacher are doubly ignorant, not only of their structured resistances but as well of the knowledge of what it is that resists in the other. Given this doubled structure of ignorance in a pedagogical encounter, each then must listen for the silence in the other, helping each other to knowledge that is inaccessible. This knowledge is not *in* the teacher; it cannot be given. It is only to be acquired in the conversation between the teacher and students as coinvestigators of each other's resistances. This is not just calling for an exchange of views in a classroom, but rather a direct acknowledgment that "the position of the teacher is nothing other than the one who learns; of the one who teaches nothing other than the way he [*sic*] learns."[40]

This effort at formulating an adequate dialogic pedagogy has in this chapter been directed toward rescuing the viability of "teaching theory," particularly theory with a potential to disrupt taken-for-granted ways of thinking about and practicing education. Such an effort is in my view still very much worth our concern. For the purpose of such teaching is nothing less than, to appropriate and paraphrase a bit of Buber's writing,[41] to keep pain awake, to awake desire through the realization that the world today is not an immutable fact and that dreams of possibility are radical in that they speak of a world not yet but still to be. This is the first task of everyone who regrets the obscuring of eternity. It is also the first task of the genuine educator in our time.

NOTES

1. Qtd. in Shoshana Felman, "Psychoanalysis and Education: Teaching Terminable and Interminable" 63 (*Yale French Studies,* 1982): 21–44. The quotation p. 30.

2. Philip Corrigan, "Social Forms/Human Capacities: Further Remarks on Authority and Difference," in *Social Forms/Human Capacities: Essays in Authority and Difference* (London: Routledge, 1990): p. 228.

3. Hanna Gelke, "The Phenomenology of the Wish in *The Principle of Hope,"* *New German Critique,* no. 145, Fall 1988, pp. 55–80. See, of course, Ernst Bloch, *The Principle of Hope* (Cambridge, Mass.: MIT Press, 1986): pp. 77–114.

4. Raymond Williams, *Keywords* (Flamingo: London, 1983): pp. 316–18. It is significant that theory is here distinct from practice but not opposed to it.

5. Courses are not the only site of educational work in my university. Other important contexts include individual meetings with students in faculty offices and thesis committee meetings, as well as personal discussions in hallways, the cafeteria, and the local pub. I have chosen to emphasize the context of "a course" because its ritualized and public character most clearly illustrate the argument of this paper. However, the dynamics of the fear of theory are present—and perhaps most easily confronted—in the other contexts of educational work as well.

6. There is a danger in using the concept of fear in that we so often take for granted that emotions are located in the dynamics of an individual psyche. I reject this view and as the argument in this chapter will show, locate the experience of fear as fundamentally social. There is no intention here to victimize with a self-referencing blame that posits personal emotional inadequacies that may be a block to learning.

7. In using the phrase "pedagogic action" I am deliberately referencing the work of Pierre Bourdieu and Jean-Claude Passeron (*Reproduction in Education, Society and Culture* [Beverly Hills: Sage, 1977]), in which such action is seen as a form of symbolic violence. This anticipates some of my arguments about the provocations of theory as well as the requirements for a pedagogy that can transcend the status of a form of symbolic violence.

8. Magda Lewis, *Without a Word: Sources and Themes for a Feminist Pedagogy* (Ph.D. diss., University of Toronto, 1988); Michelle Fine, "Silencing in Public Schools," *Language Arts* 64 (1987): pp. 157–75.

9. For a presentation of this dynamic see Franz Kafka's letter to Robert Klopstock in which he reinterprets the biblical account of the binding of Isaac in Franz Kafka, *Parables and Paradoxes,* ed. Nahum Glatzer (New York: Schocken, 1971).

10. While "ressentiment" is an important theme in several of Nietzsche's works, see in particular *The Genealogy of Morals* (Friedrich Nietzsche, *The Birth of Tragedy and the Genealogy of Morals,* trans. F. Golffing (Garden City, N.Y.: Doubleday, 1956). The dynamics of "ressentiment" are extremely important for understanding the cultural politics inherent in the rise of totalizing and fascist social forms. See, for example, Fritz Stern, *The Politics of Cultural Despair: A Study of the Rise of Germanic Ideology* (Berkeley: University of California Press, 1961).

11. Of course, there are attempts to designate jargon as specialized or professional language without any emotional or adversarial intent in its usage. This

neutralization of sign is clearly not an adequate rendition of what students mean when they speak about theoretical jargon.

12. Noelle Bisseret, *Education, Class Language and Ideology* (London: Routledge and Kegan Paul, 1979).

13. Raymond Williams, *Keywords* (London: Flamingo Press, 1983): p. 175.

14. Kathleen B. Jones, "On Authority: Or Why Women Are Not Entitled to Speak," in Irene Diamond and Lee Quinby, eds., *Feminism and Foucault: Reflections on Resistance* (Boston: Northeastern University Press, 1988), p. 122.

15. Henry Giroux, *Theory and Resistance in Education: A Pedagogy for the Opposition* (South Hadley, Mass.: Bergin and Garvey, 1983).

16. Michel Foucault, *Power/Knowledge: Selected Interviews and Other Writings, 1972–1977*, trans. C. Gordon (New York: Pantheon Books, 1980).

17. In a recent set of discussions on antiracist education, several teachers suggested that the only way OISE could be relevant to them was to supply research findings through which they could justify their practices to their colleagues and administrators.

18. Valerie Walkerdine, *Surveillance, Subjectivity and Struggle: Lessons from Pedagogic and Domestic Practices*, Occasional Paper no. 11 (Center for Humanistic Studies: University of Minnesota, 1987), p. 6.

19. Philip Corrigan, "Social Forms/Human Capacities: Further Remarks on Authority and Difference," p. 199.

20. Note the institutional or self-policing nature of the boundaries of a particular educational practice are often unreflectively taken for granted. Any form of judging others or oneself as unworthy or incapable of participating in a particular educational form is simultaneously an implicit affirmation of that form. This includes all admission procedures.

21. Foucault designates these twin processes: "objectivization" and "subjectivization." Together they provide quite powerful tools for illuminating how it is that taken-for-granted procedures can be understood as classist, racist, and sexist.

22. Teresa de Lauretis, "Issues, Terms, Contexts," in de Lauretis, ed., *Feminist Studies/Critical Studies* (Bloomington: Indiana University Press, 1986), pp. 4–5.

23. Ibid., p. 8.

24. V. N. Volosinov, *Marxism and the Philosophy of Language* (New York: Seminar Press, 1973). See particularly chap. 2, Part 1.

25. For an elaboration of this notion see Richard Teridman's "Introduction: Symbolic Resistance" in his book *Discourse/Counter-Discourse: The Theory and Practice of Symbolic Resistance in Nineteenth-Century France* (Ithaca, N.Y.: Cornell University Press, 1985).

26. Linda Alcoff, *Signs* (1988): pp. 434–35.

27. Jokes about theoretical language need not be seen as a form of rejection of a given discourse. Many students will literally play with a new discourse both as a means of defusing its potential threat and as a way of constructing the sense and sensibility that a new position may afford.

28. For some students the result of such an exclusion is a marginalization in relation to that mythic graduate student "figure in dominance": the full-time student with plenty of funding and a spouse to take care of the family who can sit at

OISE all day reading and talking to professors and other students about the nuances of the new knowledge she—but more likely he—is discovering. This is a marginalization in part enforced by the way OISE defines the doing of graduate schooling but as well is enforced by larger social inequities that emerge on the multifaceted ground of everyday life.

29. There is a trivial sense in which a text is uncomprehendible, as when students find a text with a series of unfamiliar words that need explanation. This is easily dealt with. However, more often the assertion of incomprehensibility has more to do with following the argument of a text and sensing the issues that are being addressed and how and why they might be important. The latter is what I mean by being able to take up a position within a given theoretical discourse.

30. Students sometimes will contend that language subordinates them. It is never simply this, but rather a particular language use within a given social form.

31. See Bluma Litner, *Exploring Critical Revision as a Process of Empowerment* (Ph.D. diss., University of Toronto, 1990).

32. A paradigmatic display of this process is illustrated in Lewis Gilbert's 1983 film *Educating Rita* (Columbia Pictures).

33. Bourdieu and Passeron, *Reproduction in Education, Society and Culture.* (See n. 7.)

34. Mikhail Bakhtin stresses here that the assessment, or valuing, of theory is not a judgment on its content but is constituted in an act of *"priznanie,"* or acknowledgment. This is imparting a tone to meaning by becoming responsible for it, taking the responsibility for making knowledge morally meaningful. See Gary Saul Morson and Caryl Emerson, eds., *Rethinking Bakhtin: Extensions and Challenges* (Evanston, Ill.: Northwestern University Press, 1989): p. 15.

35. Felman, "Psychoanalysis and Education." (See n. 1.)

36. The erotic character of the pedagogical encounter and its narcissistic elements and how these are implicated in the power dynamics of teacher-student relations are discussed in chap. 4 of this book.

37. Qtd. in Felman, p. 37.

38. Ibid., pp. 37–38.

39. Lacan is again qtd. in Felman, p. 31.

40. Ibid., p. 37.

41. Martin Buber, *Between Man and Man* (New York: Macmillan, 1965): p. 111. See also the surrounding "Education of Character," pp. 104–17.

6

Beyond the Racist Text: Jewish Applause for a Yiddish Shylock

Texts have ways of existing that even in their most rarefied form are always enmeshed in circumstance, time, place and society—in short, they are in the world, and hence worldly. Whether a text is preserved or put aside for a period, whether it is on a library shelf or not, whether it is considered dangerous or not: these matters have to do with a text's being in the world, which is a more complicated matter than the private process of reading.

Edward Said[1]

A few years ago I was indulging in a favorite pastime, browsing the selection in a local bookshop. In a large stack of remaindered editions I came across Lulla Rosenfeld's *Bright Star of Exile: Jacob Adler and the Yiddish Theatre*.[2] Leafing through its pages, I was quite astonished to learn that in 1901 in New York City Jacob Adler, one of the greatest Yiddish actors of his time, appeared as Shylock in an enormously successful all-Yiddish production of the *Merchant of Venice*.

A restricted sense of possibility is often the result of social amnesia and an ignorance of history. I knew little of the history of Yiddish theater and thus it was initially startling and difficult to imagine a Yiddish theater troupe playing *The Merchant of Venice* on the Lower East Side to an exclusively Jewish audience and receiving unanimous acclaim. I suspect this reaction was not entirely idiosyncratic. Like numerous North American Jews, my knowledge of and response to *The Merchant of Venice* was formed under conditions not of my own choosing and has left me with a strong sense of ambivalence about the play and its place in a curriculum of literary study.

I remember being assigned to read the *The Merchant of Venice* about the same time that I was studying for my Bar Mitzvah. Like the thousands of Jewish youth before and since, I experienced the awful ambiguity and pain fueled by the double bind of self-affirmation and rejection.[3] While I participated in a religious and cultural ritual designed to reinforce and integrate my Jewish identity, I attempted to distance myself from Shylock and his daughter Jessica (the play's Jewish characters). Shylock, of course, has been historically interpreted as one of Shakespeare's quintessential villains whose villainy and Jewishness appear indissolubly bound together. Jessica, Shylock's daughter, seeks only the love of Lorenzo, abandoning both her father and her identity as a Jew. During the course of studying the play, I grew to resent this text that seemed to fix me to these subjects of Christian scorn and Jewish apostasy. When asked to memorize a section of the play for recitation to my mainly non-Jewish classmates, I succumbed to the desire for invisibility, choosing the minor role of Salarino. I had no wish to emphasize through any imaginary Christian-Jewish dialectic my public school–produced "Otherness." Needless to say, I was glad when we moved on to *Silas Marner.*[4]

I make no claim here that my response was the singular Jewish response, as if all Jews comprehend this text in the same way. However, I do wish to begin with the observation that my response was and is common enough to allow me to assert with a good deal of certainty that no contemporary Jewish theater group in North America would choose to perform this play for its Jewish audiences.[5] Based on this premise, Jacob Adler and his Yiddish production of *The Merchant of Venice* currently stand out in sharp relief as a historical and cultural oddity, an anomalous event that for me holds a certain fascination. How can this event be accounted for? What were the conditions that made it possible?

In this chapter I argue that a consideration of these questions is a matter of neither idle curiosity nor parochial interest. Rather, a consideration of the anomalous character of Adler's production is of value precisely because it is helpful in addressing the very contemporary and important question of how textual interpretations are produced, authorized, and sustained. This question has gained currency with the unraveling of traditional notions of literary sanction, the consequences of which have been to raise new questions as to the very basis of cultural authority. In schools, media, publishing—the various points of practice where struggles over contending forms of cultural politics are taking place—formerly suppressed interpretations and excluded narratives are now being put forward for consideration. The very notion of a literary canon is being challenged by coalitions of teachers, parents, and students contesting traditional notions of the literary value of texts that have been included in course curricula on the basis of their assumed intrinsic merit. At times these struggles have spilled beyond the walls of the academy. In some districts, texts have been submitted to the judgment of courts and public commissions as to their appropriateness for inclusion in curriculum. Most recently in Ontario, the Ontario Human Rights Commission was asked to report on the appropriateness of *The Merchant of Venice* for inclusion in public school curriculum.

Thus we are beginning to see that how literary interpretation is done matters a great deal. As Daniel Cottom observes, "No way of reading is wrong except as it may become so under specific political conditions. Therefore, these conditions must be treated as the subject of sociohistorical differences within any literary theory that would not blindly identify itself with an imaginary law."[6] What can no longer be sustained within this view is any notion that the relation between a text and reader is a strictly private affair. Texts and readers always come together historically, and it is this historicity of the act of comprehension that precludes an exclusively personalist approach to understanding reader response. Grasping the implications of this view for rethinking notions of pedagogy would seem an urgent task given the inevitable engagement of educators in contemporary issues of cultural politics. Thus it is with an eye toward grasping these implications that I want to pose as a problem the articulation of what Michel Foucault[7] would call "the conditions of possibility" of Adler's Yiddish version of *The Merchant of Venice*. This will be an attempt to engage in a "history of the present," to help provide an understanding of the grounds and limitations of the current struggles over what should constitute the form and substance of a "cultural literacy" on which to build our future.

What I will provide is narrative that indicates how both Adler's performance-text and the consequent positive audience response can be accounted for. Following this, I will suggest how such a narrative can be taken up in a theoretical discourse that will allow us to develop a pedagogical perspective consistent with the project of expanding currently authorized notions of human possibility. It should be stressed that I am not interested in exploring what would count as an acceptable interpretation of *The Merchant of Venice* nor in arguing its merits as an ideal dramatic or literary form. Neither am I interested in the question of the essential greatness of Adler's performance as Shylock. Rather, I am interested in fully recognizing and exploring both the production of a particular audience for *The Merchant of Venice* and Adler's performance-text as inevitably located and caught up in the concrete material and social relations that defined the occasion of their appearance in the world.

YIDDISH THEATER AS REVOLUTIONARY CULTURAL FORM, 1862–1901

That Adler's 1901 all-Yiddish version of *The Merchant of Venice* was a success there is no doubt. The house was packed, the audience applause thunderous, and the Yiddish press laudatory. Indeed, this performance was so successful that it attracted the attention of "legitimate" theater interests, and Adler was invited to play the part of Shylock on Broadway (in Yiddish) with an all-English-speaking cast. How, then, should one go about understanding the conditions that made this success possible? Taking Jameson's advice to "always historicize,"[8] what is required is an excursion into the development of Yiddish theater.

This is not the place for a comprehensive history of Yiddish theater, nor is it possible to present a complete sociocultural analysis of the community ethos within which Jacob Adler presented his version of *The Merchant of Venice*. However, for the historical construction being attempted here it is necessary to selectively develop an understanding of both concerns in order to understand the particular configuration of audience and performance-text that was the historical circumstance of Adler's production.[9]

Yiddish theater must be understood as a particular aesthetic form that emerged within a very vital and historically specific Jewish cultural revolution. During the nineteenth century the Jews of Europe and Russia experienced for a time the lessening of restrictions on Jewish participation in civil society. With increased access to secular forms of education and a greater range of employment opportunities, Jewish interest in contemporary art, science, politics, and culture grew. There arose in community after community *maskilim*; men—and less often women—who were committed to forging a new Jewish life outside the confines and superstitions of the ghetto. This was the movement known as the *haskalah*. As this movement developed in Russia under the comparatively liberal regime of Czar Alexander II (1855–82), there began to emerge new and quite revolutionary Yiddish cultural forms. In 1862 a 16-year-old Avrom Goldfaden, soon to be famous as a playwright and impresario within Yiddish theater, appeared in a school production of a comic melodrama written by one of the Russian *maskilim*. This was the first known production of any modern Yiddish play.

The inception of Yiddish theater must be understood as a fundamentally radical event in the process of a Jewish cultural revolution. Jews had historically lacked any theater tradition. Such practices were considered vulgar and to be shunned within a life devoted to God, community, and family. While a form of Jewish theater had flourished since the Renaissance in the guise of the *purimspiel*, such performances were limited to one brief yearly holiday and were most often loosely organized within what from outside the culture might be called a type of Rabelaisian carnival.[10] Thus Yiddish theater was located within an emerging discourse that emphasized "the new," "the modern,"[11] and which (with various degrees of ambivalence) broke with what many at the time saw as a sense of limitation and suffering attached to traditional Jewish life.

The theme of early Yiddish productions emphasized not only the pride of the Jewish people rather than their sufferings but as well the "twin dangers" of the era of the *haskalah*. Rosenfeld writes:

Throughout all the early pieces . . . the Jew is seen as standing between twin dangers—the temptation to assimilate into the immoral non-Jewish world around him and on the other hand, the peril of sinking into bigotry, darkness, and superstition. Goldfaden's hero always represents progress and enlightenment; his antagonist, usually of the older generation, is capable of any absurdity or villainy in the service of his bigoted faith.[12]

Such representations and their realization in everyday life were part of the formative experiences of Jacob Adler. Adler, born in Odessa in 1855, was never a learned *maskil* although he had a deep admiration for learning and particularly for Russian literary culture and theater. His sense of the *haskalah* came from the Jewish street life of Odessa with its mix of concerns of social justice and industrial life and its ridicule and dismissal of the unworldly, strictly observant Jews who seemed the antithesis of Adler and his friends. It was among such street life that early Yiddish theater found its audience and developed its performers. Not long after Adler turned to acting, Yiddish theater was flourishing throughout Russia. This cultural activity, however, came to an abrupt halt with the assassination of Alexander II in 1882. His son, Alexander III, reversed the social reforms of his father, and the new regime became an era of brutal repression and terrifying pogroms that initiated a period of mass immigration to the West. On August 7, 1883, by governmental order Yiddish theater was forbidden throughout Russia. The Yiddish actors left quickly, hoping to find audiences in London, Paris, and New York.

According to Irving Howe,[13] the first Yiddish stage production in New York was held on August 12, 1882. A troupe of six men and two women, supported by local musicians and a choir, put on one of Goldfaden's plays. While the established German-Jewish business community and the local orthodox synagogues were embarrassed and scandalized by the very presence of a Jewish theater, the actors soon saw the potential in the increasing numbers of Yiddish-speaking immigrants beginning to arrive. Indeed, what they saw were Jews eager to break with the discourse of the ghetto and more than willing to support a theater of their own as part of the condition of entry into "the new world."

As New York Yiddish theater developed during its first decade, it took on a unique quality of its own. Irving Howe in his summary chapter on Yiddish theater suggests:

Performances tended to be long, usually lasting until midnight. Jewish audiences relished the details, often demanded that songs be repeated, took special amusement from couplets denouncing rival theatre companies, shouted denunciations of villains, and showed no displeasure with the mixture of tragedy and vaudeville, pageant and farce—nor even with the intrusion of personal affairs in the midst of performances ("occasionally an actor would invite the public to his wedding, or inform his audience about his relations with his wife"). Remembering how hard it had been to earn their few pennies, the audiences liked to feel they were getting a "full" evening. For lovers of Yiddish, the language of these plays were excruciating: "high" characters [gave] speeches in *daytshmerish,* a heavily Germanized and pompous version of Yiddish, while reserving *kuglshprakh* (pudding language, the Yiddish street vernacular) for the "low" characters.[14]

However, toward the end of the century three major events happened to alter the character of the development of New York Yiddish theater. First, Jewish immigration rose quite rapidly. It supplied lively and articulate voices for a Yiddish intelligentsia and a Yiddish labor movement, both of which became solidly entrenched on the Lower East Side. In the midst of a growing political and literary culture that included novelists, journalists, poets, and philosophers, Yiddish newspapers began to appear labeling the then-current Yiddish theater as *shund* (trash) and calling for a better theater. What was being articulated was a discourse within which a new audience would be created. This discourse engendered a commonality, producing shared meanings among diverse groups of working people and intellectuals, anarchists and socialists and Zionists, rich and poor. It was a discourse within which recent immigrants could remember the *shtetl* and Odessa nights, be proudly Jewish, and as well fiercely embrace their new home as wondrous space of modern possibility.

The second major event to alter the development of New York Yiddish theater was the arrival of Jacob Adler in 1887. After a period of initial hardship and then eventual success in London, convinced more than ever of the importance of improving the quality of Yiddish theater and raising its intellectual standards, at this time Adler was already a well-known and respected figure within contemporary Yiddish culture. The addition of his voice and more importantly his talent, energy, and practice further articulated the discourse of a *beser teyater*—a better theater. This discourse, which drew on European standards of cultural authority, was clearly more than a wish for theatrical difference. Constituted within an ongoing Jewish cultural revolution, it was an attempt to organize, support, and sustain a movement away from what was seen as parochial modes of thought and existence. It was an attempt to create a new Jewish worldview within forms that borrowed from what was then seen as the epitome of cultural civilization.

The third event of central importance in the transformation of Yiddish theater was the addition of Jacob Gordin to the growing Yiddish intellectual circle. Arriving in New York in 1891, Gordin had been a farmer, a journalist on Russian newspapers, a worker in the Odessa shipyards, and an actor in a traveling Russian company. Born into the Jewish bourgeois merchant class in the Ukraine, he had been brought up in the spirit of the *haskalah* while staying immersed in spirit of Jewish tradition. His talents as a writer were well recognized, as was his devotion to the literary and political ideas of Leo Tolstoy.

Gordin was the first Yiddish playwright to write serious dramatic works totally in Yiddish. As mentioned earlier, previous Yiddish theater had used a mixture of *daytshmerish* and street Yiddish reserving the "high form" for those characters expressing nobility and fine sensitivity. Gordin rejected this approach and instead gave his audiences a full range of characters who spoke the same language heard in homes, the sweatshops, political meetings, and the streets. It was a language practice that became an essential part of the discourse of a *beser teyater* and indeed was intended to sustain the Yiddish cultural revolution that was about to reach full bloom. Soon after Gordin's arrival, Adler and Gordin met in a wine cellar on the East Side. Adler spoke as usual of his great need for better dramatic material. As Adler relates the story,

I had in my pocket a German play . . . I gave this to Gordin, saying, "Here is a ready-made subject." . . . Gordin, with a fine gesture, gave the book back to me with the words, "If I write a play for you, it will be a Yiddish play, not a German play with Yiddish names."[15]

Thus began the pivotal collaboration between Adler and Gordin. Their first production, *Siberia,* was hailed as a significant departure; art had arrived to replace *shund.* However it was the second production, *The Yiddish King Lear,* that was to secure Yiddish theater as integral to the more encompassing cultural revolution. In 1892, in a move way from an exclusive reliance on completely new Yiddish plays, Gordin reset Shakespeare's *King Lear* in the Russia of the nineteenth century. His Lear was not a king, but a Jewish merchant of wealth and authority, a patriarchic type familiar to Russian-Jewish audiences. Prior to this performance Adler submitted the following notice to the Yiddish press:

The Union Theatre under the sole artistic direction of Jacob P. Adler, has been reorganized with the aim of driving from the Yiddish stage all that is crude, unclean, immoral, and with the purpose of lifting the Yiddish theatre to a higher level.[16]

It was reported that the audience for *The Yiddish King Lear* was excited and tense. The entire intelligentsia had turned out, and what they saw they loved; both Gordin and Adler experienced thunderous triumphs.

As the decade continued, Adler continued to play not only original scripts from Gordin but as well Yiddish translations of such plays as Shakespeare's *Othello*. Not to be outdone, other great Yiddish actors responded with new, more serious scripts and additional translations of dramas such as *Hamlet*. When Adler played *The Merchant of Venice* in 1901, it was to an audience shaped by unique historical moment.

JACOB ADLER'S SHYLOCK

But still, a Yiddish Shylock? Prior to Adler, there had been sympathetic characterizations of Shylock; most notably the portrayals by Edwin Booth and Henry Irving.[17] But this was a different venue. Indeed, both artist and audience were already positioned within the intertextuality of a Yiddish cultural revolution. Adler's audience came already knowing that Adler personified Jewish pride both in many of his roles and in his life (he had become a genuinely public and princely figure on the East Side). In other words, he was one of their own and they came looking for a particular rendition within which Shylock had to be understood as the hero of the play. Adler did not let them down.

Indeed, what Adler wished to convey was that Shylock from the beginning was governed by pride rather than revenge. He saw Shylock desiring to humble and terrify Antonio in return for the insult and humiliation Shylock has suffered at Antonio's hands. In *The Bright Star of Exile*, Rosenfeld reported that "when Adler brought his knife and scales into court and whetted the knife against his shoe, his audience laughed, knowing well it was not they who thirsted for blood."[18] In Adler's view, Shylock's desired climax was to refuse the pound of flesh with a gesture of divine compassion. When the verdict goes against him, Adler showed the merchant crushed because he has been robbed of this opportunity, not because he lusts for Antonio's death. After Shylock is commanded to give up his fortune and turn Christian, Rosenfeld describes Adler's Shylock as tottering and delivering the words "Give me leave to go from hence, I am not well" in the tone of a man near death. She goes on to portray Gratiano's jeering final lines as brutally forcing Shylock down to the very earth, crouching, sobbing, the very picture of the terrified ghetto Jew.

But the moment passes. He begins to right himself again, to find himself again. He rises, shakes the dust of the court and its justice from his sleeves, and in the full pride of his history and his race, makes his exit.[19]

That this interpretation "worked" with its audience seems beyond contention. After this performance Yiddish critic Alter Epstein wrote:

Not always does he humble himself! . . . Not always does he bow his head before the mighty ones of the earth! There comes a moment when the emperor like figure rises to its height and we see him in his true magnificence. And how we thrilled, how fierce the beating of our hearts as, arms folded on his breast, with a burning glance of scorn, he slowly left the hall![20]

DISCOURSE AND WORLDLINESS

What, then, can we learn from this story, this history of a particular conjunction of performance and audience? How might we begin to theorize this event to move from the particularities of a localized Jewish cultural revolution to a broader consideration of issues in literary interpretation and cultural politics?

First of all, it is useful to stress Edward Said's remark that "texts have ways of existing that even in their most rarefied form are always enmeshed in circumstance, time, place and society." What Said is emphasizing here is a text as a form in which "worldliness, circumstantiality, the text's status as an event having sensuous particularity, as well as historical contingency, are considered as being incorporated in the text, an infrangible part of its capacity for conveying and producing meaning."[21] What I have tried to show in this brief historical account is the way Jacob Adler's Yiddish production of *The Merchant of Venice* can be understood as a "text-in-the-world" by considering the conditions of possibility for such a performance. This analysis has been more demonstrative than comprehensive. Thus considerations of factors such as the availability of economic and material resources necessary for Adler's version of "high" Yiddish theater have not been considered here. Rather, I have chosen to emphasize how by the time of the performance in 1901 actor and audience had been coconstituted in a "discourse" that was articulating a Yiddish cultural revolution.

It is this notion of a constituting "discourse" that I now want to consider. When I referred to the conditions of possibility that were implicated in Adler's performance-text and its reception, I concretely displayed a particular constellation of social forms, material conditions, and institutional arrangements. This constellation, the manifestation of a Jewish cultural revolution, constituted a particular mode within which were produced expressive practices consistent with that revolution (in literature, journalism, theater, and everyday conversation in workshops, homes, and on the street). But to move beyond the particularities of Jewish life in turn-of-the-century New York we must move to a more general level of discussion.

I wish to designate as a "discourse" that crystallization of form and function, within a set of "conditions of possibility," which organizes a particular mode of production of the symbolic. In other words, discourses imply particular ways of articulating and employing forms of signification (textual, gestural, iconic) that set a frame of reference within which we define, organize, and regulate a particular sense of ourselves and relation to others and our physical world.[22] What discourses imply is a mode of governance over the productivity of practices of expression and comprehension. They enable particular forms of textual production and the particular interpretive schema through which a "reading" of a text (play, photograph, and so on) takes place. As discourses always refer back to their conditions of possibility, they should be understood as historically determinate. That is, they are constituted within the activity of men and women struggling to impose and resist particular social forms and material circumstances.

Thus it is anything but the case that the notion of "discourse" references something lifeless and disembodied. What is essential to grasp is that discourses are not "out there" to be adopted or to be subjected to. Rather, they are integral to our very being in the world. While we are able to make sense of our world through these discourses, this does not mean we are simply determined by our circumstances. Such a conclusion would be a perversion of historical understanding. What must be clear is that while we are already always enmeshed in a particular constellation of juxtaposed and concatenated, contradictory, and complementary discourses, it is because we are so enmeshed that we are open to and capable of attempting changes in their configuration.

DISCOURSE AND TEXTUAL INTERPRETATION

How, then, might we apply this conception of discourse to the issue of textual interpretation? Focusing on the notion that a discourse references a mode of production of the symbolic, the writing and distribution of a text can be described as constituted by sets of practices produced within a limited range of rules and ordering procedures for employing a differentiated set of images and signs. In this view texts are not ahistorical facts, but very real traces of discursively ordered and regulated productive practices.[23] This is not, however, to reduce the meaning of texts to the discursively determinate resources of their moment of production but rather to recognize that the writing and circulation of texts are not independent of history. This history enters into our comprehension of texts but does so only in relation to how we are currently constituted as reading subjects. Thus it is important to immediately emphasize that whatever their discursive origins, given the fact that we encounter texts, as Said would say "in-the-world," texts are always apprehended within socially regulated discourses. These discourses provide the schemata that enable comprehension and establish intertextual links with previously encountered traces. Bennett has stressed a similar notion. He argues for the importance of the concept of a "reading formation." By this he means a discursively produced set of determinations that connect

texts and readers in specific relations to one another in constituting readers as reading subjects of particular types and texts as objects-to-be-read in particular ways. This entails arguing that texts have no existence independent of such reading formations. . . . [Neither texts nor readers] can be granted a virtual identity that is separable from the determinate ways in which they are gridded onto one another within different reading formations.[24]

This concept is meant to blur the distinctions between notions of texts, readers, and contexts. It implies that interpretation is codependent not only on the textual trace but as well on its relation to the socially and historically ordered discourses that enable comprehension. In other words, this way of thinking about comprehension emphasizes that texts have no fixed referent for their meaning. What is being rejected here is a view of reading as organized through intratextual processes (often thought to represent "the text-itself") specified as independent of a discursive formation that (variably and historically) coconstitutes readers and texts-to-be-read.

This position emphasizes the inherent instability of textual meaning. In this light, practices that attempt to offer the truth about a text are perhaps best understood as a bid to hegemonically fix textual meaning. Methodologically, such hegemonic efforts often include establishing the terms of reference for what might be called "literary competence." Within this perspective a distinction is often made between readings that are sometimes referred to as "adequate, insightful, and mature" and those that are considered "naive, simplistic, and self-serving." Putting aside for the moment the question of who is to judge such notions as adequacy and maturity for whom, I want to focus on one of the commonplaces of literary training. This is the assumption that a competent reader requires the capability to establish a "critical distance" from one's more immediate, lived, worldly apprehension of a text. For example, readings of either the text or performance-text of *The Merchant of Venice* that downplay the dramatic eloquence of the text in favor of a response that renders it an anti-Semitic tract are often judged as one-dimensional, naive, and self-serving. Such readings are commonly diagnosed as failing to achieve "critical distance." This often means that the reader has failed to read a text "on its own terms" and has instead read into it her or his own more immediate preoccupations. Such readers are lectured or scolded for forgetting that Shakespeare's coterminous signification of "Jew" and "villainy" was produced within a taken-for-granted Elizabethan anti-Semitism that has no legitimate referent in contemporary life. Thus such readers are judged as failing to grasp the forms employed by Shakespeare within their proper historical context, thereby missing the transcendent "truths" in the text.

What I do *not* wish to argue here is that the concept of critical distancing has no place in education. Indeed, I view critical distancing as essential for any educational project committed to helping people venture beyond what they already know. Teaching interpretation is an important means of both adding to and interrogating the value of the existing discursive resources of readers. However, the demands of critical distancing, the hegemonic fixing of the range of valued interpretations, and the pretension that one can get back to the "text itself" strip us of our ability to hear what is at stake in an initial, immediate, very worldly, and passionate reading. They can become forms of miseducation that result in acts of symbolic violence on those they intend to help. It is for this reason that I have become increasingly concerned with the question of how we understand and respond to disagreements over textual meaning. What do we hear, and what is inaudible to us in the response of the Other? Can the theoretical perspective on the relationship between interpretation and discourse discussed above help us to hear differently?

HEARING THE OTHER WHO DISAGREES

I will begin this discussion by widening the referent of the "controversial text" beyond my initial concern with *The Merchant of Venice.* To do so, I wish to introduce another example of a textual engagement that has been received with considerable surprise by my students. This is the eloquent and powerful reading of Joseph Conrad's *Heart of Darkness* by the Nigerian novelist Chinua Achebe.[25] Achebe reads *Heart of Darkness* as a racist text and in the process insists on a very different signification of Africa and of intertextual referents of "blackness." In this reading Achebe uncovers Conrad's text as dependent upon a set of parallel oppositions: white/black, Europe/Africa, civilization/demonic. He demands that they be judged against an alternative mode of production of the symbolic that gives voice to those who have been suppressed within a self-justifying colonialist discourse.

For students trained to read the universal "truths" in Conrad's text, Achebe is quite discomforting. Acknowledging his brilliance and scope, they know he cannot be charged with an intellectual immaturity that would limit his ability to read *Heart of Darkness* as a transcendent masterpiece.[26] Thus is constituted a moment of contradiction pregnant in its pedagogical possibilities. As previously embedded regimes of truth are called into question, students want to know (and here I quite deliberately quote the words of Marvin Gaye) "what's going on?" The pedagogical response is to ask of what value Achebe's view of Conrad's text is to us.[27] What do we hear in his reading?

One of the initial impulsive responses to Achebe is to hear him reading Conrad from a position that mitigates the cost of the psychic and social displacement engendered by engaging in a self-negating discourse. In other words, the charge would be that Achebe is too close to the surface level of Conrad's text and must distance himself from the portrayal of Africa that Conrad makes available to him. My own reading of *The Merchant of Venice*, which I reported at the beginning of this chapter, might likewise be seen as invested (at least in part) with the same dynamic. While incredibly patronizing and totally insufficient, such a point of view at least acknowledges the violence inherent in a discourse that renders difference into a justification for marginalization and dominance. What is insufficient about the above observation is that it converts what is potentially a socially insurgent interpretation into a prophylactic exercise of psychic self-protection, thus greatly distorting what we are able to hear in what Achebe is saying.

Another response to Achebe is to hear him attempting to define the truth of Conrad's text. This might be understood as an attempt to rehegemonize our evaluation of Conrad from master storyteller to racist writer, perhaps in the process knocking him off high school and university reading lists. If we hear Achebe this way, we then set ourselves the problem of trying to decide whether we agree with the truth claims Achebe is making about the text. This may or may not have been Achebe's intent, but to hear him in this way is again too limited, failing to recognize the nature of the insurgency in Achebe's reading.

These common ways of hearing a literary response, as reflective of the psychodynamics of the respondent or as a truth claim about a text that must be adjudicated as to its validity, are in fact quite depthless. To hear Achebe more deeply requires a different way of listening, one I think suggested by some of the theoretical resources introduced above. In relation to the caution that meanings cannot be fixed to texts, one might regard Achebe as attempting to fix the range of meanings of *Heart of Darkness* without regard for the historical and variable determinations that make particular readings possible. What is not at issue in this view is that Conrad can be read in multiple ways. That texts are polysemic and signs multiaccentual is a basic premise of the relation between discourse and interpretation I am offering here. Achebe's view does not render "incorrect" the conventional interpretation, which reads Conrad's text as a statement that the universal savagery in all humanity is never quite tamed and, hence, capable of returning anytime. But then where does this leave us? Does not the refusal of the desire to adjudicate the truth of Achebe's assertions or at least individualize his response leave us adrift in a relativism that challenges nothing and takes us nowhere?

I think not. In relation to the agenda of a pedagogy of possibility, what is far more productive pedagogically is to ask ourselves, discursively, what makes Achebe's reading possible and why we (and/or others) have never quite read *Heart of Darkness* that way before. Within this perspectival shift, Achebe's reading can be heard as pointing to the historically constituted discourse from which Conrad draws his rhetoric. It is a discourse that structures and is structured by very real racist, colonialist relations among particular groups of people, a historical legacy we are still living. This discourse, as a mode of production of the symbolic, is a set of signifying conventions that ultimately must be shared by writer and readers in order for the text to be comprehensible at all. Thus when we read Conrad and render invisible the discursive grounds on which a case for the universal truth of this text is asserted, we are effacing our own taken-for-granted situatedness in a formation that Achebe insists we call into question. In hearing Achebe this way, we can begin to glimpse the discursive terrain that he and Conrad share with us (and at a very simplistic level allows us to comprehend enough of Conrad's story and Achebe's response to talk to each other about them). What is shared is that which we already know about, what I will in abbreviation call the discourse structuring and structured by the long *durée* of economic and moral colonialism. At one level we all more or less *know about* the same thing; but at another level, listening to Achebe carefully, we can also begin to learn that we *know it (and embody that knowing) very differently.* Thus the insurgency in Achebe's reading. It ruptures the taken-for-granted grounds of our own understanding and teaches us that the scars and wounds of history cannot be erased within our search for universal truths. It teaches us further that if as a species we are to have a common life together, we must define these relations by means of discursive resources not hegemonically based on the categories of Western civilization.

Thus we are thrown headlong into the question of considering the educational and political importance not of the meaning or value of a given literary text, but of the modalities of production of its meaning and value. What we are confronted with is the very basic question of the value we wish to accord to the discourses and corresponding "conditions of possibility" implicated in a particular reading.[28] In this view, we are forced as readers to recognize an inevitable moral and ethical accountability that we share in regard to our own readiness to interrogate and shift the grounds of our own readings. This then begins to point the way to some new questions for educational practice.

BEYOND THE RACIST TEXT

I shall now turn more directly to the pedagogical implications of the view of textual interpretation I have been exploring. What individual and communal aims might such implications address? On the one hand, we might take the central aim of textual study as self-referential. That is, through a study of one's responses to text, one can be helped to locate oneself (one's perceptions, beliefs, desires) within the very "worldly" discourses that constitute a person's way of being in the world.[29] This would be done with the intent of raising questions as to the commitments, ethics, limitations, and possibilities of such discourses. This effort would be part of a pedagogical project that is concerned with helping students to come to a better understanding of who they are, how their history has been constituted, and how this knowledge can open up possibilities for change and enhancement, not only of their own lives but the lives of others as well. It must be stressed that such a position does not mean that the only pedagogically valid readings are those produced from within the discourses available to students on the basis of their everyday existence. This uncritical celebration of "the student voice" is clearly a reactionary educational position. Rather, what we must work toward in our practice is a pedagogy within which complementary readings are made available as the basis from which a person's own discursive potentialities and constraints can be assessed and judged.

There is, however, another, perhaps more communally focused aim that should be emphasized as well. This aim relates to what is at stake when we encounter people who have what I will call "insurgent readings" of a given text (such as Achebe's reading of *Heart of Darkness*). As teachers it is imperative that we achieve some clarity as to what is at stake when we support or resist others in questioning dominant or conventional interpretations. Within the theoretical frame I have been considering, we might begin to see that certain insurgent readings are enabled by discursive regimes that directly contest the meaning produced in dominant discourse and that this very insurgency has a primary educational significance. In other words, we miss the significance of parental and student objections to texts such as *The Merchant of Venice* or *Heart of Darkness* if we see such disputes as disagreements over the proper meaning of a text. Rather, the question to be asked from an educator's point of view is what discourse is regulating an insurgent reading and whether it would be desirable and possible to support that as a counterdiscursive position. It is in this sense that we can recognize how such events call us to account for the moral and ethical basis of our pedagogical project.

If we agree that an insurgent discourse should be nourished (and there are circumstances where we may not), minimally we can make the readings constituted within that discourse available in our classroom. At times these may be provided by the students in a class; at times voices that would otherwise not be heard would have to be provided. These would be the voices of those who have been dominated, displaced, and silenced. This is one justification, for example, of including African, Asian and East Asian, Arab, Latin American, and Caribbean criticism in course content. But more is required here than the engagement with an insurgent reading such as Achebe's or, in his own way, Adler's. If we wish to help articulate counterdiscursive positions from which students may begin to define practices that challenge existing social forms, more than insurgent readings are necessary. Important as they are, insurgent readings are not an adequate basis for exploring the power inherent in a counterdiscourse. For example, an insurgent reading of *Heart of Darkness* might help clarify how nonwhites have been systematically structured into positions of inequality, but it would fail in illuminating the social possibilities enabled by the regime that made the insurgent reading possible. This means that beyond the provision of complementary readings, teachers will be called to account for how they respond to the existence of discourses that challenge hegemonic forms of thought and practice. If we are to support such challenges, then the variety of textual forms made available within a counterdiscourse will have to be made accessible so that they can be assessed for their potential in expanding the forms of expression of our human capabilities.

In all likelihood, such a pedagogical option will mean altering both traditional curricular content and conventional notions of authority vested in the assertions of knowledge/power that often characterize much of what stands for acceptable teaching. As we move toward a different version of "teaching the text," we will have to contest the provision of meaning based on institutional authority. This authority is conferred by either an academic discipline, a social status, or a state that contracts classroom personnel to name preferred meanings, meanings often placed into a hegemonic relation with others that may be constructed. If as teachers we can find a way to articulate a radically different form of practice, we will be in a prime position to develop what I have previously considered as a necessary alliance among a variety of people engaged in forms of cultural work (see Chapter 3). In this case, educational work must be recognized as taking place across multiple sites, so that teachers, parents, writers, dramatists, and producers of visual media are all coordinated in making clear how dominant social forms may be challenged.

What I have been arguing is that theorizing the problem of "controversial text" through the notion of discourse allows us to see that insurgent readings are not simply struggles over the sign—what a given text means—but actually struggles over forms of life, struggles over how people's identities will be constituted and history lived. What is not at issue is whether a text is to be judged as racist or sexist. Indeed, to formulate the question in this matter is to miss the point, condemning particular authors and publishers while forgetting the material grounds and discursive practices that make such texts intelligible in the first place. What must be remembered is that there are no racist or sexist texts-in-themselves. Rather, there are exclusionary, violent, and oppressive writings and readings produced and regulated by discourses that assert a "truth in the world." It is these discourses that can and must be contested, overturned, and supplanted with a discourse capable of embracing a plurality of possibility. *This position in no way ignores the potential of existing texts to reinforce and continue to produce racist and sexist discourses.* Thus the argument cannot be taken as a license for the free distribution of textual bigotry. The fact that in the late 1920s a production of *The Merchant of Venice* in Vienna ended in a riot during which several Jewish members of the audience were murdered and that Jewish prisoners in concentration camps were forced to enact the play is testimony both to the force of a racist discourse within which the performance-text could be constituted and engaged. It also bespeaks the fact that the existence of the text has helped to articulate the conditions for a genocidal discourse.

For the above reasons I do think that as educators we can act responsibly when we consider withdrawing and replacing certain texts for study.[30] But if we do this, it should be clear what it is we are trying to accomplish. The withdrawal or replacement of a text may or may not be the best way to contest the discourses that anchor racist and sexist practices. There is, for instance, the option of working with such texts, to uncover the intertextual relations in which they are embedded and the discursive grounds of their genesis and comprehension. There can be no rules as to which option to pursue. The practice of pedagogy cannot be developed in a formulaic manner, for teaching is, first and foremost, a practical activity that must respond to the contingencies of particular classroom encounters. However we choose to proceed, if we center specific texts as if they were the heart of the issue, we may be missing the mark. What is necessary is that we direct our concern to both the conditions of possibility that make a given text a viable threat to a progressive future and those which will sustain us in containing such threats.

SO HOW WOULD YOU TEACH THE MERCHANT OF VENICE?

No text can exist outside the historical contingencies and relationships that produce the discourses within which it is enunciated and comprehended. The question is whether this notion will be acknowledged and considered in textual study or ignored or suppressed. Throughout this chapter there has been an implicit subtext that relates to the notion of how one might teach using a text that has been implicated in the reproduction of forms of discrimination and dominance. Certainly, my centering of *The Merchant of Venice* is not innocent in this regard. Thus it is appropriate after so many words, to try to answer the pragmatist's question: So how would *you* teach *The Merchant of Venice*?

First of all, I would most likely retain the use of the text, doing so not for reasons of literary merit but in acknowledgment of the traditional place of *The Merchant of Venice* in public schooling. In Ontario there has been a 100-year canonization of Shakespeare as *the* author essential to literary study.[31] It is this process of canonization that must be rubbed against the grain through raising questions about the adequacy of previous judgments and interpretations. This means making concrete that the evaluative process of canonization is not so much a matter of recognizing the abstract truth value of a text as it is assessing how well a text performs desirable functions for particular people at particular times.[32] To address this aim requires helping students uncover how it was that *The Merchant of Venice* was placed in the curriculum in the first place, seeking out what claims were made on its behalf and on the behalf of the Shakespearean canon. Second, I would include as part of the study of *The Merchant of Venice* a range of performance-texts and documented receptions of the play. This would encompass traditional Shakespearean productions as well as those like Jacob Adler's, that of Israel's Habima Theatre, and the forced renditions by Jewish prisoners in Nazi concentration camps. The aim here would be to try to make evident the various conditions of possibility implicated in particular performances and their reception. Finally, I would want to make evident to the class as a whole the multiple forms of student interpretation of the play, challenging students to trace the meanings and pleasures in their own readings to the discursive grounds on which they were formulated. By focusing on these discursive grounds, I would attempt to help students interrogate the limits and possibilities of their own and others' ways of making sense of the world in relation to plausible notions of a desirable future.

We cannot ignore or suppress counterdiscursive readings within the guise of a judgment of a "failed or inadequate reading." However, neither can we be content to celebrate difference as simply the articulation of the individual "student voice," acknowledging a reader's individual "point of view" as if the historical and political accent of this voice were simply inaudible. What must be made both audible and visible are *the conditions of possibility* not only of the articulations of particular texts but as well, the articulations of particular readings. Such "conditions of possibility" must be confronted for what they are, struggles to define a "regime of truth" within which life is to be lived. Such regimes will then require interrogation and judgment regarding the notions of human possibility that they support, challenging our students and ourselves to consider which mode of reading defines a true horizon of hope.

NOTES

1. Edward Said, *The World, The Text and The Critic* (Cambridge: Harvard University Press, 1982), p. 35.

2. Lulla Rosenfeld, *The Bright Star of Exile: Jacob Adler and the Yiddish Theatre* (New York: Crowell, 1977).

3. Since its formation in the 1920s, the Toronto Jewish Congress has regularly

received complaints from Jewish parents and students about the teaching of *The Merchant of Venice* and consequent abuse of Jewish students. (Bernie Farber, personal communication).

4. For a discussion of the dynamics of being recognized in one's Otherness, see E. Anderson and E. Lee, *Selection and Positive Use of Literature Containing Controversial Issues* (North York, Ontario: North York Board of Education, 1989); Roger Simon, "Being Ethnic/Doing Ethnicity," in Jon Young, ed., *Breaking the Mosaic* (Toronto: Garamond Press, 1987).

5. This is not true, however, for Israel. The Habima Theatre produced *The Merchant of Venice* as early as 1936 amid great controversy. Speculation on why the play might be produced for a Jewish community in Israel and not in the Diaspora would take us into a discussion of conditions that produced the modern diasporaic Jewish identity, a concern beyond the boundaries of this volume. For an interesting recent discussion see Leonard Fein, *Where Are We? The Inner Life of America's Jews* (New York: Harper and Row, 1988).

6. Daniel Cottom, *Text and Culture: The Politics of Interpretation* (Minneapolis: University of Minnesota Press, 1989), p. 13.

7. Michel Foucault, *Power/Knowledge* (New York: Pantheon Books, 1970).

8. Fredric Jameson, *The Political Unconscious: Narrative as a Socially Symbolic Act* (Ithaca, N.Y.: Cornell University Press, 1981).

9. The historical arguments of this paper are based on Rosenfeld, *Bright Star;* Ronald Sanders, *The Downtown Jews: Portraits of an Immigrant Generation* (New York: Harper and Row, 1969); and Irving Howe, *World of Our Fathers* (New York: Harcourt Brace Jovanovich, 1976).

10. Mikhail Bakhtin, *Rabelais and His World* (Cambridge: MIT Press, 1968).

11. In this sense the *haskalah* was part of a larger discourse of modernity that emerged in the mid-nineteenth century.

12. Rosenfeld, *Bright Star,* p. 44.

13. Howe, *World of Our Fathers,* p. 461.

14. Ibid., p. 464.

15. Rosenfeld, *Bright Star,* pp. 260–261.

16. Ibid., pp. 263–64. The notion of "lifting . . . theatre to a higher level" was not unique to Yiddish communities. For an understanding of the economic and cultural dynamics informing the development of "high culture" in late-nineteenth-century America see Lawrence W. Levine, *Highbrow Lowbrow: The Emergence of Cultural Hierarchy in America* (Cambridge: Harvard University Press, 1988).

17. For an interesting account of how performances of Shylock have varied and how such performances might be seen as constituted within their own historical epochs, see Toby Lelyveld, *Shylock on Stage* (London: Routledge and Kegan Paul, 1961).

18. Rosenfeld, *Bright Star,* pp. 303–4.

19. Ibid., p. 305.

20. Ibid.

21. Said, *The World, the Text, and the Critic,* pp. 35, 39.

22. For a clear and comprehensive introduction to this framework for understanding the relation between language and literary production, see Catherine Belsey, *Critical Practice* (New York: Methuen, 1980); Richard Terdiman, *Discourse/Counter-Discourse: The Theory and Practice of a Symbolic Resistance in Nineteenth-*

Century France (Ithaca, N.Y.: Cornell University Press, 1985; Chris Weedon, *Poststructuralist Literary Theory and Feminist Practice* (Oxford: Basil Blackwell, 1987).

23. Of course, not every text is produced within a monological discursive regime. It is important to stress that the productivity of writing and reading is often organized within multiple and often contradictory discourses. Indeed it is often these contradictions that critical pedagogical practice will seek to make manifest and exploit.

24. Tony Bennett, "Texts in History: The Determinations of Readings and Their Texts," in D. Attridge, G. Bennington, and R. Young, eds., *Poststructuralism and the Question of History* (Cambridge: Cambridge University Press, 1987), pp. 70–71.

25. Chinua Achebe, *Hopes and Impediments: Selected Essays, 1967–1987* (London: Heinemann, 1988). Achebe is reading Conrad against the grain of Western "civilization." Such readings produce irritation within centers of Eurocentric power. See, for example, Craig Raine's review of Achebe's essay, "Conrad and Prejudice," *London Review of Books, 22 June 1989,* and the subsequent exchange of letters in response to this review.

26. Such a response is indeed blatantly logocentric in its credentializing of Achebe's reading of Conrad on the basis of Achebe's stature as a novelist who has received critical acclaim in the West. It is important to note that it is on this basis that many people will take Achebe's reading seriously, while simultaneously dismissing similar remarks made by students or parents.

27. While for reasons of maintaining a certain linearity of argument, I will gloss the issue of who is "us," it is too important to simply ignore. As we are all implicated in the discourses of Western racism, how we are so implicated of course varies. Hence, there is no single "us" for whom Achebe writes. The task is to clarify how the demands of discourse out of which Achebe writes will alter our practice.

28. This is equally true for other readings against the grain of texts like *Huckleberry Finn, The Taming of the Shrew,* and, most recently, Salman Rushdie's *Satanic Verses.*

29. Henry Giroux, "Textual Authority, Voice, and the Role of English Teachers as Public Intellectuals," in S. Aronowitz and H. Giroux, eds., *Postmodern Education: Culture, Politics and Social Criticism* (Minneapolis: University of Minnesota Press, 1990).

30. To raise the question of censorship in relation to curricular context is a red herring. As all curriculum is a particular choice of content from a vast set of possibilities, notions of inclusion, exclusion, withdrawal, and replacement are essential parts of curricular practice.

31. See Robert Morgan, *English Studies as Cultural Production in Ontario, 1860–1920* (Ph.D. diss., University of Toronto, 1987) for a genealogy of the English studies in Ontario schools. In this study Morgan links the canonization of Shakespeare to the importance of asserting the centrality of Ontario to the British Empire.

32. Barbara Herrenstein Smith, "Contingencies of Value," *Critical Inquiry* 10, no. 1 (1983): pp. 1–35.

7

What Schools Can Do: Designing Programs for Work Education That Challenge the Wisdom of Experience

Roger I. Simon and Don Dippo

Schools alone cannot solve the problems facing youth today. Yet few working in education are willing to absolve themselves from the responsibility they feel for those they teach. The question persists: What, if anything, should we be doing in schools to help transform the restricted and uncertain future many youth face?

The answer to this question will depend on how we understand schools, both as state institutions and as sites of complex social processes. Our view of schooling is one that rejects a reductionist economic determinism. That is, we reject as overtly simplistic the view that schools are inherently conservative institutions whose primary function is to support existing forms of social and economic relations. This is a perspective advanced in many studies of the impact of educational attainment on occupational status and social mobility.[1] It is a "black-box" view of schools with little understanding or appreciation of the diverse, complex, and often contradictory practices that make up the everyday life in classrooms, hallways, staff rooms, and school yards.

In order to consider what might be done in schools to help transform future possibilities for youth, we would do well to view schools as a site of cultural production. Consider, through an extended analogy, what this might mean. In *A Philosophy of the Future*, Ernst Bloch explored the utopian impulse of daydreams.[2]

Dreams come in the day as well as at night. And both kinds of dreaming are motivated by the wishes they seek to fulfill. But daydreams differ from night dreams; for the daydreaming "I" persists throughout, consciously, privately, envisaging the circumstances and images of a desired, better life. The content of the daydream is not, like that of the night dream, a journey back into repressed experiences and their associations. It is concerned with, as far as possible, an unrestricted journey forward, so that instead of reconstituting that which is no longer conscious, the images of that which is not yet can be phantasied into life and into the world.[3]

What significance does Bloch's analysis of daydreams have for education? In a sense, both share a common project: the production of, in Bloch's words, "images of that which is not yet." Without a perspective on the future, conceivable as a desired future, there can be no human venture. As an introduction to, preparation for, and legitimation of particular forms of social life, education always presupposes a hopeful vision. In this respect a curriculum and its supporting pedagogy are versions of our dreams for ourselves, our children, and our communities. But such dreams are never neutral. They are always *someone's* dreams, and to the degree that they are implicated in organizing the future for others, they always have a moral and political dimension. It is in this regard that schools must be understood as sites of cultural politics and, thus, that any discussion of schooling must include a discussion of educational practice as a form of cultural and political work.[4]

As sites of cultural politics, schools are places where a sense of identity, place, worth, and above all value, is informed and contested through practices that organize knowledge and meaning. Our image of ourselves and our world provide us with the concrete sense of what is possible and what is desirable. Therefore, what is vital is that we engage young people in the process of questioning their future identities and possibilities.

CRITICAL PEDAGOGY AND WORK EDUCATION

Our work in Ontario has been with high school cooperative education programs. These are programs of extended partial work entry in which students spend up to two-thirds of the time allocated for a course working in a workplace within their community. The remaining one-third course time is spent in school in studies that relate to their workplace experiences. The range of workplaces used for such programs is quite broad: they include small businesses, large corporations, government offices, and social service agencies. Within broad Ministry of Education guidelines, the purpose and format of such programs vary from school to school. It remains an open question as to what and how students learn in such programs and in what respects different conditions and arrangements influence student learning.

It is in this context that we are trying to develop a critical pedagogy of work education. This is a pedagogy that begins with the premise that while students need to learn about the "realities of work" and develop marketable skills, the primary task of work education *is not* to prepare students to meet the needs of employers nor to ensure a student's immediate economic survival. We are interested in education for work and not simply training for jobs. Therefore we ask what knowledge, skills, and abilities do students need in order to understand and participate in changes that are taking place in the work world? This, we assert, is a question of cultural politics. Helping students to understand the economic, social, and cultural relations that shape their sense of what is possible and desirable influences the extent to which they are able to define an expanded range of possibilities for the future.[5]

It is important to connect this concern to our sense of the purpose of a critical pedagogy. For us a critical pedagogy is centrally concerned with the moral and analytical task of assessing whether specific social forms encourage and make possible the "realization of differentiated capacities, or whether they disable, deny, dilute and distort those capacities."[6] As well, critical pedagogical practice is concerned with the educational and political tasks of constructing new forms that would expand the available range of social identities and possibilities. These twin tasks we view as both the problem and the project: to expand what it is to be human. It is at once a moral, educational, and political agenda that requires our efforts in schools and our alliance with other transformative projects taking place in workplaces, families, churches, local government councils, and elsewhere in our communities.

This chapter will discuss what might be done within school programs such as cooperative education that would enable students to develop a perspective from that they might be better able to take their dreams for reality and define images of "that which is not yet." The educational agenda for such an effort is broad and complex, one that deserves much deliberation. Here, however, we will limit our focus to a fundamental task required by anyone seeking to transform positivist and individualist notions of learning and competence: the task of challenging the wisdom of experience.

CHALLENGING THE WISDOM OF EXPERIENCE

One of the first steps in reformulating such programs as cooperative education in the service of a critical pedagogy is to challenge the prevailing wisdom that experience is the best teacher. All too often this way of thinking leads to a separation between what goes on at work and what happens in school. Work experience itself is taken for granted as complete or self-contained and is ignored in the classroom in favor of general employability skills, career guidance exercises, or regular shopwork. But much more fundamentally, we must challenge the very character of experience, make clear its variety of forms, and explore the differing implications of each form for the design of work experience programs.

We depart here from simple notions of constructing pedagogy on the basis of student experience. Critical pedagogy, we agree, centers student experience. However, while speaking or writing one's experience can be both empowering and a mode of resistance to silencing social forms, experience is not an unproblematic notion. We must avoid the conservatism inherent in confirming that which people already know. Experience should never be celebrated uncritically. Rather, student "voices" should be encouraged while simultaneously facilitating the interrogation of such voices.[7] This defines one of the central problems of critical pedagogy: how to acknowledge student experience as a legitimate aspect of schooling while being able to challenge both its content and form during the educational process.

In an attempt to make clear the complex and multifaceted nature of "experience" within any "experiential education" program, we have defined (based on our in-depth research with students, parents, teachers, and employers) four primary ways in which work experience can be understood. Each version of experience has different implications for thinking through the ways in which the practice of work education should be accomplished. We do not argue that these categories are exhaustive or mutually exclusive; rather, the point here is that the emphasis any given program places on one or more of these notions of experience will determine the nature of the cultural politics supported by such a program.

1. Experience is information and techniques one acquires by participating in new and different situations. Becoming familiar with a new situation in part entails learning what to expect from others and what is expected by others. Employers often value this version of experience. This is what they mean when they say that experience is valuable because it gives students exposure to the "real world" and "teaches them what it is really like out there."[8] In addition, experience as the acquisition of knowledge and techniques also includes practical learning, that is, learning what to do and how to do it. Usually this kind of learning is consistent with an extension of the knowledge the teacher expects the placement to provide. Instances of this kind of practical learning are commonly reported among students.[9] Here Derek, a student placed in a machine shop, gives a lengthy example of learning how to sharpen drill bits:

You just put it against the grinding wheel at a certain angle . . . and when he was showing me, I always used to keep the drill bit up and it should be on a slope—a downward slope as you sharpen it, right. And you just run the drill bit up the grinding wheel. And when he used to tell me how to sharpen it, he'd say,

"Run the drill bit up the grinding wheel" and then I'd do it and it would sharpen just perfect, eh. Sometimes I'd get confused on the angles 'cause you have to look at it by eye, you know, it just goes by eye. And then I got this measuring tool and I could tell it would be perfect every time I did it, right. You have to use your own hand to guide it, right. And he'd show me how to rest my hand, and you know I was really tense at first to do it and he says, "Rest your hand and just take your time," eh. Usually you go up the grinding wheel all the time and you'd have to turn it too, eh. Like there was a trick to it, and every time I'd do it, it would go up, but I wouldn't quite turn it, eh, and you have to have the same motion. And now, when I was in machine shop today, I was doing it and it was perfect. It just came! Just like the way he showed it to me the first time, you know. And it's amazing! I like learning something like that.

Sometimes this kind of practical learning conflicts with the knowledge the teacher expects the placement to provide. Here Jennifer discusses what is expected at the nursing home where she works. She describes a form of situated, practical knowing that transgresses the boundaries of officially sanctioned school knowledge, a knowledge that idealizes nurse-resident relations.

The nurse asked me to take her [an elderly resident] down, so I was taking her down. All of a sudden she starts to scream and I'm doing, "Oh, great." I don't need it, so I'm standing there, "What do you want me to do?" And the nurses are yelling at her because she knows better than to do that, and like, it's for her own good. . . . So she was screaming and the nurses said, "Just leave her." And they were yelling at her. The charge nurse was yelling at her, like, because she knows better than to do that. [In a later interview] You know Doris and Mrs. Morgan, they fight. It's terrible. The two of them will just go at it and one of them will slap the other and I'll just go, "Stop that now!" Like I'll, I, I've gotten to the point where I will yell at them, because I know that they're not supposed to do that. And the nurses' aides will yell at them and whatever, so I figure, well, if I see it going on, I might as well yell at them too.

Jennifer's experience exemplifies the potential disjuncture between official school knowledge and what "it is really like out there." Practical knowledge of techniques and expectations are important; both provide for a sense of competence structured on the terms of existing economic and cultural relations. However, discrepancies between school knowledge and practical workplace learning should not be taken uncritically; rather, they provide an agenda for pedagogical work. They allow both students and teachers to explore the socially constructed and economically determined character of the work practices of a particular business or institution.[10]

2. *Experience is a personal characteristic that one has as a result of participating in real work.* This version of experience refers to the acquisition and possession of valued personal contacts, work habits, attitudes, and skills

that can be used informally, put on a résumé, or reported in a job interview. Here experience is understood as an asset, and having experience is what makes one valuable in the labor market. The accumulation of such assets is the process of commodification of self, something students quite explicitly state as one of their reasons for enrolling in cooperative education (e.g., "I developed a more mature attitude, and it'll be a good reference for me in the future").

Students who are not particularly satisfied with their work placements often use this version of experience as a justification of last resort. Consider Angela, a student interested in becoming a nursery school teacher. Her parents, however, want her to go into nursing. Angela registered for a co-op placement in pediatric nursing, hoping to satisfy both her parents and herself. For circumstantial reasons beyond her control, her desired placement never materialized, and she was placed in adult rehabilitation, where she often worked with elderly patients. Angela said about her placement:

I came and spoke to Mrs. Johnson [the teacher responsible for Angela's co-op placement] and asked her if she could get me another placement. . . . But they were all filled up. So . . . then I said I'll stay with this for a while because I'm learning a lot here, right, and I am getting volunteer experience and, well, working with people. It's good experience too! I've never had volunteer work before, right. So this is my first volunteer work and some places . . . they [employers] do like it if you have volunteer work, right, so this helps.

Many industrialized countries use this version of experience as a key feature of policy intended to address a "solution to the youth unemployment crisis." The assumption is that by subsidizing employment through work experience programs (instead of making hard decisions about fundamental social and economic transformation), they will provide youth with the necessary experiences to get jobs when the economy improves and provides new and expanded employment opportunities. It is within this framework that policy makers in Ontario argue "co-op works" because "it's tough to get a job without experience."

What is the issue here for us as teachers? As long as youth continue to face competitive pressures in obtaining employment, we cannot simply turn our backs on their efforts to survive and "make it" within an antipathetic and atomizing economic system. Commodification of self is part of the reality of getting a job. But surely our responsibilities extend beyond training students in commodification techniques. Commodification of self must be understood as a historical and social process shaped by the particular forms of employment available in a certain time and place. In other words, commodification requires coming to terms with a process that restricts and distorts. It encourages those capacities that fit prevailing social forms while those capacities seen as useless are ignored or repressed. This is not a process many students take lightly. If we are to encourage the expansion of human possibility, we need to help students comprehend how existing social forms of employment became dominant and what it would take to construct alternative possibilities.

3. *Experience is a challenging situation that is to be endured or undergone.* This way of viewing experience focuses on the idea of testing or proving oneself. It is based on the assumption that a person who has undergone the "ordeal" becomes different or better. Students sometimes call such events *"real-life* experiences," differentiating them from the dependency characteristic of childhood and indicating that such events contain exhilarating and anxiety-producing challenges. It is a version of experience culturally associated with the theme of "growing up." This version of experience is often cited as the basis of the claim that cooperative education programs are related to improvement in self-concept. The following excerpts are taken from a journal written by Michael Holt, a student who was placed at a local radio station.

Sept. 26   Every day is getting better. Today I successfully operated *all* of the many controls for "Newswave" and was very impressed with myself. The best part is TODAY—18,000 people heard my name and voice. Tomorrow I will be co-hosting for one hour (amazing!). In the morning I actually wrote two news stories for the program (and typed). My afternoon was spent with Jim Jones, Program Director, as we went to pick up equipment (sound). My day was the best.

Oct. 16   What a hectic, busy day. I started off writing news and being minutes behind schedule. I was rushed and unorganized. Immediately after "Newswave" (which went fine), the DJ was late, and I had 3 seconds to put a record on to avoid having "dead air." Immediately after that I was to engineer a future show. I rushed and made several dumb little, and I emphasize "little," errors. To make a long story short, I made and corrected every possible mistake; I did do all of this under pressure and for the first time editing, I did a perfect job. What a good experience. Rushing doesn't pay. I learned a lot about editing and production today, all on my own.

Nov. 3   I'm hearing that I'll be getting an on-air shift very soon. I'm sort of very worried about doing a good show and saying the right things and playing the right music. All the same, I think I can pull it off. I'm looking forward to it. IT'S GOING TO BE SOOO BLOODY EXCITING! YAHOO!

Nov. 14   It was "BLOODY EXCITING." It was the Michael Holt Show for 2½ hours today. I had to select all of the music and mix it as best I could. I received a lot of compliments on my show. Some just said, "Great show, Mike. Loved the music." I felt very comfortable. I talked quite frequently but not for any great length of time. "Newswave" went flawless 100%. I'm hiding the fact that right now I'm exhausted. I mean 9:30 P.M. and I'm lying in bed. That's never happened before. Good night.

This is a version of experience quite different from the first two. Its value is not defined in terms of a potential exchange relation in the marketplace but rather is defined by its significance in relation to the project of expanding human possibilities. It is a version of experience that stresses the point that possibility can be defined through the simultaneous transformation of *both* circumstances and selves.

Of course, not all job placements offer such experiences. Indeed, we are in the process of developing an analysis of how various work processes enable some forms of student participation and disable other forms. In our view teachers designing work education programs must develop their ability to "read" the existing social relations and practices of the work site for the particular possibilities they articulate as social forms. This "reading" requires teachers to understand worker and student behavior differently than many teachers commonly do. For example, it is often said that a student has a "good attitude" when he or she comes to work early, asks questions, shows interest, looks for things to do, and so on. Our analyses suggest that seeing these practices as a "good attitude" essentializes what in reality is an organized social relation. In other words, what the student does in the workplace is taken as evidence by the teacher that the student has certain qualities, while in fact, what is being observed is a particular practical congruence between a specific set of student capacities and the existing requirements of an already-established social form.

Understanding how to find and define social forms that allow a sense of challenge and possibility is something that we argue should be a part of the design of work education programs. We reject the assumption that any experience in and of itself is a worthwhile educational occasion. A critical pedagogy here requires an ongoing attempt to provide students with access to forms that organize the transformative potential of experience.

4. *Experience is the knowledge and understanding one accomplishes or develops in the way in which one makes sense of a situation or set of events.* This notion of experience is considerably different from the previous three. Here the notion of experience is made problematic; it is not something obvious that speaks for itself but rather an understanding that is constructed as a particular interpretation of a specific engagement with material and people over time. It is on this basis that we argue that cooperative education, by placing students in work situations, creates an educational occasion in which students necessarily confront ideas, terms, procedures, relations, and feelings in order to make sense of their presence in the workplace. How students do this—how they accomplish experience—depends in part on the beliefs, ideas, assumptions, and values they bring with them, but also on the context and content of reflection and analysis that we may be able to provide in our co-op programs.

This version of experience affirms the importance of what Michel Foucault called the indissoluble link between knowledge, power, and truth.[11] No experience is simply given. How we think and talk about our world shapes our understandings of why things are the way they are, which images of "that which is not yet" are possible and desirable, and what needs to be done for things to be otherwise.

To utilize the educational potential of this fourth version of experience we advocate a specific approach to the in-school component of cooperative education. Such an approach would offer concepts and a language that would help students interpret work-related situations and relations. It would provide an opportunity for students to engage with new ideas and frameworks that challenge their taken-for-granted ways of thinking about working. In other words, a critical pedagogy of work education would here intervene in the way students commonly, and often uncritically, accomplish work experience.

IN-SCHOOL PEDAGOGY AND ACCOMPLISHED EXPERIENCE

Cooperative education, as experiential learning, obviously relates to all four notions of experience, and clearly all four are relevant to the design of co-op programs. In this regard it should be recognized that what co-op teachers *do* undoubtedly influences the quality of experiential learning in every respect. This includes (1) obtaining work placements and establishing a working relationship with people at a workplace, (2) monitoring student performance while on the job, and (3) organizing the substance and process of the in-school component. All three aspects are important. However, given the limitations of space, the remainder of this chapter will focus on the in-school component and some of the difficulties of trying to use work experiences in a classroom context.

Through our research, we've come to believe that the educational benefits of any work experience program are enhanced when students are given the opportunity to talk together about their jobs. They need to reflect upon and analyze what they saw, heard, and did at work; how they felt about what was happening; and how they understood then and understand now their exposure to the work world. This requires working with the meanings, values, attitudes, feelings, questions, understandings, and misunderstandings students have about their work placements. When we ask students to consider their own work experiences, we are not suggesting the task is simply to tell stories or relive episodes at work. Rather, the agenda is to initiate a process within which students compare and contrast, analyze and discuss, the "stories" they tell about work. We are asking students to understand why and how they accomplish experiences as they do. This means working *on* and *with* experiences and coming to grips with the possibility and implications of

viewing experience as a social and historical construction. A critical pedagogy of work education requires paying attention to, and sometimes
challenging, some of the commonsense ways of thinking about experience. It also means looking for ruptures, contradictions, and forms of
counterdiscourse with which to challenge existing forms of ideological
hegemony.

What does it mean to challenge ideological hegemony, to work on and
with student experience, and to call into question commonsense ways of
thinking? The following excerpt is transcribed from an informal small
group discussion with several male students enrolled in a vocational
high school who have taken co-op placements in conjunction with their
"major shop," upholstery. Consider a portion of one student's "story,"
Don's account of his experience working in a small factory producing relatively inexpensive furniture:

I didn't like it because I don't like mass producing at all, because, uh, the place I
was working at . . . I was there for a whole term . . . and the furniture sure
looked nice, you know. It really looked good. But you wouldn't believe what was
in it! Like, they would just be slapping it all together, you know, bam-bam-bam.
And charging a lot of money for 'em. There was no quality there, you know what
I mean? But a custom shop—not all the time but most of the time—there's more
quality there. . . . See, a lot of the material we had there, like, Harv was a
cheap-o. He was cheap as cheap can get. He would be buying rolls of material
which he'd get at the cheapest price he could, and he'd be giving it to his sales-
men to sell, you know, "Sell this, it's not the greatest material, it's kind of cheap,
but sell it," you know, 'Cause we'll charge 'em twenty-five bucks a yard when
he's paying $3.50 for it kind of thing, right. Seriously, I thought he was cheap. He
would be buying foam and, uh, he bought a big roll of lining that goes under-
neath a couch—he bought a roll, he musta got it cheap, but he bought a whole
roll of lining and it was all covered in oil. Believe it or not there was oil, like
splashes all over it, all over the whole roll. And you'd have to roll out about ten
yards until you find maybe three feet of clean, partially clean, light grey type of
thing, and then you have to pull out more and more. I mean he was cheap! You
know, he was trying to keep the money down, he was trying to—the quality of
work—he was really putting down the quality. And he was, he wasn't just, uh,
he was really cheap.

There was one guy there, he was there for about a week just before I left, and
he was from Newfoundland, and he came up to me, he goes, "So you really like
upholstery?" And I go "Yeah, you know, I really like it." He goes, "Why?" He
goes, "Where did it all start?" And I go, you know, "It started when I made my
own, my first couch, at home," right. And, uh, he goes, "Hey, I'll tell you,
you're crazy 'cause upholstery is going right out." He said, "I hate upholstery,
and I never forgave my dad for putting me in upholstery. I think you're crazy to
go into upholstery." And he was really putting it down. "So why the hell are you
working in an upholstery shop, right?" He's going, "Well, that's all I can do." So
I go, "Well, go out and shovel, you know, garbage if you want but stop putting

down people," right. And he was really going on, putting it down so bad, and that I'd be, you know, sick-o if I went into the business type of thing, eh. But that really, I just brushed it off, but you know, another guy, the guy I worked with, Larry, he said he wouldn't let none of his kids go into upholstery. That it was just too hard to make money. He said it just hurts you, like, he says he hasta go twice a year to get needles in the arms "cause he does so much pulling it wrecks his arms. He says he has to go down and get needles and that."

In working with transcripts like this one over the past several years, we've come to recognize common patterns that restrict the way people make sense of experiences. Here we will focus on several that are evident in the preceding transcript.

Many students, not just Don, tend to locate explanations for events in terms of personalities instead of situations: "Harv was a cheap-o"; "The boss is a jerk." Such assessments are not always negative; for instance, we commonly hear such comments as "The people at my office are so friendly." For us the issue is not that people aren't cheap, jerks, or friendly but rather that such qualities are contextual and are continually organized, produced, and regulated within relationships. It is not that friendliness and unfriendliness are unimportant but rather that students need to be able to see how a particular organization of work allows certain kinds of social relations to exist, relations within which people express their thoughts and desires as organized and structured by those relations. From the point of view of a critical pedagogy of work education, such reconceptualizations are important because they give students a sense that alternative social arrangements might open up enhanced possibilities. At the very least, this is a perspective within which students can consider explanations of their experience beyond the individualizing and often possibility-narrowing assumption that events can be totally accounted for by a presumed fixed character structure.

Another tendency we have found in student reflections on their work experiences is their use of workplace specifics as "evidence" to support taken-for-granted assumptions about "the way it is out there." Generalizations, in such instances, confirm rather than challenge what students already "know" about work. For Don it is important to understand the range of "realities" that define upholstery work. His assessment of furniture manufacturing is based on the particulars of the situation he was in and some assumptions about the differences between mass production and custom building. Yet not all furniture manufacturing plants are like the one at which Don worked. Many (possibly most) are, and the important question for Don to ask is why. A pedagogy adequate for challenging and deepening Don's understanding of his work experience would have to address the social organization of production processes and its structuring economic context. Because the existing pedagogy naturalizes student experience, the issue was never taken up in a way that could provide Don with a basis for expanding his horizon of comprehension. His experience led him to assume a rather limited range of possibilities of how upholstery work might be done; he accepted this range as self-evident and natural, as simply "the way things are."

Related to this limitation is another common problem, the failure to recognize how much of our own histories and assumptions shape our ability to make sense of the world. Certainly, Don's experiences in the school upholstery shop had an influence on his understanding of what was going on at his work placement. School shops like upholstering and woodworking are commonly organized around individual projects in which skills development, a sense of craft, and quality are stressed. Little wonder, then, that exposure to large-scale manufacturing contradicts Don's understanding of what upholstering *is* and *should be*. So strong is his ideal (and so constricted his vision) that he cannot see or hear the "bad news" embodied in the pain and disillusionment of experienced workers: "I just brushed it off." Yet these, too, are a part of the reality of upholstering work, a reality that must be confronted if it is ever to be transformed so as to enhance human dignity.

As important for making sense of their experiences as are the knowledge and understandings that students "bring to" their workplaces, so are the knowledge and understandings that they don't bring and have not yet had the occasion to develop. These "gaps" can be the source of serious misunderstanding when experience is left to "speak for itself." Consider Derek once again. In terms of developing proficiency and a sense of competence in the use of tools and materials, his workplace experience was invaluable. However, to the extent that work education programs focus exclusively on the technical relations of production, they deny students the opportunity to develop insights into the social relations within which technique is embedded. This prevents students from understanding how technical and social competence codetermine the opportunities and satisfactions possible in particular work situations.

After a few weeks on the job, Derek's co-op placement in an electrical supplies manufacturing plant was put in jeopardy because the company was preparing to lay off some of its regular employees. The personnel manager announced that the placement would end until he was able to recall all the workers on layoff. He further commented that he was having "a hell of a time" keeping the two students in the shop. "Hotheads" in the union were insisting that the students be let go because they were doing productive work that could be done by union members. However, the manager argued that the company had made a commitment to train the students. Subsequently, the union shop committee agreed to let them stay until the term finished but not to take any more after that. The personnel manager elaborated on the situation from his point of view:

If they [the union members] were smart, they wouldn't open their traps. But I understand why they do. You see two guys out there who are throwing out production [the co-op students] so, the thing is, some of their co-workers are being laid off. I'm only doing it [eliminating co-op] because the union has said they'd like it done because everyone is bitching out there. We don't want to upset our employees.

With regard to Derek, the personnel manager said,

There is this one redheaded kid out there right now on the milling machine and the lead hand thinks he's a dream. He's better than any guy we've got as far as operating is concerned. The company is getting a break with this particular student. We are getting production . . . he's not holding up production . . . he's giving production. That's why we're so happy. . . . If I could hire this redheaded guy right now, he would have a job tomorrow.

So the situation was this: the union was concerned about student productivity while members were on layoff; the personnel manager and the lead hand were raving to the students and the teacher monitor about how well the students were doing. How did Derek make sense of what was going on? Here is what he said about his own output:

They'd make me do over a hundred. I'd do over a hundred in a day, right. These things, they'd take a long, well, they took about five minutes for each one, like, I ran them off quite fast. . . . What they do is, they just pull up a crate there and it's full, just stacked, right. And you do that 'til it's finished.

Commenting on the pace of work, Derek continued:

People, you know, they were just taking their time. They'd do it as the day goes, right. They wouldn't rush it. They just do the right job and take their time. But I was doing it quite fast at first, but then I started slowing down and working at my own pace again, right.

Though he was never confronted directly by other workers regarding his work pace, Derek learned about working too fast by paying attention to what other workers said about Glen, the other co-op student. Glen was a "legendary" machine shop student who worked fast and with flair, but according to Derek,

The workers, they didn't like that, when he was working like that, eh. They said, "You know, you shouldn't be working like this." One guy said openly, well, like one guy was talking to me about him, right, he goes, "this guy thinks he's really good and he's working too fast," you know. He goes, "We like to stay at a steady pace but he's taking things too far," right.

The sense of this worker's objection to the way Glen worked is not fully understood by Derek, who still saw advantages to working faster than the others: "He [Glen] has all the tools, and you know, it's good to be like that 'cause he's going to be going somewhere in the future, right. He'll have a good job."

Derek constructed his understanding of the other workers' apprehension of co-op students this way:

They could have somebody doing our job and getting paid for our job that we're doing. People were getting laid off, and if we weren't working there, maybe we'd save somebody else from getting laid off 'cause we were doing quite a bit of work, you know. Like me and Glen, when we were doing stuff, we'd mass produce so many things.

Derek's account of an argument between Glen and another regular employee is instructive:

Glen was arguing with one of them at first, eh. One of the guys, he was really mad 'cause he's been there a long time and he does his work at a certain limit, right. He doesn't overdo, he doesn't underdo, he just stays at the same thing where everybody's pleased, right. Like Glen, he was doing more than that guy. Like, they [personnel] would hire him [Glen] and they'd let some guy like that go, that's been working there a long time, if they see some guy that's working really fast, you know. That's what they were scared of, eh.

How does Derek regulate his own practice to mediate these contradictory versions of how fast to work?

At first I'd mass produce quite, like a lot more than you'd normally do, right. I'd really stick to it, you know, because a lot of people, they'd just take their time, do one at a time. But at first, I just kept doing them, all the time. I never had a break or nothing. I just kept working and working, right. And then I just started slowing down and I just worked, I'd work fast, you know, but I'd go to the washroom or I would go have a drink of water and you go back and you just start doing the same thing again, right, for a long, whatever, a couple of hours 'til you had your lunch or something like that. . . . . I stayed at my own pace, like, I slowed down a bit, but I kept up more than I should . . . just a bit more, you know. Just to keep them pleased, that I'm really trying my best, right.

Quite clearly, Derek does not understand this situation as one of "rate busting," nor does he identify the collective interest such a concept implies. Rather, he understands workers' objections in individualistic terms: If *he* (Derek/Glen) works fast, *they* (regular employees) might get laid off, and *he* (Derek/Glen) might get hired. "That's what they were scared of, eh." However, the resources that organized Derek's understanding are flawed: this is simply not the case. The personnel manager would hire the "redheaded kid" *if he could,* but the union contract specifies he can not.

Whether we, as teachers, agree or disagree with the modified piece-rate structure or the system of seniority or the practice of closed shops, it is important for students to understand how these systems work, why they're in place, and whose interests they protect. We cannot assume that this kind of knowledge and understanding will "come" to them simply by being exposed to the "realities" of the work world. In this instance it didn't, but it might have, had the in-school component of Derek's co-op program not taken experience so much for granted.

In addressing the problematic character of student experiences we have in no way intended to diminish the importance of such experiences as a point of reference for doing critical pedagogy. However, just as student experiences are central to our project, so is the effort to challenge the taken-for-granted character of such experiences. This leads us to re-emphasize in these closing remarks the centrality of the pedagogical problem of both legitimating student experiences as appropriate curriculum content and at the same time working to challenge such experiences. Solutions to this problem must be found if we are to foster in our students an expanded sense of human possibility. This is why we have insisted that any design of a true education for work—an education that would help students to eventually be able to define "that which is not yet"—must address experience as both a process of meaning production and a basis for the educational work of social transformation.

NOTES

1. Two classic studies of the impact of educational attainment on occupational status are, in Canada, John Porter, Marion Porter, and Bernard Blishen, *Stations and Callings* (Toronto: Methuen, 1982) and, in the United States, Christopher Jencks et al., *Inequality* (New York: Basic Books, 1972).

2. Ernst Bloch elaborated at length on the utopian impulse of daydreams in his masterwork, *The Principle of Hope* (Cambridge, Mass.: MIT Press, 1986). This work was written during the 1940s and 1950s and has only recently become available in English. See particularly vol. 1, his section on "Anticipatory Consciousness."

3. Ernst Bloch, *A Philosophy of the Future* (New York: Herder and Herder, 1970).

4. Roger I. Simon, "Empowerment as a Pedagogy of Possibility," *Language Arts* 64, no. 4 (1987): pp. 370–81.

5. Roger I. Simon, "Work Experience as the Production of Subjectivity," in David Livingstone and Contributors, *Critical Pedagogy and Cultural Power* (South Hadley, Mass.: Bergin & Garvey, 1987); Magda Lewis, "The Construction of Femininity Embraced in the Work of Caring for Children," *Journal of Educational*

Thought 22, no. 2A (October 1988): pp. 259–68; Don Dippo, "Critical Pedagogy and Education for Work," in P. Harris-Jones, ed., *Making Knowledge Count: Advocacy and Social Science* (Montreal: McGill-Queens University Press, 1989).

6. Philip Corrigan, "In/forming Schooling," in Livingstone, *Critical Pedagogy and Cultural Power*, p. 33.

7. Henry Giroux, "Radical Pedagogy and the Politics of Student Voice," *Interchange* 17, no. 1 (1986): pp. 48–69.

8. Sylvia Smitas, *Employer and Employee Perspectives of Secondary School Business Courses Offered Through Cooperative Education* (M.A. thesis, University of Toronto, 1984).

9. The interview excerpts reported in this chapter are taken from an extensive ethnographic study of student experiences in cooperative education programs. This research was supported by the Social Sciences and Humanities Research Council of Canada under grant numbers 410-81-0906, 410-83-0770, and 410-84-0109.

10. For an extended discussion of the curricular importance of contradictions between official school knowledge and real working knowledge see Roger I. Simon, "But Who Will Let You Do It? Counterhegemonic Approaches to Work Education," *Journal of Education* 165, no. 3 (1983): pp. 235–56.

11. Michel Foucault, *Knowledge/Power*, trans. C. Gordon (New York: Pantheon Books, 1980).

8

Remembrance as a Source of Radical Renewal

Guilt, like innocence, is never a collective affair but a personal one. But together we bear the responsibility for what we will do in the present with our past heritage.[1]

President Richard von Weizäcker

"There is no document of civilization which is not at the same time a document of barbarism. And just as such a document is not free of barbarism, barbarism also taints the manner in which it was transmitted." In a flash of recognition, these words of Walter Benjamin[2] illuminated the photograph I had just uncovered. I had been flipping the pages of an old family photograph album. It had belonged to an RCMP (Royal Canadian Mounted Police) officer who had served with "the Force" during the first half of the twentieth century and thus contained numerous portrayals of "behind-the-scenes" life as a "Mountie." There in a large black-and-white glossy print was an RCMP photographer taking the picture of a bulky, impassive First Nations man in full headdress, sitting with arms folded in front of a teepee (see Figure 1). To one side of this man stands an RCMP officer, hands folded behind his back and legs spread, watching the photographer (perhaps posing as well?). On the other side, a second officer is kneeling and watching the seemingly stoic subject of the composition. A photograph of a photograph being taken.

This print has become emblematic for me. It stands as a document of civilization that portrays the process of making documents *for a civilization* and in doing so, reveals itself as a document of barbarism. Nor did

Figure 1

its original mode of transmission escape a similar taint.[3] Cloistered in a family album kept hidden on a back shelf of a dusty armoire, available only for private reminiscence and unintended for any public sphere, the limitations which structured the viewing of this photograph were complicitous with its barbarous content. What Benjamin advised us to do with such images is wrest them from the context and codifying structures of the victors and rulers in order to reinsert them in new constellations that will help illuminate the present as a moment of radical possibility. In this sense and for this purpose, Benjamin advocated that we *"brush history against the grain"* (emphasis added).[4]

My intent here is to expand on Benjamin's metaphor in an effort to clarify and explore how it might help inform a practice of representation and presentation of knowledge consistent with the aspirations of a pedagogy of possibility. What follows is decidedly *not* a recapitulation of Benjamin's writings nor an attempt to interpret their significance and limitations. Rather, I have read Benjamin as an educator,[5] searching for fragments amid his thoughts that, in juxtaposition with my own concerns, might crystallize in an open path to the future.

Philosopher, art critic, essayist, and cultural historian, Walter Benjamin wrote during the period between the two world wars. Much of his most provocative work was accomplished during the last eight years of his life in a precarious state of exile and flight from fascist Germany. On the surface, a concern with Benjamin's often difficult and, at times, arcane writing may seem a bit too esoteric for a book centrally concerned with questions of pedagogical practice. Yet I think Benjamin's work worthy of attention by educators because within what was an overriding concern with the formulation of a dialectical cultural practice, he began to formulate the epistemological outlines of one aspect of what might be recognized as a pedagogy of possibility. This was a practice that did not require the obliteration of the past and its replacement with a new "truth," but rather a fundamental reconfiguration and rereading of the documents of tradition in a way that might help "reveal the present as a revolutionary moment."

It is in this context that we can view Benjamin as very much concerned with the effects of particular modes for the production and transmission of written, spoken, and visual expression and representation. Embracing in some limited respects a positive relation to modernity (at least in relation to its suppressed utopian potential), Benjamin was centrally preoccupied with the fundamental shift in perception and experience that he thought had emerged within the era of consumer capitalism. Such had become the mode of transmission and reception of cultural objects and memories that he feared the utopian impulses retrievable in tradition and remembrance were in danger of being overpowered by the requirements of an "ever-present" present. In response, Benjamin was searching for a practice from within which one could "wrest tradition from the conformism which [in every era] is about to overpower it."[6] In this sense, for Benjamin the mode of inheritance of cultural objects was not a matter of indifference, a concern that aligns him with our interests as educators.

In the terminology of everyday school life, one might say that Benjamin was concerned with curricula practice, with how one might construct and present representations of the world beyond immediate experience so as to dialectically engage that experience and enable the articulation of new human possibilities. As I have emphasized in Part I, this theme has been too often ignored in contemporary discussions of progressive education. While highlighting important aspirations such as enhancing the democratic character of schooling and implementing a dialogic, problem-centered education, such discussions seem to relegate issues of the construction, presentation, and representation of knowledge to regressive forms of transmission pedagogy. This chapter is intended to recenter these concerns for a critical pedagogy, a pedagogy capable of both affirming *and* challenging the immediacy of our everyday experiences. Those of us working within this mode are attempting to construct curriculum and teaching practices that enable students to call into question existing "truths" and imposed limits on the exercise of human capacities, while simultaneously envisioning new possibilities for themselves and their communities. In this sense our goal is to "teach against the grain." How can Benjamin's notions help in the formulation of such perspectives?

For Benjamin, to "brush history against the grain" was always to do so from within a particular historical conjuncture *and* from a position within what he called "now-time"—the current moment, within which a radically redemptive sense of possibility is always present. Indeed any consideration of the educational implications of Benjamin's thought must eventually address the question of what the concept of "now-time" might mean for a pedagogical outlook. For the moment however, suffice it to say that "to brush against the grain" constitutes a practice infused with historical contingency and the utopian impulse of the "not yet." As indicated above, Benjamin's strategy was not to obliterate the past but to radically reconfigure the relationship between the past and present. This meant challenging the existing modes of inheritance of our views of our selves, others, and our environment with new patterns and forms of presentation, representation and association. In the following section of this chapter I will discuss Benjamin's conception of the "dialectical image" and consider its relation to pedagogical practice. Subsequently, I will discuss in depth the notion of "now-time" and then comment on the importance of the construction a critical pedagogy of remembrance.

Before proceeding however, I wish to add a supplementary note. A remarkable feature of the decade of the 1980s was the rich explosion of cultural practices exploring "tradition" as a resource for identity politics. This politics has been invaluable in challenging existing racist and sexist social forms and has spurred renewed interest in exploring pluralisms that avoid reduction to a conservative individualism or cultural separatism. In this light, one might suggest we hardly need a pre–World War II European philosopher to explore such issues. There is a point here. I have no intent of posing Benjamin and his sense of tradition as the Eurocentric authority within which issues of remembrance and renewal should be defined. Yet this does not mean Benjamin should be ignored. I admit to a long-standing fascination with the man and his work. There are aspects of his thinking and frame of reference that have always vitalized my thinking and helped to clarify my intuitions. This, then, is my attempt to work through what certain aspects of Benjamin's work might mean for my project. To do this in a way true to the partial perspective from which I write, I will have to confront a problem Benjamin sought to avoid. While his work was infused by the particularities of specific dimensions of Judaism, Benjamin felt that his theological concerns had to remain mostly hidden. This for me, has become an untenable position. I will not escape the responsibility for a degree of explicitness in relation to my own theological impulses. This poses a difficult challenge: how to write from within my location as a Jew engaging his own tradition, while writing for an audience, whether secular or still embracing some form of spiritual or religious ethos, whose primary interests and responsibilities lies in a public form of educational practice. There are no easy solutions.

DIALECTICAL IMAGES AND PEDAGOGICAL PRACTICE

In complex societies, emancipation means the participatory transformation of administrative decision structures. Is it possible that one day an emancipated human race could encounter itself within an expanded space of discursive formation of will, and yet be robbed of light in which it is capable of interpreting its life as something good? The revenge of a culture exploited over millennia [by] the legitimation of domination would then take this form: Right at the moment of overcoming age-old repressions, it would harbor no violence but it would have no content either. Without the influx of those semantic energies with which Benjamin's rescuing criticism was concerned, the structures of practical discourse—finally well established—would necessarily become desolate.[7]

Jürgen Habermas

Beyond the immediacy of firsthand experience, the modes of presentation and transmission of information, narratives, and images within various communication technologies articulate propositions through which one attempts to comprehend "how the world works" and what one's place is within it. In other words, what is offered are regulating forms of discursive regimes and image repertoires that orient us to ways of attending to what is to be heard and seen as well as perceived and interpreted. Particular sets of such forms can take on a hegemonic character. When set into dominance, they direct attention to particular concerns and aspirations while simultaneously leading us to suppress, ignore, and pass by issues and features that might be disruptive to the interests of those in a position to define the terms on which everyday life is lived. One phenomenological measure of such dominance is the shock that occasions the seeing of a picture or the reading or hearing of a story that disrupts taken-for-granted modes of comprehending events that have occurred beyond one's immediate experience.

Benjamin had a fascination for images that could provoke, shock, and disrupt. Whether in visual, aural, or written form (or some combination of these modalities), such images encode vivid, often emotionally charged embodiments of sets of concrete relations that elicit semantic and affective associations with the potency to arouse astonishment and thoughtfulness. Of particular interest to Benjamin were images that were counterevidential and could serve as a source of questions and critique of all-too-familiar explanations.[8] Images, seen in this light, were not to be employed as forms for aesthetic contemplation but as spurs to action. In a typical synthesis of imperative and slogan, Benjamin made his concern clear.

Only images in the mind vitalize the will. The mere word by contrast, at most inflames it, to leave it smoldering, blasted. There is no intact will without exact pictorial imagination. No imagination without innervation.[9]

Innervation, the provocation of action that would expand the range of human possibility, was the expressed concern of much of Benjamin's cultural practice. It was through the construction of what Benjamin called "dialectical images" that he felt one might be able to engage in a form of remembrance which, rather than being an empty nostalgia for times past, could illuminate moments of radical possibility that remain scattered like the shards of the broken vessels of creation throughout the present. The construction of dialectical images had a political and pedagogical intent: to enable the past to be perceived in a way that made the present visible as a moment within which people could act to alter the material grounds and social terms on which their lives were lived. Thus I think it of considerable interest to attempt both a recovery and application of Benjamin's design for a critical practice.

His work prematurely and permanently disrupted by war, Benjamin nevertheless left some indication as to how to redeem fragments of the past through their juxtaposition with those of the present to form images whose innervative semiotic character embodied dialectical moments of both destruction and construction. Given the linear conventions of writing, I shall consider each of these moments separately. However, it is important to keep in mind that these moments are not analytically independent. Benjamin's dialectical images were monadic in character, their elements fusing not a in seamless "harmonizing perspective,"[10] but into constellations of unreconciled, mutual referentiality. As I will attempt to illustrate, the pedagogical potential of such images lies in this referentiality, a dynamic that articulates a simultaneous semantic deferral and engagement of each moment with the other.

Within a dialectical image, the moment of destruction preserved a fragment (that is, a text or object) but exploded the cultural apparatus within which it was encoded. This meant radically calling into question the normalized discursive fields and cultural practices that provide the spatial and temporal logic within which a given historical fragment acquires a particular taken-for-granted sense. This was the moment of shock. Not a shock calculated to either thrill or impassion while eliciting a flight from the idea nor one so severe that it might induce an immobilizing trauma. Rather, Benjamin's interest was in the construction of images that could

"arrest fleeting phenomena and start thought in motion, or, alterna-
tively, shocking [taken-for-granted] thought to a standstill and setting reified objects in motion by causing them to lose their second-nature
familiarity."[11] In this sense the moment of destruction within a dialectical
image attempts to bring time to a halt, exposing the present as not simply a transition from one moment to the next. Consider what this might
mean in reference to the picture of the taking of the photograph of a First
Nations man shown earlier. This photograph by itself is not yet a dialectical image but, through its potential destructive force, embodies one moment in its realization.

As with all pedagogies, shock effects are contingent on the viewing
subject and the circumstances within which such images are engaged.
Images are neither simply self-evident nor monological.[12] They cannot be
said to elicit determinate, predictive responses, and clearly their pedagogical employment must incorporate considerations as to the context in
which they are apprehended. However, this is not to say that images
such as the photograph referred to above are without effects. To try to
make clear the destructive potential of the photograph (and hence to begin to clarify the complex monadic quality of a dialectical image), I shall
begin with my own double-layered response. First of all, despite my familiarity with the constructed, ideological character of all documentary
photographs, this print of "a picture being taken" registers a shock that
arrests my ease at an unreflective fascination with images that seem to
speak so clearly of the "way things were." Taken-for-granted views of
photographs usually attend to them as copies of reality, truthful documents of times past. Whether in the form of hegemonic histories supplied in textbooks or in the form of countermemories provided by radical
documentarians, taken-for-granted presentations of historical images are
used to assert knowledge claims about the truth of the past.[13] A photograph of the process of doing documentary photography breaks this illu-
sion.

This has not been lost on the critical assessment of documentary
forms, forms which include representations of people of the First Nations of America. For example, in an incisive critique of an exhibition of
Robert Flaherty's photographs of Inuit people of the southern Arctic, Peter Wollheim points out that the portraiture common to Western Europe,
which emphasized the individual personality in presentations of facial
details, was complicit with the reproduction of the myth of the "noble
savage."[14] Wollheim's article itself is a good example of text that disrupts
the substance and transmission of Flaherty's photographs.

The rupturing of my unreflective gaze requires that I give attention to
the conditions for and practice of the construction of what is about to be
presented as a "document of civilization." What this attention com-
mands is what is normally forgotten, the stories of how it was that the

particular document of reality came to be produced in a particular way. This, then, is the second level of my response to the RCMP photograph. The reflexivity that calls into question the truth of this photograph also calls out beyond it. Hence its destructive potential is not sealed within the fragment but is further mobilized as it fuses with texts more current in my life (texts that emanate from among other places, most recently the Mohawk barricades at Oka, Quebec).

The rupture of the image as a statement of "the way it was" is not without its unwanted insights, especially if one has an investment in a particular mode of the transmission of tradition, one filled with smoothly polished anecdotes, artistically refined and imbued with decades of forgetting.[15] In Canada, those of us (even without historical naiveté) who have become attached to the "dream image"[16] of the Mounties as a fair and honorable force for justice are jolted by a fragment in which "the Force" can be recognized as the military arm of an occupying colonial power. Such images assert a truth that threatens to dissolve barriers erected to keep identities safely within the bounds of the existing social order. Such images are meant to make apparent "those rough and jagged places at which the continuity of tradition breaks down [revealing] "cracks" [that provide] a hold for anyone wishing to get beyond these points."[17]

For many people of the First Nations of the Americas, images such as that presented by the RCMP photograph are neither novel nor shocking. On the contrary, their familiarity is simultaneously enraging and depressing. Such images are (perhaps) not meant for people of the First Nations but rather those of us who have not yet fully awakened from the nightmarish dream of the European enlightenment.[18] However, more than wakefulness is required if such "shocks" are to help illuminate moments within which one might proceed with a project of possibility (see Chapter 2). Indeed, Benjamin recognized that such negations were not enough. Thus he stressed the required constructive moment in the formation of a dialectical image. After the historical fragments were blown free of codifying structures that entrapped them, it was necessary to catch them up again in new sets of discursive relations. The elements of the past were to be rescued and redeemed, drawn together in new constellations that connected with the present.[19]

The intent is not to collapse past and present but to hold them together in a mutually referential tension. Such tension is to be expressed in a constellation that provokes new meanings and arrests or "fissures" what Benjamin considered "the catastrophe"; that "things just go on." In this sense dialectical images are not just empirical extensions into space but as well, set fragments moving through historical time. It is the dialectical relation, constituted in the superimposition of fleeting images, present and past, that makes both moments suddenly come alive in a time pregnant with radical possibility.

A brief but vivid example of the juxtaposition central to the notion of a dialectical image can be seen in the antitheses Benjamin noted between bomb-dropping airplanes and Leonardo da Vinci's utopian anticipation for the "flight of man." Da Vinci expected "that [man (sic)], having raised himself into the air [would] look for snow on the mountain summits, and then return to scatter it over city streets shimmering with the heat of summer."[20] In contradistinction, Benjamin witnessed the awesome technological prowess of the German Luffwaffe as its capabilities were demonstrated in cinematic "newsreels" that displayed the death and destruction of the Spanish Civil War. The sky filled to the horizon with planes simultaneously dropping hundreds of bombs was a fresh and astounding sight. Here Benjamin brought together the utopian and the real in an attempt to compel the recognition of technology's potential *and* the study of history for the reasons that technology nonetheless came to terrorize humanity.[21] This was a study intended to inform the rage of a humanity betrayed and mobilize the struggle to grasp the ground on which the range of human possibilities are to be regulated and realized.

With this example in mind, consider how one might extend the RCMP photograph into a dialectical image. Several months after Brian Mulroney was first elected prime minister of Canada, he traveled to Wall Street to address business leaders in the United States. His message was straightforward: Canada was "open for business." After his speech was reported in the Toronto newspaper *The Globe and Mail*, Tony Hall of the Department of Native Studies at the University of Sudbury wrote the following letter to the editor.

"Canada was not built by expropriating retroactively other people's property," Prime Minister Brian Mulroney has told business leaders in the United States. . . . He is wrong. This is precisely how Canada was built.

The expropriation of Indian and Inuit lands by newcomers for their own economic purposes is a fundamental fact at the basis of the country's history. In large parts of Canada—in most of British Columbia, the Yukon, the Northwest Territories, Quebec and the Maritimes—there has never been any formal agreement on the part of indigenous people to share their ancient homelands.

In those parts of Canada covered by treaties—basically Ontario and the Prairie provinces—the terms of these sacred agreements between the Crown and the Indian nations often remain unfulfilled.

Now the Prime Minister is taking steps to open Canada, including what remains of Indian and Inuit resources, yet further to exploitation by the most economically aggressive power in the world. Before so self-righteously proclaiming Canada's moral aversion to theft of property, he should examine more closely the status of the territorial rights he feels entitled to place on the auction block.[22]

A Canadian prime minister addressing leaders of another nation about a just and honorable history that all people living in Canada might recognize remains today a utopian image (contrast this with the moral legitimacy that accompanied Vaclav Havel's address to a joint session of the U.S. Congress). Since the summer of 1990, Canadians have witnessed more visible and militant First Nations protests over land appropriations and unresolved land claims. The irony in Mulroney's speech has grown stronger. However, this irony need not lead to a despairing cynicism. Indeed, such irony makes possible the question of what we (you and I) would have to do to provide the basis for the utopian speech a prime minister *could* give.

The practice of a dialectical historical imagination is one resource for answering such questions. The "dream image" of a prime minister speaking of a just and honorable Canadian history, juxtaposed with the previously presented RCMP photograph, provokes a pedagogical call for an elaboration of how conquest and coercion were manufactured into the often told "official" story of "Indian" consent and government beneficence. This story has hidden untold suffering produced through government failures to confront and resolve questions of native claims to sovereignty. It is also a story of an inability or unwillingness of many Canadians to adequately assess the respect and moral commitments due people of the First Nations. Perhaps from the vantage point of "now-time," the reconsideration of how such stories were written might inform what must now be done to assert a project of possibility for all communities of people living above the forty-ninth parallel.

"NOW-TIME" AND THE ETHICAL IMAGINATION

Benjamin's notion of a dialectical image recognizes an inevitable claim the present has on the past. Yet this still leaves unanswered the question of how such claims are to be made. Should not such constructions be dismissed as epistemologically arbitrary? Are not dialectical images formed through a play of "found images" manipulated so as to produce a deliberate form of propaganda that should be rejected as a decontextualized misrepresentation of historical fact? Neither is the case. Benjamin was quite clear on this; the constellations of signs that formed a dialectical image were to derive their warrant from an ethical imagination historically constituted and embodied within a theologically informed "now-time" (what in German Benjamin called *Jetzt-zeit*).

The concept of "now-time" requires considerable qualification concerning the notion of the "present," which is superimposed on the past. The "present" is not to be understood as the empirical present, the given state of things. Rather, the representational work of a dialectical image was to lay claim on the past from within a utopian ethical dimension.[23] From this location the dialectical visioning that Benjamin sought could not be confused with a romantic and restricted notion of nostalgia. Benjamin's interest was in a form of rescue or redemption of the past, a practice of remembrance implicating us in the very possibility of such redemption. He wrote:

The past carries with it a temporal index by which it is referred to redemption. There is a secret agreement between the past generations and the present one. Our coming was expected on earth. Like every generation that preceded us, we have been endowed with a *weak* Messianic power, a power to which the past has a claim.[24]

Here, then, is the crux of the problem of "now-time." What is this weak Messianic power with which "we have been endowed"? In what sense can the notion of a messianic "now-time" become a resource for radical renewal and enhanced human possibility?[25]

Within traditions of Jewish rabbinical literature and philosophy such questions are not new. In fact, they express an enduring practical theological problem whose roots are in the physical and spiritual oppression Jewish communities have experienced over the centuries. If the possibility of a messianic era is seen as totally unconnected with material history—as many traditional sources would avow—then hope would be left to "break through fate as if from above,"[26] and consequently the concept would have little practical importance. On the other hand, there is another notion of messianic hope within tradition "that does not require one to adopt the Exodus model of divine intervention in order to aspire to radical changes in human history."[27] This is made clear in the thought of the great twelfth-century rabbinical scholar Moses Maimonides. In Maimonides' assessment of the messianic era one will not have eliminated the problems of the human condition. Rather, as David Hartman explains,

One will only have created an order that is capable of dealing adequately with those problems. It will be the optimal reality for the implementation of the Sinai covenant, but human nature itself will not have been redeemed. The potential for evil and sin will not have been eliminated. Human freedom, with the consequent possibility of choosing evil, will remain. . . . The difference is merely that the range of opportunities for expressing the human powers of love will have been greatly expanded because the majority of human energies will not be exhausted in the battle to survive.[28]

In this view the messianic moment is a normative category within history. The hope eminent in this perspective springs from a dedicated responsibility for the realization of an ethical-spiritual commitment, not from a simple yearning for the time of ultimate peace and resolution. It is the realization that the fullness of that ethical-spiritual commitment will require a social, economic, and political reality within which we can enact freedom and dignity.

This sheds some light on the importance of how dialectical images are to be constructed. The past is articulated to a "now-time" that is not simply the standpoint of the present but rather a standpoint of responsibility for and commitment to the project of bringing about the conditions necessary for the messianic age. Once the messianic promise is understood, not as a myth but as historical possibility, from this point on, time can be said to exist in two simultaneous registers.[29] The first is the register of secular history, which defines an empirical present. The other, continuously a rational possibility, is the standpoint of "hope" (as defined in Chapter 1). It is the possibility of connecting these two registers that is the "weak messianic power with which we have been endowed." This endowment is only possible through the nexus of the social and the sacred, through the practice of historical and material analysis infused with the commitments engendered by the centrality of the spiritual-ethical in human affairs.[30]

A precise example of what such a practice might look like is well illustrated in the work of the contemporary German artist Klaus Staeck. During the period of reconstruction after the Second World War, the government of West Germany allowed the immigration of large numbers of "foreign" workers. While providing a source of cheap labor for difficult physical work, these workers bore the brunt of considerable discrimination in relation to their reception in German communities and the systematic lack of legal protection that would have mitigated their economic exploitation. In 1972–73 there were approximately 4 million non-German workers and their families in Germany, mainly Italians, Turks, and East Europeans. At this time the German economy entered a serious recession. In response, the government proposed a series of measures establishing quotas for the number of workers living in specific regions and restricting the movement of what were then being called *Gastarbeiter* (guest workers).

In 1974, Staeck produced a poster called *Fremdarbeiter*, which demonstrates the importance of clarifying the notion of the present from which claims on the past are made (see Figure 2). Literally, a *Fremdarbeiter* is a "strange worker," one who is out of place or not of this place. In more contemporary terms, it refers to one who is constructed and positioned as "Other" within combined relations of power/difference. However, in Germany the word has additional connotations. During the Nazi regime, *Fremdarbeiter* was the term used to refer to slave labor, both in the concentration camps and in the regular war plants. After the war the term was deemed unacceptable and *Gastarbeiter* became the euphemistic substitute.[31] In Staeck's poster, pictured in tones of black and white, are two men emptying garbage into a garbage truck. The worker in the foreground seems to be wearing a uniform one might associate with incarceration. On the jacket of this worker, over the heart, where it appeared on similar-looking uniforms thirty years earlier, is the Jewish Star of

David. Yet this star is striped with the colors of the Italian flag. Visually following the line of this worker's left arm, one sees that he is shown holding two garbage pails, one of which is stamped with an identification number. The uniform, the Star, and the identification number all gesture toward a past so as to concretely create a constellation in which a present image is dialectically grasped in relation to an earlier one.

In Staeck's poster, iconic features of the Holocaust are ripped from their context through the mode of dialectical juxtaposition. From the vantage point of someone who has studied the events of Jewish history from 1933–45 and pondered the still vital question of what practices might best sustain the remembrance of the unique "events" of this era, I anticipate objections to Staeck's image. Simplifying for the sake of brevity, one might object that to decontextualize such symbols as the Star and the identification tattoo and use them as a way of formulating a relation of correspondence between the Holocaust and contemporary racist practices is both to diminish the magnitude of the evil symbolized by Auschwitz and to oversimplify history in the extreme. If Staeck's image is taken as a claim of historical correspondence, I would agree with this objection. Such an interpretation is indeed plausible if the present's claim on the past is viewed as being made solely within the secular present. However, if claims on the past are seen as being made from that register Benjamin called "now-time," a different reading is possible.

Rather than seeing a claim of historical correspondence, the images of the Jews of Auschwitz and Germany's contemporary "guest workers" are held in a mutually referential dynamic tension. In this constellation and through this tension, past text and present image are illuminated by a redemptive light. This light emanates from an ethical-spiritual source that makes visible the necessity for a worldly utopia to be guaranteed by actions that must be taken in the present, actions designed *to prevent any possible correspondence* between the Jewish victims of Fascism and the "guest workers." This is one way in which to understand Benjamin's remark that "to articulate the past historically does not mean to recognize it 'the way it really was.' It means to seize hold of a memory as it flashes up at a moment of danger." Clearly, we all live in an empirical present that must be grasped and acknowledged. However, we also live within an ethical present whose forward-pressing hopefulness is its most precious feature. A critical educational practice that suppresses either register cannot help but fall prey to either a cynical deconstructionism or a wishful futurism.

A CRITICAL PEDAGOGY OF REMEMBRANCE

Remembrance is the practice in which certain images and stories of a collective past are brought together with a person's feelings and comprehension of their embodied presence in time and space. Indeed, perva-

Figure 2
Source: "Fremdarbeiter," Nr. 56a Klaus Staeck (1975), edition Staeck. 69 Heidelberg 1. Reprinted with permission.

sive struggles over how remembrance should be done attest to its importance in the life of human communities. This struggle has taken place and continues to take place not only in the realm of what constitutes an accurate historical record and what images and stories are worth remembering but as well in the consideration of what it might mean to learn from the past, given our situated standpoint in the present. A good part of this struggle takes place through institutional mediation. That is, as sites of representation and presentation of versions of a collective past, schools, cinema, broadcast media, publishing, galleries, conferences (all sites of cultural production) are constantly the locus of practices that attempt to provoke particular practices of remembrance.

A pedagogy of possibility, one intended to enhance the expression of human dignity and secure the renewal of life on our planet (see Chapter 2), cannot remain indifferent to the spiritual desire to understand our presence in both historical and cosmic time. Neither can it remain indifferent to political projects (explicit or not) that structure particular attempts to influence how remembrance will take place. In this chapter I have been attempting to explore the heuristic value of Benjamin's concept of a dialectical image for the task of reconceptualizing a pedagogy of remembrance. Informed by this notion, such a practice would consider how one might locate and represent images and stories of the past that connect to the present in a way that reveals a present irradiated with the anticipation of radical possibility.

Benjamin understood the curriculum problem. An empirical-ethical present must recognize the past as its own concern, the difficulty being that the past has to be discovered by the present in a way that was never intended, because the present could have never been predicted. This sets a twofold teaching agenda, helping people develop an understanding of their empirical-ethical present and exploring how this present might inform and be informed by a particular sighting of the past. This requires teaching that enables people to see stereoscopically into the depths of historical shade. Stereoscopic images are three-dimensional, works created not from one image but from two. On their own historical facts are depthless and distancing. To create the depth and draw the historical record into relation with us, we must provide the other half of the picture from images developed in our own "now-time."[32]

Living in the Americas in the late twentieth century, the salience of this agenda is becoming more and more manifest. In May 1973 in Extremadura, Spain, a meeting of academics and government officials prescribed a commemoration to be conducted in 1992 as a celebration of the "half-millennium of the discovery [sic] of America."[33] Since that time, attempts to provoke similar celebratory practices of remembrance have been planned in most countries on our northern and southern continents. Such plans have not gone unnoticed by members of indigenous communities. As Jose Barreiro put it,

The impetus to "celebrate" Columbus as metaphor for discovery and to identify colonization as the exalted method of civilization has deep currents in Ibero-American and other European thinking. Indians can recognize it and yet recoil from it, as the reality of the conquest and subsequent victimization endured are too obvious. . . .

Celebrating the Columbus Quincentenary as a discovery, or even a celebration of an encounter between two distinct civilizations, European and American, begs the question of who was here standing on the shore? What has happened to them? What is their perspective on that momentous event and its repercussions? What are those Indian opinions now?[34]

Since the mid-1980s, the people of the First Nations of the Americas have begun to formulate plans for their own practices of remembrance. As coordination grows, it is becoming clear that not only will images and stories missing from the "official record" be put into view, but there will be an attempt to put forward a past that recognizes the current conjuncture as a moment of revolutionary possibility for indigenous peoples. This means recognizing the possibility of securing self-governing communities from which to define one's own possibilities and contribute in globally valued ways to a sane and life-renewing culture.

Yet 1992 counterdiscursive practices of remembrance cannot remain limited to First Nations communities. Those of us whose ancestors arrived in the Americas after Columbus have been living the privilege initiated by that event, but at a cost in human and environmental terms that has been staggering. We too are faced with the challenge of re-visioning our collective past from the standpoint of our empirical-ethical present. As cultural workers faced with the task of teaching against the grain of a received historical tradition,[35] perhaps we may find Benjamin's insights helpful as we think through a pedagogy of remembrance that might contribute to the radical renewal of the terms of reference of our daily lives.

ANOTHER VERSION

Yet for me 1992 has an additional resonance. There is another "quincentenary" to remember. On March 30, 1492, King Ferdinand and Queen Isabella signed a degree expelling all Jews (more than 150,000) from Spain within a period of four months. After virtually a hundred-year period of expropriation, torture, auto-da-fé and mass conversion, Spain was suddenly *"Juden-frei."* As a postbiblical collective tragedy, this event was dwarfed in its proportions only by the Holocaust. While the "quincentenary" of the expulsion of the Jews from Spain undoubtedly calls for practices of remembrance, what it must not do is supplant the importance of a reconsideration of Columbus's arrival in the land now called the Americas. As a white, Ashkenazi Jew whose family immigrated to

North America from the Russian Pale, I know that this migration was made possible by the conquest initiated by Columbus. While I resist being absorbed into an amorphous, homogenized construction of whiteness, I cannot fail the responsibility of considering what I/we do in the present with our past heritage and our current privilege. But perhaps the real challenge here is to avoid the historical separation of these two five-hundred-year-old events and to grasp, without losing the specificity of either, their shared significance. After all, the conditions of possibility for both were secured by the totalizing power of a truth told within the twin orbits of imperial majesty and fascist religiosity. Remembering both events together may strengthen our efforts in refusing and transforming the legacy of this heritage.

חזק חזק ונתחזק

Be Strong, Be Strong, And Let Us Strengthen One Another.

NOTES

1. President von Weizäcker made this remark while speaking to the Czech people fifty-one years after Hitler entered Prague Castle to announce the takeover of Czechoslovakia (*London Times*, March 16, 1990, p. 9).

2. Walter Benjamin, "Theses on the Philosophy of History," in *Illuminations*, trans. Harry Zohn (New York: Schocken Books, 1969), p. 256.

3. "The mode of inheritance of cultural objects is not a matter of indifference. Instead, it is the central problem pertaining to those works and their interpretation." Susan Buck-Morss, "Walter Benjamin—Revolutionary Writer (I)" *New Left Review*, no. 128, July–August 1981, pp. 50–75.

4. Benjamin, "Theses on the Philosophy of History," in *Illuminations*, p. 257.

5. I am greatly indebted to Susan Buck-Morss for helping me understand the importance for education of Benjamin's writings. Her volume *The Dialectics of Seeing: Walter Benjamin and the Arcades Project* (Cambridge: MIT Press, 1989) has been singularly influential in the development of this chapter.

6. Walter Benjamin, "Theses on the Philosophy of History," in *Illuminations*, p. 255.

7. Jürgen Habermas, "Walter Benjamin: Consciousness Raising or Rescuing Critique" (Cambridge: MIT Press, 1983), p. 158.

8. Ackbar Abbas, "On Fascination: Walter Benjamin's Images," *New German Critique*, no. 48 (Fall 1989): pp. 43–62.

9. Qtd. from Benjamin's *One Way Street* in Buck-Morss, *The Dialectics of Seeing*, p. 290.

10. Ibid., p. 67.

11. Ibid., p. 106.

12. At times, Benjamin seemed to insist that such images could speak for themselves. See, for example, Adorno's criticism of what he understood as Ben-

jamin's position on the self-evidential quality of a dialectical image in Fredric Jameson, ed., *Aesthetics and Politics* (London: New Left Review Books, 1977).

13. For excellent discussions of some of the limitations and problems of the educational documentary form see Robert A. Rosenstone, "History, Memory, Documentary: A Critique of *The Good Fight, Cineaste* 17, no. 1 (1989): pp. 12–15; and Abigail Solomon-Godeau, "Who is Speaking Thus? Some Questions about Documentary Photography," in her *Photography at the Dock* (Minneapolis: University of Minnesota Press, 1991).

14. Peter Wollheim, "Robert Flaherty's Inuit Photographs," *Canadian Forum*, November 1980, pp. 12–14. For a different assessment of Flaherty, see Richard Barsam, *The Vision of Robert Flaherty: The Artist as Myth and Filmmaker* (Bloomington: Indiana University Press, 1989).

15. Marie-Luise Gaettens, "The Hard Work of Remembering: Two German Women Reexamine National Socialism," in Frieda Johles Forman, ed., *Taking Our Time: Feminist Perspectives on Temporality* (Oxford: Pergamon Press, 1989), p. 77.

16. Benjamin in no way wished to dismiss the innervative potential of dream images. For an elaboration of his use of the concept "dream image" see Buck-Morss, *The Dialectics of Seeing*, particularly chap. 5.

17. Ibid., p. 290.

18. Nightmares and the Enlightenment are both complex phenomena. I am not implying that the legacy of the Enlightenment has been without redemption. I only wish to stress that the practices of "civilization" developed and exported from Europe between approximately 1700 to 1914 have not been unproblematic given the moral project outlined in Part I of this book.

19. Buck-Morss, "Walter Benjamin," p. 56.

20. Buck-Morss, *The Dialectics of Seeing*, p. 245.

21. Ibid., p. 245.

22. Tony Hall, "PM Should Study Land Rights before Moralizing, Reader Says," *The Globe and Mail*, December 14, 1984, p. 7.

23. Note here the similarity of Benjamin's thought to that of Ernst Bloch. For the importance of a utopian ethical dimension for education see chap. 1.

24. Benjamin, "Theses on the Philosophy of History," p. 254.

25. I here diverge from Benjamin. My own attempt to address the meaning of "now-time" is a faint echo of the contemporary writings of Rabbis Joshua Abraham Heschel and David Hartman.

26. This is the phrase used by Habermas (p. 149) in his appreciative critique of Benjamin's position.

27. David Hartman, *A Living Covenant: The Innovative Spirit in Traditional Judaism* (New York: Free Press, 1985), p. 254.

28. Ibid., p. 251.

29. Buck-Morss, *The Dialectics of Seeing*, p. 242.

30. The recent concern over the importance of the spiritual dimension of human existence has provided a series of interesting discussions of the possible tensions that lie between a historical and religious consciousness. Such tensions are often constructed through the assumption that the realm of the spiritual lies in religious commitments to aspects of life that transcend history. For an introduction to these issues see the special issue, "The Last Modern Century," of *New*

Perspectives Quarterly 8, no. 2 (Spring 1991). Benjamin, in my view, offers insights that attempt to resolve this tension.

31. Jacob Mey, *Whose Language? A Study in Linguistic Pragmatics* (Amsterdam: John Benjamins, 1985), p. 136 n.

32. Buck-Morss, *The Dialectics of Seeing,* p. 292.

33. Jose Barreiro, "View from the Shore: Toward an Indian Voice in 1991," *Northeast Indian Quarterly,* Fall 1990, pp. 4–20.

34. Ibid., pp. 8, 11.

35. For examples of educators who have recognized the importance of the quincentenary and have taken up the challenge of a critical practice of remembrance, see Bill Bigelow, Barbara Miner and Bob Peterson, eds. "Rethinking Columbus," Milwaukee, WI: Rethinking Schools, Ltd., 1991.

Bibliography

Abbas, Ackbar. "On Fascination: Walter Benjamin's Images." *New German Critique* 48 (Fall 1989): 43–62.

Achebe, Chinua. *Hopes and Impediments: Selected Essays 1967–87*. London: Heinemann, 1988.

Aiken, Susan Hardy, Karen Anderson, Myra Dinnerstein, Judy Lensink, and Patricia MacCorquodale. "Trying Transformation: Curriculum Integration and the Problem of Resistance." *Signs* (Winter 1987): 255–75.

Alcoff, Linda. "Cultural Feminism vs. Poststructuralism: The Identity Crisis in Feminist Theory." *Signs* 13, no. 3 (1988): 405–36.

Apple, Michael. *Teachers and Texts: A Political Economy of Class and Gender Relations in Education*. New York: Routledge, 1986.

Aronowitz, Stanley. "On Narcissism." In *The Crisis in Historical Materialism*, 1st ed. New York: Praeger, 1981.

Aronowitz, Stanley and Henry Giroux. *Postmodern Education: Politics, Culture and Social Criticism*. Minneapolis: University of Minnesota Press, 1990.

Bakhtin, Mikhail. *Rabelais and His World*. Cambridge: MIT Press, 1968.

Barreiro, Jose. "View From the Shore: Toward an Indian Voice in 1991." *Northeast Indian Quarterly* (Fall 1990): 4–20.

Belsey, Catherine. *Critical Practice*. New York: Methuen, 1980.

Benjamin, Walter. "Theses on the Philosophy of History." In *Illuminations*. Translated by Harry Zohn. New York: Schocken Books, 1969.

Benjamin, Walter. "The Author as Producer." In *Reflections: Essays, Aphorisms, Autobiographical Writings*. New York: Harcourt Brace Jovanovitch, 1978.

Benjamin, Walter. "The Destructive Character." In *Reflections: Essays, Aphorisms, Autobiographical Writings*. New York: Harcourt Brace Jovanovich, 1978.

Bennett, Tony. "Texts in History: The Determinations of Readings and Their

Texts." In *Post-Structuralism and the Question of History,* edited by D. Attridge, G. Bennington, and R. Young. Cambridge: Cambridge University Press, 1987.

Benton, Ted. "Marxism and Natural Limits: An Ecological Critique and Reconstruction." *New Left Review* 178 (November/December 1989): 21–86.

Berger, Thomas. *Fragile Freedoms: Human Rights and Dissent in Canada.* Toronto: Clarke Irwin, 1981.

Bigelow, Bill. "Discovering Columbus: Re-reading the Past." *Language Arts* (October 1989).

Bloch, Ernst. *The Principle of Hope.* Cambridge: MIT Press, 1986.

Bauman, Zygmunt. *Modernity and the Holocaust.* Ithaca: Cornell University Press, 1989.

Bisseret, Noelle. *Education, Class, Language and Ideology.* London: Routledge and Kegan Paul, 1979.

Bobo, Jacqueline. *"The Color Purple:* Black Women as Cultural Readers." In *Female Spectators: Looking at Film and Television,* edited by E. Deidre Pribram. London: Verso, 1988.

Bourdieu, Pierre and Jean-Claude Passeron. *Reproduction in Education, Society and Culture.* Beverly Hills: Sage, 1977.

Briskin, Linda. "Feminist Pedagogy: Teaching and Learning Liberation." *Feminist Perspectives* (Canadian Research Institute for the Advancement of Women, Ottawa) 19 (August 1990): 12–14.

Britzman, Deborah P. "Who has the Floor? Curriculum, Teaching and the English Student's Struggle for Voice." *Curriculum Inquiry* 19, no. 2 (1989): 143–62.

Buber, Martin. *Between Man and Man.* New York: Collier Books Macmillan, 1965.

Buck-Morss, Susan. "Walter Benjamin—Revolutionary Writer." *New Left Review* 128 (July/August 1981): 50–75.

Buck-Morss, Susan. "Benjamin's Revolutionary Pedagogy." *New Left Review* 128.

Buck-Morss, Susan. *The Dialectics of Seeing: Walter Benjamin and the Arcades Project.* Cambridge: MIT Press, 1989.

Bulkin, Elly, Minnie Bruce Pratt, and Barbara Smith. *Yours in Struggle: Three Feminist Perspectives on Anti-Semitism and Racism.* Brooklyn: Long Haul Press, 1984.

Carr, Wilfred, and Stephen Kemmis. *Becoming Critical.* Philadelphia: Falmer, 1986.

Clifford, James. *The Predicament of Culture: Twentieth-Century Ethnography, Literature and Art.* Cambridge: Harvard University Press, 1987.

Connell, Robert W. *Teachers' Work.* Boston: Allen and Unwin, 1985.

Corrigan, Philip. "Race/Ethnicity/Gender/Culture: Embodying Differences Educationally." In *Breaking the Mosaic,* edited by Jon Young. Toronto: Garamond, 1987.

Corrigan, Philip. "In/Forming Schooling." In *Critical Pedagogy and Cultural Power,* edited by David Livingstone et al. Toronto: Garamond Press, 1987.

Corrigan, Philip. *Social Forms/Human Capacities: Essays in Authority and Difference.* London: Routledge, 1990.

Cottom, Daniel. *Text and Culture: The Politics of Interpretation.* Minneapolis: University of Minnesota Press, 1989.

Crean, Susan, and Marcel Rioux. *Two Nations.* Toronto: James Lorimer, 1983.

Cunningham, Frank. *Democratic Theory and Socialism.* Cambridge: University of Cambridge Press, 1987.

Curtis, Bruce. *Building the Educational State in Canada West.* Philadelphia: Falmer Press, 1988.

Davin, Anna. "Imperialism and Motherhood." *History Workshop Journal* 5 (Spring 1989): 9–65.

de Lauretis, Teresa. *Alice Doesn't: Feminism, Semiotics and Cinema.* Bloomington: University of Indiana Press, 1984.

de Lauretis, Teresa, ed. *Feminist Studies/Critical Studies.* Bloomington: University of Indiana Press, 1986.

Dehli, Kari. "Women and Class: The Social Organization of Mothers' Relations to Schools." Unpublished Ph.D. Dissertation, Ontario Institute for Studies in Education, University of Toronto, 1988.

Deleuze, Gilles. *Foucault.* Minneapolis: University of Minnesota Press, 1988.

Dippo, Don. "Critical Pedagogy and Education for Work," In *Making Knowledge Count: Advocacy and Social Science,* edited by P. Harris-Jones. Montreal: McGill-Queens University Press, 1989.

Ellsworth, Elizabeth. "Why Doesn't This Feel Empowering? Working Through the Repressive Myths of Critical Pedagogy." *Harvard Educational Review* 59, no. 3 (August 1989): 297–324.

Ehrenreich, Barbara. *Hearts of Men: American Dreams and the Flight from Commitment.* New York: Anchor Press, 1983.

Fein, Leonard. *Where Are We? The Inner Life of America's Jews.* New York: Harper and Row, 1988.

Felman, Shoshana. "Psychoanalysis and Education: Teaching Terminable and Interminable." *Yale French Studies* 63 (1982).

Fine, Michelle. "Silencing in Public Schools." *Language Arts* 64 (1987): 157–75.

Flax, Jane. "Re-membering the Selves: Is the Repressed Gendered?" *Michigan Quarterly Review* (Special Issue: "Women and Memory") 26, no. 1 (Winter 1987): 92–110.

Foster, Hal. "Against Pluralism." In *Recordings: Art, Spectacle, Cultural Politics.* Seattle: Bay Press, 1985.

Foucault, Michel. *Discipline and Punish.* New York: Vintage Books, 1979.

Foucault, Michel. *The History of Sexuality.* Vol. 1. New York: Vintage Books, 1980.

Foucault, Michel. *Power/Knowledge: Selected Interviews and Other Writings 1972–1977.* Translated by C. Gordon. New York: Pantheon Books, 1980.

Foucault, Michel. "The Subject and Power." In *Michel Foucault: Beyond Structuralism and Hermeneutics,* edited by H. Dreyfus and P. Rabinow. Brighton, Sussex: Harvester Press, 1982.

Freud, Sigmund. *Civilization and Its Discontents.* London: Hogarth Press, 1957.

Freire, Paulo. *The Pedagogy of the Oppressed.* New York: Herder and Herder, 1970.

Gaettens, Marie-Luise. "The Hard Work of Remembering: Two German Women Re-Examine National Socialism." In *Taking Our Time: Feminist Perspectives on Temporality,* edited by Frieda Johles Forman. Oxford: Pergamon Press, 1989.

Gallop, Jane. "The Immoral Teachers." *Yale French Studies* 63 (1982).

Gates, Henry, Jr. "The Master's Pieces: On Cannon Formation and the Afro-American Tradition." *South Atlantic Quarterly* 89, no. 1 (Winter 1990).

Gelke, Hanna. "The Phenomenology of the Wish in the Principle of Hope." *New German Critique* 145 (Fall 1988): 55–80.

Giddens, Anthony. *Central Problems in Social Theory: Action, Structure and Contradiction in Social Analysis.* London: Macmillan, 1979.

Ginsburg, Alan, and Sandra Hanson. "Gaining Ground: Values and High School Success Final Report to the U.S. Department of Education." Washington, D.C.: Government Printing Office, 1985.

Giroux, Henry. *Schooling and the Struggle for Public Life: Critical Pedagogy in the Modern Age.* Minneapolis: University of Minnesota Press, 1988.

Giroux, Henry, and Roger I. Simon. "Popular Culture as a Pedagogy of Pleasure and Meaning." In *Popular Culture, Schooling and Everyday Life,* edited by Henry Giroux and Roger I. Simon. South Hadley, Mass.: Bergin and Garvey, 1989.

Goldhaber, Michael. *Reinventing Technology: Policies for Democratic Values.* New York: Routledge and Kegan Paul, 1986.

Goodson, Ivor, ed. *International Perspectives in Curriculum History.* London: Croom Helm, 1987.

Goodson, Ivor, ed. *School Subjects and Curriculum Change.* London: Falmer Press, 1987.

Goodson, Ivor, ed. *The Making of Curriculum.* London: Falmer Press, 1988.

Gordon, Anita, and David Suzuki. *It's a Matter of Survival.* Toronto: Stoddart, 1990.

Goethe, Johann Wolfgang von. *Faust.* Translated by Barker Fairley. Toronto: University of Toronto Press, 1970.

Grant, George. *Empire and Technology: Perspectives on North America.* Toronto: House of Anansi, 1969.

Greene, Maxine. "The Passion of the Possible: Choice, Multiplicity and Commitment." *Journal of Moral Education* 19, no. 2 (May 1990): 67–76.

Haber, Clive, and Roland Meighan, eds. *The Democratic School: Educational Management and the Practice of Democracy.* Ticknall, Derbyshire: Education Now Publishing Cooperative, 1989.

Habermas, Jürgen. "Walter Benjamin: Consciousness Raising or Rescuing Critique." In *Philosophical Political Profiles.* Cambridge: MIT Press, 1983.

Haraway, Donna. "Situated Knowledges: The Science Question in Feminism and the Privilege of Partial Perspective" *Feminist Studies* 14, no. 3 (1988).

Haraway, Donna. *Primate Visions: Gender, Race and Nature in the World of Modern Science.* New York: Routledge, 1989.

Harding, Sandra. *The Science Question in Feminism.* Ithaca: Cornell University Press, 1986.

Harlow, Barbara. *Resistance Literature.* New York: Methuen, 1987.

Hartman, David. *A Living Covenant: The Innovative Spirit in Traditional Judaism.* New York: The Free Press, 1985.

Hebdige, Dick. "Some Sons and Their Fathers." *Borderlines* 11 (Spring 1988).

Haug, Frigga. "Daydreams." *New Left Review* 162 (March/April 1987).

Heidegger, Martin. "The Question Concerning Technology." In *Basic Writings.* New York: Harper and Row, 1977.

Henriques, Julian, Wendy Holloway, Cathy Urwin, Couse Venn, and Valerie Walkerdine. *Changing the Subject: Psychology, Social Regulation and Subjectivity.* London: Methuen, 1984.

Heschel, Abraham J. *The Prophets*. Philadelphia: Jewish Publication Society, 1962.

hooks, bell. *Talking Back: Thinking Feminist, Thinking Black*. Toronto: Between the Lines Press, 1989.

Howe, Irving. *World of Our Fathers*. New York: Harcourt Brace Jovanovich, 1976.

Jameson, Fredric, ed. *Aesthetics and Politics*. London: New Left Review Books, 1977.

Jameson, Fredric. *The Political Unconscious: Narrative as a Socially Symbolic Act*. Ithaca: Cornell University Press, 1981.

Jenks, Christopher, et al. *Inequality*. New York: Basic Books, 1972.

Jones, Kathleen B. "On Authority: Or Why Women Are Not Entitled to Speak." In *Feminism and Foucault: Reflections on Resistance*, edited by Irene Diamond and Lee Quinby. Boston: Northeastern University Press, 1988.

Kafka, Franz. *Parables and Paradoxes*. Edited by Nahum Glatzer. New York: Schocken, 1971.

Kearney, Richard. *The Wake of Imagination*. Minneapolis: University of Minnesota Press, 1988.

Laclau, Ernesto. "Interview." *Strategies* 1, no. 1 (1989).

Laclau, Ernesto, and Chantel Mouffe. *Hegemony and Socialist Strategy: Towards a Radical Democratic Politics*. London: Verso, 1985.

Lawrence, Jerome, and Robert E. Lee. *Inherit the Wind*. New York: Bantam, 1975.

Lelyveld, Toby. *Shylock on Stage*. London: Routledge and Kegan Paul, 1961.

Levine, Lawrence W. *Highbrow Lowbrow: The Emergence of Cultural Hierarchy in America*. Cambridge: Harvard University Press, 1988.

Lewis, Magda. "The Construction of Femininity Embraced in the Work of Caring for Children." *Journal of Educational Thought* 22, no. 2A (October 1988): 259–68.

Lewis, Magda. "Without a Word: Sources and Themes for a Feminist Pedagogy." Unpublished Ph.D. Dissertation, Ontario Institute for Studies in Education, University of Toronto, 1988.

Lewis, Magda, and Roger I. Simon. "A Discourse Not Intended for Her: Learning and Teaching Within Patriarchy." *Harvard Educational Review* 56, no. 4 (November 1986): 457–72.

Litner, Bluma. "Exploring Critical Revision as a Process of Empowerment." Unpublished Ph.D. Dissertation, Ontario Institute for Studies in Education, University of Toronto, 1990.

Lorde, Audre. "The Uses of Anger: Women Responding to Racism." In *Sister Outsider: Essays and Speeches*. New York: The Crossing Press, 1984.

Lusted, David. "Why Pedagogy?" *Screen* 27, no. 5 (September–October 1986): 3.

Lyotard, Jean-François. *The Postmodern Condition: A Report on Knowledge*. Minneapolis: University of Minnesota Press, 1984.

Mey, Jacob. *Whose Language? A Study in Linguistic Pragmatics*. Amsterdam: John Benjamins, 1985.

Morgan, Robert. "English Studies as Cultural Production in Ontario 1860–1920." Unpublished Ph.D. Thesis, Ontario Institute for Studies in Education, University of Toronto, 1987.

Morson, Gary Saul, and Caryl Emerson, eds. *Rethinking Bahktin: Extensions and Challenges*. Evanston: Northwestern University Press, 1989.

Nicholson, Linda J., ed. *Feminism/Postmodernism*. New York: Routledge, 1990.

Nietzsche, Friedrich. *The Birth of Tragedy and The Genealogy of Morals.* Translated by F. Golffing. Garden City, N.Y.: Doubleday and Company, 1956.

Osbourne, Ken. *Educating Citizens: A Democratic Socialist Agenda for Canadian Education.* Toronto: Our Schools/Our Selves Educational Foundation, 1988.

Peller, Gary. "Reason and the Mob: The Politics of Representation." *Tikkun* 2, no. 3 (July/August 1987).

Popkewitz, Thomas, ed. *Critical Studies in Teacher Education: Its Folklore, Theory and Practice.* London: Falmer, 1987.

Popkewitz, Thomas, ed. *The Formation of School Subjects: The Struggle for Creating an American Institution.* New York: Falmer, 1987.

Porter, J., M. Porter, and B. Blishen. *Stations and Callings.* Toronto: Methuen, 1982.

Raine, Craig. "Conrad and Prejudice." *London Review of Books* (June 22, 1989).

Rajchman, John. *Michel Foucault: The Freedom of Philosophy.* New York: Columbia University Press, 1985.

Robbins, Bruce. "The Politics of Theory." *Social Text* 18 (Winter 1987/88).

Rosaldo, Renato. *Culture and Truth: The Re-Making of Social Analysis.* Boston: Beacon Press, 1989.

Rosenfeld, Lulla. *The Bright Star of Exile: Jacob Adler and the Yiddish Theatre.* New York: Crowell, 1977.

Rosenthal, Michael. *The Character Factory: Baden-Powell's Boy Scouts and the Imperatives of Empire.* New York: Pantheon,1984.

Rosenstone, Robert A. "History, Memory, Documentary: A Critique of the Good Fight." *Cineaste* 17, no. 1 (1989): 12–15.

Rosler, Martha. "In, Around and Afterthoughts [On Documentary Photography]." In *Three Works.* Halifax: The Press of the Nova Scotia College of Art and Design, 1981.

Rowe, Ella. "Desire and Popular Culture: The Ego Ideal and Its Influence in Production of Subjectivity." Unpublished paper, Ontario Institute for Studies in Education, University of Toronto, 1984.

Said, Edward. *The World, the Text and the Critic.* Cambridge: Harvard University Press, 1982.

Sanders, Ronald. *The Downtown Jews: Portraits of an Immigrant Generation.* New York: Harper and Row, 1989.

Sartre, Jean-Paul. *Search for a Method.* New York: Alfred Knopf, 1963.

Scheffler, Israel. *On Human Potential: An Essay in the Philosophy of Education.* Boston: Routledge and Kegan Paul, 1985.

Shor, Ira, ed. *Freire for the Classroom: A Sourcebook for Liberatory Teaching.* Portsmouth, N.H.: Boynton/Cook, 1987.

Simon, Roger I. "But Who Will Let You Do It? Counter Hegemonic Approaches to Work Education." *Journal of Education* (Boston) 165, no. 3 (1983): 235–56.

Simon, Roger I. "Empowerment as a Pedagogy of Possibility." *Language Arts* 64, no. 4 (1987).

Simon, Roger I. "Work Experience as the Production of Subjectivity." In *Critical Pedagogy and Cultural Power,* edited by David Livingstone et al. South Hadley, Mass.: Bergin & Garvey, 1987.

Simon, Roger I. "Being Ethnic/Doing Ethnicity." In *Breaking the Mosaic: Race and Ethnicity in Education,* edited by Jon Young. Toronto: Garamond Press, 1987.

Simon, Roger I., Don Dippo, and Arleen Schenke. *Learning Work: A Critical Pedagogy of Work Education.* New York: Bergin & Garvey, 1991.

Smitas, Sylvia. "Employer and Employee Perspectives of Secondary School Business Courses Offered Through Co-operative Education." Unpublished Masters Thesis, Ontario Institute for Studies in Education, University of Toronto, 1984.

Smith, Barbara Herrenstein. "Contingencies of Value." *Critical Inquiry* 10, no. 1 (1983): 1–35.

Solomon-Godeau, Abigail. *Photography at the Dock: Essays on Photographic History, Institutions and Practices.* Minneapolis: University of Minnesota Press, 1991.

Stern, Fritz. *The Politics of Cultural Despair: A Study of the Rise of Germanic Ideology.* Berkeley: University of California Press, 1961.

Teriman, Richard. *Discourse/Counter-Discourse: The Theory and Practice of Symbolic Resistance in Nineteenth-Century France.* Ithaca: Cornell University Press, 1985.

Trinh, Minh-ha. *Woman Native Other.* Bloomington: Indiana University Press, 1989.

Unger, Roberto Mangabeira. *Passion: An Essay on Personality.* New York: The Free Press, 1984.

Volosinov, V.N. *Marxism and Philosophy of Language.* New York: Seminar Press, 1973.

Walkerdine, Valerie. "On the Regulation of Speaking and Silence: Subjectivity, Class and Gender." In *Language, Gender and Childhood,* edited by Carolyn Steedman, Cathy Unwin, and Valerie Walkerdine. London: Routledge and Kegan Paul, 1985.

Walkerdine, Valerie. "Video Re-Play." In *Formations of Fantasy,* edited by Victor Burgin, Cora Kaplan, and James Donald. London: Methuen, 1986.

Walkerdine, Valerie. "Surveillance, Subjectivity and Struggle: Lessons from Pedagogic and Domestic Practices." Occasional Paper No. 11, Center for Humanistic Studies, University of Minnesota, 1987.

Walsh, Catherine E. *Pedagogy and the Struggle for Voice: Issues of Language, Power and Schooling for Puerto Ricans.* New York: Bergin & Garvey, 1991.

Walzer, Michael. *Interpretation and Social Criticism.* Cambridge: Harvard University Press, 1987.

Weedon, Chris. *Feminist Practice and Poststructuralist Theory.* London: Blackwell, 1987.

Welch, Sharon. *Communities of Resistance and Solidarity.* New York: Orbis Press, 1985.

Weiler, Kathleen. *Women Teaching for Change: Gender, Class and Power.* South Hadley, Mass.: Bergin & Garvey, 1988.

Weiler, Kathleen. "Freire and a Feminist Pedagogy of Difference." Unpublished Manuscript, 1990.

White, Roger, and David Brockington. *Tales Out of School: Consumers' Views of British Education.* London: Routledge and Kegan Paul, 1983.

Williams, Raymond. "Resources for a Journey of Hope." In *Toward 2000.* London: Penguin Books, 1983.

Williams, Raymond. *Keywords.* Flamingo: London, 1983.

Williams, Raymond. *Resources for Hope.* London: Verso, 1989.

Willinsky, John. *The Triumph of Literature/The Fate of Literacy.* New York: Teacher's

College Press, 1991.

Wollheim, Peter. "Robert Flaherty's Inuit Photographs." *Canadian Forum* (November 1980): 12–14.

Young, Iris Marion. "The Idea of Community and the Politics of Difference," In *Feminism/Postmodernism,* edited by Linda Nicholson. New York: Routledge, 1990.

Index

ABOUT THE AUTHOR

ROGER I. SIMON teaches in the Department of Curriculum at the Ontario Institute for Studies in Education. Simon has conducted research and written extensively in the areas of critical pedagogy and cultural studies. In 1991 he received the Ontario Colleges and Universities Faculty Associations [OCUFA] Excellence in Teaching Award. Simon's recent publications include *Learning Work: A Critical Pedagogy of Work Education* (with Don Dippo and Arleen Schenke) (Bergin & Garvey, 1991) and *Popular Culture, Schooling and Everyday Life* (with Henry Giroux) (Bergin & Garvey, 1989).

DATE DUE

FEB 2 4 1997	
MAY 1 3 2003	
OCT 3 0 2005